Images of Post-Soviet Kazakhstan
A Cosmopolitan Space with Borderland Anxieties

Images of Post-Soviet Kazakhstan
A Cosmopolitan Space with Borderland Anxieties

Suchandana Chatterjee

Maulana Abul Kalam Azad Institute of Asian Studies
Kolkata

in association with

KNOWLEDGE WORLD

KW Publishers Pvt Ltd
New Delhi

The **Maulana Abul Kalam Azad Institute of Asian Studies** (MAKAIAS) is an autonomous body under the Ministry of Culture, Government of India. Based in Kolkata, it was registered as a Society under the West Bengal Registration of Societies' Act of 1961 on the 4th of January 1993, with Prof. Nurul Hasan, the then Governor of West Bengal, as the President of the Society. It is funded by the Department of Culture, Government of India.

MAKAIAS is a centre for research and learning with a focus on social, cultural, economic and political / administrative developments in Asia from the middle of the 19th Century onwards, with special emphasis on their links with India, and also on the life and works of Maulana Abul Kalam Azad.

ISBN 978-93-86288-02-8
e-book ISBN 978-93-86288-03-5

KNOWLEDGE WORLD
Published in India by

Kalpana Shukla
KW Publishers Pvt Ltd
4676/21, First Floor, Ansari Road, Daryaganj, New Delhi 110002
Phone: +91.11.23263498/43528107
Email: knowledgeworld@kwpub.com • www.kwpub.com

2011 FIP BA BEST PUBLISHERS AWARD (ENGLISH)

Printed and Bound by Bhavish Graphics.

Contents

Acknowledgements

This study has evolved in a number of ways for which I am grateful to my Kazakh friends. I thank Svetlana Kovalskaya, Gulnara Nadirova, Ablet Kamalov, Elena Bainazarova, Laura Yereksheva, German Kim and Yulia Goloskokova for their research inputs. Each of them shared ideas that helped me understand the diverse approaches about Kazakhstan's past and present. Elena and Yulia are incredible fellow travellers who introduced me to the old world and new world charm of Almaty and Astana, Kokshetau and Borovoe. In Atyrau, two young friends, Nurbergen and Aidar, consultant with Tengiz Chevroil and Civil Engineer with Atyrau Oil and Gas Company respectively, have been my enthusiastic research guides. I am truly impressed by these two young men who are not just professionals engaged in foreign companies or state-owned energy projects, but are also Kazakh nationals who have not forgotten their glorious Soviet past. I was lucky to be introduced to them by the Calcutta-based engineer, Sumantro Chattopadhyay who was in Atyrau in the early 2000s when India's engineering companies were engaging senior engineers in foreign collaboration projects in Central Asia, especially Kazakhstan. The Caspian oil project was a formidable entity and Indian engineers like Sumantro belonged to that league. I am grateful to Sumantro for his narrative of a prosperous provincial city situated between Asia and Europe.

I owe my understanding of bordered conscience to Ablet Kamalov, the Uyghur historian in Almaty. He took the initiative of introducing me to the Uyghur and Dungan communities in the microregion of Zarya Vostoka, in Almaty oblast. I was deeply touched by the warm reception arranged by the families in the neighbourhood. I was their privileged guest just after Ramadan in 2013.

During my research trips, I was fortunate to get support and advice from the Indian Embassy in Astana. Ambassador Ashok Sharma and his team including Rakesh Banati, Satyanjal Pandey, Sunando Chakraborty have been extremely helpful and guided me with suggestions about site visits in the neighbourhood of Astana.

I am grateful to MEA's Eurasia Division for supporting MAKAIAS's Regional ICCEES Conference initiative and for extending financial support towards my participation in IXth ICCEES Congress in Makuhari in August 2015. Such an event provided the opportunity of interacting with scholars working on themes relevant to my subject of research.

I thank Maulana Abul Kalam Azad Institute of Asian Studies for supporting this project.

My family continues to be my greatest support. Som and Mimi have grown up to appreciate the intricacies of social science research. Sukalyan continues to be the optimist and has mentored me at the most difficult stages of my research.

Introduction

On cosmopolitanism

Cosmopolitanism has become a renewed field of enquiry since the 2000s. A very simple meaning of cosmopolitanism is "a way of being in the world"[1] and as a willingness to engage the Other. The idea of cosmopolitanism has evolved from Kantian philosophical tradition.[2] Over time, questions have been raised about Kantian philosophy of Enlightenment and the concept has been reframed in the light of social and cultural contexts that transcend bounded and nation-state formulations. The idea has expanded to include a wide range of social and cultural theories stretched across cultures and disciplines—philosophy, sociology, political theory and anthropology: e.g., "rooted cosmopolitanism,"[3] rootless cosmopolitanism" and "cosmopolitan patriots,"[4] "vernacular cosmopolitanism,"[5] "aesthetic cosmopolitanism"[6] and so on. With such changes in methodological approaches to cosmopolitanism, the term came to denote a social position in which individuals and communities tend to have meaningful attachments. Today, the impression about cosmopolitanism is multiple allegiances to peoples, places and traditions that lie beyond the boundaries of the nation-state.[7]

There are various strands in cosmopolitanism. Cosmopolites can be of various kinds even though cosmopolitanism is generally associated with elite behaviour. Steven Vertovec and others have conceived of cosmopolitanism as a habitual concept whereby culture is a toolkit.[8] These scholars, even while trying to move out of the ethnic lens, are somewhat rigid in their approaches about fixed cultural differences. Theirs is a stereotypical projection of cosmopolites as wealthy and elite groups of privileged people who experiment with consumerism and "brands." Their cosmopolitanism reflects commodification and consumer culture. Here is an image of cosmopolitanism of the developed nations who undertake cosmopolitan tourism or visits to exotic places.

There are scholars who argue differently by proposing cosmopolitanism as a cultural condition. In their view, aesthetic cosmopolitanism, manifested in social settings, is a completely different form—found in homes, represented by people and families who develop a variety of opinions on various things—music, for instance. So, besides globally mobile people (expatriates, exiles, transnational migrants, refugees), cosmopolitans can also be people within their own homes but with varied opinions. However, there could be an appreciation of the "home plus"—i.e., when these people start visiting places and have a sense of commitment to the world as a whole.[9]

Scholars have actually tried to argue about the varieties of social settings, very often diasporic settings or lifeways of people who have migrated. In its introductory chapter, *The Ashgate Research Companion to Cosmopolitanism* offers a description about the new cultural phenomena that has appeared through mobility and interconnectedness in a global world. Current processes of transnational contact, travel and migration that enabled intensified patterns of cultural exchange are components of this expanded research about cosmopolitanism that is not merely a label to describe distinctiveness of the Other, but a category that describes cultural phenomena. So, the shift of analysis has now shifted to variety of human elements and cultural engagements. Plural histories enable cosmopolitan identities, memories and discourses that appear in both Western and non-Western historical contexts.[10] Implicit in this analysis are the Eurocentric underpinnings of cosmopolitanism that are compared and contrasted with Asian discourses of cosmopolitanism.

Multiple cosmopolitanisms also suggest "cosmopolitan sociability." Such a behaviour or attitude might well be seen among mobile people, including transnational migrants and travellers. The explanation for this "cosmopolitan attitude" is as follows: "rootedness and openness cannot be seen in oppositional terms but constitute aspects of the creativity through which migrants build homes and sacred spaces in a new environment and within transnational networks."[11] So, there are two strands of cosmopolitan sensibility here: the older one that subscribes to the nation-state project and is primarily linked to elites, intellectuals and others; and the revised concept that seems to disapprove of the nation-state perspectives and is rooted in sensibilities of the diaspora and diverse sociocultural groupings.

Asian cosmopolitanism

But there are also sociable behaviours that go beyond these binary trajectories and have a shared sense of common sensibilities. Here we need to examine

Asian discourses about plural loyalties—standing in many circles but having a common ground. Such pro-Asian sentiments have created the urge to focus on the aspect of intersection of diverse representations. This perspective takes researchers beyond the prism of binaries, i.e., exclusion versus inclusion, sameness versus difference and into the domain of cosmopolitan openness. As the discussion moves to Asian cosmopolitanisms, one needs to consider the varieties that one gets to see here. The subject of Eurasian communities in Southeast Asian historiography is one such variant. Talking about Eurasian families, reference has been made to family histories of Dutch and British families in colonial Penang in seventeenth–nineteenth centuries whose life journeys reflect multiple cultural worlds. Moving away from fixed frames like hierarchies of power that structured colonial governance, the new studies have reflected more and more on sites of Asian interaction—in this case Penang.[12] Cosmopolitan engagement reflects the idealised form of cosmopolitan relations whereby both sides take the perspective of the other seriously, and both sides engage in substantive dialogue about cultural equality and mutual respect. Dialogue among cultures was prescribed in the late 1990s by Kuan Hsing Cheng and his Indian counterpart Ashis Nandy. Pointing to the new cosmopolitanism that was located in Asia, Chen and Nandy argued fervently that the need was to "redefine" Asia not merely as the repository of the exotic and esoteric that was coveted by the West, but as *another arena* where the fates of the competing nation-states of Europe were getting decided. "Asian cultures never responded to European encroachment passively," they argued. "It is now pretty obvious that Asian civilisations, whatever else they may or may not have done, have certainly not been passive spectators of their own humiliation and subjugation. They coped with the West in diverse ways—sometimes aggressively resisting its intrusiveness, sometimes trying to neutralise it by giving it indigenous meanings, sometimes even incorporating the West as an insulated module within their traditional cultural selves."[13] Nandy and Chen have proposed alternative forms of dialogue originating in the new cosmopolitan rubric of Asia, Africa and South America in the last two hundred years. At the same time, the writers have felt the need not to juxtapose the West and Asia as contending or competing with each other, but bring both within the rubric of a dialogue as opposed to resistance and create a culturally integrated world.

Theorists of new Asian cosmopolitanism have pinned their hopes on Asia not merely as a space prone to Orientalist and imperialist designs, but as method. Such an approach not only recognises Asia as a spatial and historical category but also *accepts* it as a category of identification that needs to be worked with constantly. Therefore, the aim is not to distinguish Asian types or exemplars from Western counterparts but to be receptive to new ways of "border thinking." In fact, the thought ought to be not about Asia as a "bordered space" but as a conglomerate of Asian identities with cities in a participatory role. The idea is to wait and watch how urban aspirations across regions of Asia recognise each other and reciprocate.

In the world of cosmopolitan rethinking, the word "cosmopolitanism" connotes a variety of social settings, sociocultural processes and individual behaviours. South Asian scholars have conceptualised "lived cosmopolitanisms" and have felt strongly about empirical and analytical settings in the global South. Their arguments revolve round social relations, both past and present, in Southeast, South and East Asia and their associated littorals. Interpreting the salience of places and histories, such perspectives give attention to forms of social relations and the practice of politics that emerge in the global South. Pheng Cheah (of Malaysian origins) suggests the criticality of the post-colonial space and its influence on the intellectual's writings. Such is the case of located-ness in the post colony of the state of Kerala in India, the case of "connected histories" that Sanjay Subrahmanyam argues about and that implicitly is a critique of the Eurocentric imaginings of Asia and its geographical "disconnectedness," or perhaps the fresh imaginings of littoral Asia with suppressed histories and cultural geographies (as explained by Lakshmi Subrahmanian, is the case of connected histories of peninsular India, Singapore and Malay in the nineteenth century and as exemplified by Tamil migration from South to Southeast Asia). Biographies in the Bay of Bengal region narrate experiences of the Hadrami community (with connected histories of the Arabian and Malay worlds) and now belonging to the truncated nation-state of what once constituted the Malay world. The South Asian and Southeast Asian angles are woven together in Amitav Ghosh's *The Hungry Tide*, in which the appeal lies in the connecting—across space and time—and a new cosmopolitanism is forged. The implication is that imposition of nationalist frames on these historical and spatially interconnected formations and dispensations is erroneous.[14]

The study

I intend to frame my present project based on this gamut of impressions about cosmopolitanism. Here, I am concerned with Kazakhstan's cosmopolitan setting, and I would tend to accept that the following factors define Central Asian dynamics in the post-Soviet situation: sociocultural conditions, a world view, multiple subjects held in unison—i.e., a concentric circles' approach of a cosmopolitan world and an attitude or disposition or behaviour that is largely acquired through experience, especially travel. The study revolves round the relationship between space and transitional identity in Kazakhstan in the post-Soviet period. Emergent discourses about cosmopolitanism suggest multiple interactions in a transitional space. The cosmopolitanism of our times implies the dynamic responses of communities in transition. The diversities and heterogeneities instead of the specifics, the encounters, the networks, the challenges, the ways of living, the multitude of fates need to be considered and this is what contemporary debate on cosmopolitanism is all about. The images are of the many and not of the one and only one—not of "a circle created by cultures that are diffused from the centre but of centres that are everywhere and circumferences nowhere." So, the picture is far bigger as there are infinite ways of being and belonging. There are diverse and multiple engagements that should be looked into. The present study attempts to focus on such engagements in post-Soviet Kazakhstan, especially in the present millennium when its "competitive profile" increased, either through eastward integration or through Eurasian partnerships or through collaborative ventures with East Asia, Southeast Asia and South Asia. Several writings have tried to showcase these two profiles of Kazakhstan—the national and the international. The national profile is pitched on Nazarbayev's governance which depicts an unusual combination of urban transformation (centred round Astana and Akmolinsk oblast) and a selective treatment of its ethnic groups (preferences being for the titular nationality or the *otanlar*, which is a generic name for those belonging to the Kazakh homeland). This overly Kazakised rhetoric is frequently criticised. But what stands out is the wider milieu of a cosmopolitan Almaty which is the home of educated Russian population and the cultural elite which is juxtaposed to citified Astana that has been recommended by Nazarbayev's government as the "appropriate site" of the Kazakhs' steppe identity. The variety is also seen in the case of Uyghur neighbourhoods of Almaty, in the frontiers of Akmolinsk oblast reminiscent of Tsarist Russia's

Cossack military fortresses, in *gulag* (concentration camp) memorials near Akmolinsk/Tselinograd/Astana and in the Caspian hub Atyrau that is iconised as the oil fountain of the present century and the game changer of Kazakh economy.

Kazakh borderlands have a completely different profile. The predicaments or dilemmas of the borderlands pertain to the aspect of shared spaces that have transformed interethnic relationships in Kazakhstan. The attempt is to assess the relationship between the cosmopolitan space that Kazakhstan represents and its borderland identities. The Kazakhs' attachment to their homeland is a constant—but the question is whether that territorial reality fits into other paradigms of identity and belonging. Such questions arise in the case of Mongolian Kazakhs and Uyghurs of Semirechie—in both cases the sentiment of place is far stronger compared to the overwhelming global experiences of the mainland Kazakhs. The emotional attachment is far greater in these two cases. So, the appeal for a historic homeland for all Kazakhs is often not popular among Mongolian Kazakhs who did not move to Kazakhstan by default in the aftermath of Soviet disintegration. So, the desire for a global experience in Kazakhstan seems to be much less in the case of Mongolian Kazakhs. The Uyghurs too have a strong attachment to their place of origin, i.e., Semirechie. Compact Uyghur settlements in southeast Kazakhstan which straddles the China border are autochthonous communities with a localised Semirechien attachment—an aspect that has been studied only within the limited scope of *Uyghurovedeniya*. The intention is to go beyond the myopic view of the Uyghurs as a minority nationality of Xinjiang Autonomous Region of People's Republic of China and hence a Chinese problem. The emphasis is more on the meaningful presence of the Uyghurs as a dynamic Central Asian community originating in the Semirechie region and living in compact settlements in southeast Kazakhstan, mainly in the Almaty district. Such intricacies of the live-in experiences of Uyghur and Dungan communities have been taken into consideration in this study. The diversity unfolds in competing narratives about Kazakh cities and their social surroundings as well as the spectacle that each of these cities represents.

Cosmopolitanism in Kazakhstan has attracted widespread attention especially in the context of post-Soviet nation-building whereby commentaries on aspects such as history-writing, urbanisation, economic development, demography and migration, diaspora links, cultural identity are innumerable. Basically the interest is about the performance of post-Soviet regimes as Kazakhstan. In dealing with the "appearance" of a post-Soviet set-up, the assumption is about new forms, rather than old forms—a sudden break rather than continuity of past political and social traditions. There seems to be a polarisation of views among cosmopolitans and nationalists, but what is interesting is the extremely varied nature of these views and also the variety of interpretations about historical and contemporary events. It is the diverse opinions that make Kazakhstan's cosmopolitan setting a unique case study.

The study takes into account such variables of cosmopolitanism in Kazakhstan, defined by spatial growth of urban spaces like Almaty on the one hand and social fragmentation as an offshoot of the policy of "Kazakisation" on the other. The former trend, set in motion during the Tsarist and Soviet eras, gives Kazakhstan its competitive profile while the latter reflects the underlying social tensions. The cosmopolitan ambience of the urbanised locales is distinct from the predicaments of the Kazakh borderlands. These borderlands with big towns and cities like Shymkent (in the south), or Karaganda (in the north), are overlaid with a variety of non-titular ethnic groups like the Uzbeks, the Uyghurs and the Dungans. Their dilemmas of living portray the divergent sentiments of transnational groups. It is this divergence or diversity that has governed the character of interrelationships among ethnic groups in Kazakhstan. Transnational migration is the recurrent theme of the migration debate in Kazakhstan ever since the announcement of the *Oralman* (return of ethnic Kazakhs) programme by the Kazakh state. The economic, social and cultural impact of return migration has been examined in a major way in the case of the Uyghurs and Dungans and Mongolian Kazakhs. The analysis is not very substantial in the case of the Uzbeks of Kazakhstan. The ambiguous status of the *oralman* is also discussed as a case specific to migration studies. What has been considered is not just the Law of Migration in Kazakhstan (2011) or subsequent amendments which media reports have interpreted as causing a lot of problems to the ethnic Kazakh returnees—*oralmany*—and to the internal rural migrants to cities. Such reports pertain to how the *oralman* faces innumerable problems in negotiating the legal institutional and bureaucratic obstacles in formalising their status.[15]

Such facts also raise several pertinent questions about "belonging" and "homelessness." The Kazakhs' attachment to their homeland is a constant;

what is variable is whether that territorial reality fits other paradigms of identity and belonging. So, it is the element of hybridity that has entered the debate about "transnationalism" and "diaspora" which is extremely relevant in the context of Mongolian Kazakhs who trace their origins to Kazakh territories in western China but have been blocked from the other side of the Altai due to the creation of international borders in the 1930s that made Mongolia a Soviet ally and cut it off from Chinese Altai. In the aftermath of Soviet disintegration, the predicament of the bordering regions increased. The Mongolian Kazakhs did not move to Kazakhstan by default and the call of a return of Kazakhs (*oralmany*) to Kazakhstan did not have the desired results. The factor of emotional attachment was far greater—the emotional connection with specific landscapes was extremely strong rather than the cultural association with the Kazakhs. So, instead of an automatic shift, there seems to be an immobilisation of this transnational Kazakh group. There seems to be a stronger "place identity" than a desire to be part of the global experience. So, definitely here, one sees that the Mongolian Kazakhs have a feeling for an alternative homeland rather than a historic homeland for all Kazakhs.

The Uyghurs too have a strong attachment to their settlements in Kazakhstan. The compact Uyghur settlements in southeastern Kazakhstan that straddles the China border are autochthonous communities with a localised Semirechien attachment. The study seeks to explore the nuances of belonging of borderland communities like the Uyghurs. It takes into account the aspect of "in-between-ness" among the Uyghurs, shedding the myopic view of the Uyghurs as a minority community inhabiting the Xinjiang Autonomous Region of the People's Republic of China. The emphasis here is on the Uyghurs as a dynamic Turkic community having a meaningful presence in the Central Asian region. This aspect opens up a much more lively debate about borderland communities of the erstwhile Soviet Union and their live-in experiences rather than a China-centric paranoia about the Uyghur autonomy movement that could have a spillover effect among co-ethnics in Kazakhstan.

The Kazakh conscience

The images are of the many, and as suggested here, relate to the Kazakh conscience. The Kazakh conscience represents a repertoire of diverse opinions regarding Eurasianism, intellectuals' reformist agenda, *zhuz* legacy, people's histories. Kazakh conscience has alternated between inherited traditions and social transformation. To talk about Kazakhstan's inherited tradition, one has to step back into history and review the Steppe's northern locations that are rich with legends and stories about the Middle Horde and its illustrious chieftains. The Kazakh intellectuals' adaptation to the ideology of their colonial mentors or the negotiations between Kazakh sultans of the Middle Horde and their imperial masters is a glorified chapter in Kazakh history. But what seems to be left out in this glorified history are the tribal linkages in the Kazakh steppe and allegiance of minor allies (the Oirats for example). Some of them belonged to diverse tribal groups in west Kazakhstan that constituted a different tribal confederation, i.e., the *Kishi Zhuz* (Lesser Horde) that was headed by tribal leaders Ablai Khan and Abul Khair Khan.

Kazakh conscience is also about real life experiences reminiscent of the Soviet period. Diverse sentiments are seen among non-titular nationalities like the Germans and the Koreans who became victims of Soviet deportation. The saga of deportation comes alive with tales of banishment and exile narrated by survivors. The urban spectacle is also very different in different cities—the spatial growth of urban centres like Almaty and Astana is a stark contrast to the fringe status of oil towns like Atyrau despite the growing popularity of Tengiz Chevroil. TCO and the Kashagan oil project (now dumped by the government) are the rallying point of several western companies as well as collaborative projects that are being showcased in a major way, much to the apathy of dissenting voices in Atyrau. Also attractive is the Russian environment in northern Kazakhstan with Kokshetau, situated at the junction of the Kazakh-Siberian Railway network and emerging as the regional centre of Akmola oblast with a city *akimat* exercising authority that is beyond the President's control. It thrives as an eco-region with government's development programmes on the priority list.

The people's psyche is different in different regions of Kazakhstan. The continuity of tribal tradition is the dominant feature in the Akmolinsk oblast. Astana is at the centre of this oblast. Situated beside River Ishim and its tributary Esil it is the *Heart of Eurasia* (with depictions of steppe settlements like Bozok that originated in the medieval period and was transformed into a city "that never sleeps").[16] In Almaty, the feeling of attachment prevails among generations with live-in experience. The factor of emotional attachment is strongest in the case of the Uyghurs of Semirechie who live in compact settlements in Zarya Vostoka district of Almaty. Kokshetau, a quaint provincial town in north Kazakhstan is a living memory of Soviet past, immortalised by the regional museum *Istoriko-kraevicheskie muzei* under the patronage of Department of Culture of Akmolinsk Oblast (*Upraveleniya Kultury, Akmolinsk Oblast*) stored with memorabilia belonging to Soviet patrons of music, sports and art. Kokshetau is also immortalised as the native place of the Kazakh ethnographer Chokan Valikhanov who belonged to a noble Kazakh lineage. Memory-driven consciousness among the Kazakhs as victims of Soviet deportation come alive in Alzhir Memorial Complex in Malininka village 40 miles west of Astana where a memorial complex–the *Akmola Deportation Camp of Wives of Traitors of the Revolution*–bears testimony to broken families and sorrows of women and children of Kazakh, Uzbek, Azeri, Polish, German and Korean backgrounds who were forced into a life of seclusion in these camps in the 1930s.

Such tangled emotions unfolded right in front of my eyes—during my research trips to Kazakhstan in the past three years. Initially, like most global observers, my basic interest was in the appearance of cosmopolitanism, governed by ideologies like Eurasianism that have been nurtured for a fairly long time. Both in Astana and Almaty, such voices of cosmopolitanism are heard and seen—very strongly among academic circles and institutions like Nazarbayev University and Lev Gumilev University (in Astana), Turan University in Almaty and among limited circles in Kazakh National University (KazNu) and R. B. Suleimanov Institute of Oriental Studies in Almaty patronised by the Ministry of Science and Education. Gradually however, the Kazakh conscience representing diverse sentiments tended to unfold and these unravelled more interesting images about Kazakhstan's past and the present.

The hypothesis of this project is the cosmopolitan environment of diverse settings and not only of capital cities, Almaty and Astana. It is true that the iconic capitals have generated a lot of hope among the rich and the powerful. But, what cannot be ignored is the wider reach of Eurasian and global engagements in which western port cities like Atyrau play a prominent role. At the same time, there is creeping disillusionment among Kazakhs of the rural areas whose lives are badly affected by the regime's modernisation projects like transfer of capital from Almaty to Astana and more recently the devaluation of the *tenge*. While the euphoria among the capital's elite groups about Nazarbayev's governance persists, there is a wide variety of relational shifts between Kazakhs and Russians, Kazakhs and Germans, Kazakhs and Koreans, Kazakhs and Mongols and so on.

The present study takes into account such variables of cosmopolitanism in Kazakhstan. All these issues will be explained in the various chapters of this study.

This research underwent a transition in the course of the past three years. Initially, the concern was about a binary trajectory: Kazakh ethnic nationalism that was counterbalanced by civic nationalism featured by multiple sentiments of non-titular nationalities. Gradually attention moved to the image of "the global modern" displayed through a cosmopolitan ambience with twin properties: that of the urban environment of Almaty and Astana and that of the peripheral environment represented by Kazakhstan's minority nationalities like the Koreans, Germans, Uyghurs, the Dungans, Uzbeks etc. Even here, there are two contradictory sets of ideas—hope and despair. The iconic capitals, Almaty and Astana have generated lot of hope among the rich and the powerful. The development-related projects in Caspian port cities like Atyrau also create a lot of hope (and hype) about Kazakhstan's Eurasian engagements that also involve global partners. On the other hand, there is despair and disillusionment among minority nationalities that have been affected by governmental decrees on Kazakisation, repatriation of *oralmandar* (returnees) to Kazakhstan. The most recent example of cosmopolitan behaviour is popular reaction to the President's desire to rename his country as *Kazakh Yeli*. Issues of deportation and displacement, migration and homeland, diaspora and transnationalism are linked with the second hypothesis of cosmopolitanism. The purpose was to study this wide gamut of opinions in order to get an understanding of the identities in transition in Kazakhstan that cannot be possibly overshadowed by dominant ethno-nationalist concerns.

The chapters

The five core chapters in this study are essentially inclined towards competing narratives about Kazakhstan. Narratives flow from a variety of impressions not just about ethnicity but also a variety of non-ethnic markers of identity (like nomadic tradition), developmental dynamics, relational shifts from the Soviet to the post-Soviet periods and intra-regional complexities. Field impressions and research on the ground have substantiated such ideas.

The first and second chapters attempt a review of post-Soviet debates about history and ethnicity that have marked (and marred) identity-related issues in Kazakhstan. Sharing the views of Kazakh academicians Nurbulat Masanov and Abdumalik Nasanbayev, scholars have discussed the predominance of the Kazakh ethno-nationalist rhetoric. Critiquing the premise of ethnicity as group distinctiveness flowing from a series of genealogical claims (*shezire*), Kazakh scholars have pointed out that the label creates boundaries among groups which thereby suggest a level of internal homogeneity that is unlikely to exist. The problematic of ethnicity was matched by a related set of writings about the homeland. The homeland issue has been a persistent feature in debates that originated since the announcement of the repatriation (*oralman*) programme. So, the initial chapters have discussed how the national historical narratives in the post-Soviet period have been mostly concerned with these paradigmatic notions of ethnicity and homeland, often leaving out significant interludes in Kazakh people's history. In the second chapter about competing narratives, the discussion swings to such lapses in history-writing which also brings out interesting analogies of the Soviet and post-Soviet periods. Zifa Auezova among others, is particularly sensitive to such forgotten episodes of the generation of the 1920s-1930s—which brings out an interesting analogy of the odds of transition in the two periods—Soviet and post-Soviet. So, the genre of national histories is not the only story. Conscientious scholars have drawn our attention to several competing narratives that are completely out of tune with the ideological correctness of the emerging historical narratives. *Chapter Two* in particular pointed to such ambiguities which have practically opened the audience to larger issues about the homeland. So, not only is there recognition of new tribal histories and identities of the homeland, but also there have been interesting insights about Kazakhstan's "uncommon history" that is navigated through source-studies. This strand of history-writing is a variant that needs to be taken into account irrespective of the euphoria about post-Soviet Kazakhstan's dynamic profile that was extremely attractive to a generation that had a lot of expectations about independence and its aftermath. The interest in the subject of interethnic behaviour with respect to Russo-Kazakh relations continues to exist. The ambiguous rapport of the Russians with their two homelands—Russia and Kazakhstan produced other complications. The complications emanated from a series of other ambiguities—for example the Migration Law which assigned the oralman (returnee) status to those Kazakhs migrating to Kazakhstan from outside the Soviet Union and "repatriate" status to those who were migrating from within. Broadly speaking, the Kazakhs who attempted to return to Kazakhstan in the wake of Kazakisation were identified as a diaspora with the basic assumption that these groups of return migrants will effortlessly integrate with their ancestral homeland and co-ethnics in Kazakhstan. In most cases, their exile status has been highlighted. Now, this categorisation is not applicable to the Mongolian Kazakhs who as per Mongolian laws are not considered to be descendants of the exiles. The ethnonym "Kazakh" became the contentious issue ever since the repatriation policy was announced. The presence of "returnees" created some uneasiness among "resident Kazakhs." It is this aspect of contested relationship with the kin state representatives, in this case the Kazakhs of Kazakhstan, that has been explored in the chapter "Relational Shifts." Unlike the Russians in Kazakhstan or the Kazakhs in Mongolia, the dialectics of the homeland issue among the Uyghur community in the Semirechie (Kazakh name *Zhetysu* or the Land of the Seven Rivers) region of southeastern Kazakhstan have largely been ignored—exceptions being special issue of *Central Asian Survey* on the Uyghurs.

All these big and small games in Eurasia are pivoted round Kazakhstan's ability to steer its course through diplomatic channels while Russia continues to play the role of the regional hegemon. Kazakhstan's advantage is its post-independence economic performance that has attracted a lot of foreign investment. But this is a partial story. Kazakhstan's Chinese, Russian and Uzbek borderlands share traumatic legacies of Soviet territorial delimitation, deportation, displacement and resettlement. In the wake of independence, demographic trends have also created dislocation in the Kazakh space, especially with the outmigration of Russians to other regions of the CIS. In Mongol-Kazakh borderlands (of Bayan Olgii province for instance), place identities are related to the live-in experiences in Mongolia which is the host country. Here, the preference is of staying "immobile" which is in sharp contrast to the Kazakh metanarratives of homeland and diaspora that prescribe identity with Kazakhstan. Place identities expressed through sentiments of religiosity, kinship ties and cultural diversity have created competitive situations for the Nazarbayev regime. Such issues of concern have been described in *Chapter Four.* The concerns are localised in nature or are too distant to be taken seriously. But these do at times reflect regional stakes. For the Kazakh state that projects itself as a strong state, much of its regional options are extremely limited in nature. It has been far more successful in defusing internal dissent and unrest without the risk of a rebellion or a secessionist movement. The Kazakhs' Semirechien attachment does arouse Uyghur sentiments but these have seldom grown out of proportions or have escalated to a challenge in the nature of a Uyghur separatist movement as in neighbouring China. The Irtysh river issue and water sharing with China was a constant worry in the early years of Kazakhstan's independence especially from the viewpoint of environmental degradation faced by local villagers but this issue did not assume proportions of a nationwide stir against China. The only issue that might have somewhat dented Nazarbayev's image of governance to a certain extent is the oil workers' strike in Zhanaozen in the Mangystau region of west Kazakhstan. The ensuing riot and the state's tough handling of that particular situation on its own terms and that too on the twentieth anniversary of Kazakhstan's independence was a subject of criticism by observers worldwide. What appears to have been at stake was the country's credibility as an energy-rich state largely counting on the West's support. The government's aggressive stance towards demonstrators, media and reporters was a replica of what happened in Ukraine's Maidan in 2013-14. Three years since Zhanaozen, comparisons have been made about popular protest having a jingoistic effect on Central Asia's neighbourhood. Journalistic freedom was curbed—to the extent that Kazakhstan's oil hub—the Aktau province—filled with *oralmany* from Uzbekistan and Iran—was deliberately shut out of public gaze. The presence of Kazakh returnees on the prosperous west coast was a source of discontent—as most of these diaspora Kazakhs were unable to match the high living standards of the people working in the oil industry. As Kazakh returnees, they had to cope both ways—as Kazakhs looking for rehabilitation in their homeland and as workers eking out a difficult existence in oil rich Mangystau province. These are symptomatic about social decline which have also affected the resilience of the Kazakh people. On-the-face reports about official clampdown on demonstrators do not tell the complete story. So this chapter is about a myriad of concerns—of the people living at the edge. This is also a chapter that tells us about uncommon ancestral traditions, attitudes and popular beliefs in mountainous regions like the Altai where people are more committed to well-being and health rather than Islamic religiosity.

The *final chapter* is based on impressions of field visits to Kazakhstan. The impressions of the three annual research trips (2012-14) to this resource-rich dynamic Central Asian country have varied from time to time—oscillating between belief and disbelief, curiosity and scepticism. Curiosity was inspired by the ability of the country to position itself reasonably well within the international arena by establishing its status as a negotiator and partner in regional alliances and also by responding to domestic compulsions with regard to non-titular minority nationalities like the Uyghurs, Dungans and the Uzbeks. In recent times, Kazakhstan's adjustments with Uzbekistan in the Aral Sea water-sharing disputes also have attracted a lot of global attention.

Scepticism was aroused due to ambiguities of the Law of Migration which left certain questions unanswered. The attention shifted to other frames—and these frames reflect variations in social behaviour in the post-Soviet Kazakh space. The gamut of perspectives has been fairly wide—ranging from the nostalgia of a Soviet-trained intellectual group in Almaty's academic environs to the elitist ambitions of the noveau riche and the famous in Astana bestowed with blessings of the Kazakh government and finally to the local aspirations of young professionals in western Kazakhstan.

To sum up, Kazakhstan's post-Soviet ambience reflects a combination of the real and the unreal. What is evident is not merely a negation of old forms but rather an evolution of past norms. Looking ahead, Kazakhstan seems to be fully committed to integration and is ready to experiment with options within the CIS rubric as well as beyond. Her interest lies in treading on the path of balancing opportunities within the CIS. Introspection on such a course of action—giving Kazakhstan her best chance to strengthen her position as the most committed nation seeking and securing Eurasia's future—is necessary. This would also give her added visibility in the West as well as in the Asia-Pacific region which is perhaps the next best option after the G-8 bloc for its comparable models of growth and development. So, her best option is to ally with extra-regional actors that give credit to new leaders of the twenty-first century. One has to learn to accept that regional overtures for Kazakhstan, or for that matter, for any Central Asian country, counteracting Russian hegemony or bypassing Chinese competition will not be enough. It is also important to strike deals with a distant socialist country like Vietnam or with Malaysia that has a Muslim population which is engaged in the service sectors. And, of course, these are maritime nations whose maritime connectivity is perhaps the best rated in the world. How far Kazakhstan is prepared to expand or contract its regional options by going beyond the oil and gas options that might improve her global profile is something that might be worth exploring. In fact, Kazakhstan is not, without reason, seeking to peg her options in the ASEAN framework.

The Republic's priorities, either in terms of the new "unions" within the CIS, or from a Eurasianist perspective with glances towards the east, are voiced time and again by Astana's elite circles and the think tank in Almaty, Kazakhstan Institute for Strategic Studies (KISI). KISI's scholars are optimistic of Kazakhstan-monitored regional integration beyond the scope of the SCO. The *concluding chapter* reviews unfolding dynamics within the CIS in the context of epochal paradigms that shape not Putin's, but Nazarbayev's Presidency. So, the time has come to look beyond the Russian prism. It is Nazarbayev's last call during 2015-16 that might or might not be a serious matter for the CIS. Whether Kazakhstan intends to reap benefits through new alliances within the CIS framework that will bring non-actors like Armenia and Belarus into the field and will boost the image of CIS is something one needs to observe closely. But these are safe options—because these nations all owe allegiance to the ex-Soviet space. But what are the uncertain scenarios which Kazakhstan's think tanks are giving serious thought to?

Such speculation is non-ending. In a total recall mood, the chapter also reviews cultural mediations between the Kazakh and the non-Kazakh worlds that have inspired an entire generation of Almaty-based scholars associated with oriental learning.

Notes

1. Jeremy Waldron, "What is cosmopolitan?" *The Journal of Political Philosophy*, 8 (2), 2000, pp. 227-43.
2. In Kantian philosophy, cosmopolitanism denoted Western prescriptions of allegiance to the world community. Today, it has a resonance in a wide range of cultural, social and political currents throughout the world. But instead of European universalism which has been translated into some kind of European order, revisionist writings have focused on Asian variants of cosmopolitanism. As Delanty has pointed out, "Asian hybrid cultural forms are favourable milieus for the development of cosmopolitanism." But it would be unfair to propose that transformation in Asian societies have occurred in the light of transformation in western societies. In Asia, the plural nature of its civilisations and overlapping cultures and identities suggests a pronounced form of popular cosmopolitanism and civic cosmopolitanism. Writings about East Asian or South East Asian experiences of multiculturalism (through travel and migration, consumption and

communication) indicate changing preferences for market economics, human rights, rule of law, environmental justice, etc. These are what is called expressions of invigorated Asianism—not that confronts westernism or globalisation, but that reflects a completely new approach to culture of Asia. As Delanty approves, "postmodern culture is now an integral part of many major Asia cities where a new kind of aesthetic cosmopolitanism has come into effect." Gerard Delanty, "The cosmopolitan imagination: critical cosmopolitanism and social theory," *The British Journal of Sociology*, vol. 57, issue no. 1, 2006.

3. Mitchelle Cohen, "Rooted cosmopolitanism," *Dissent*, Fall 1992.
4. Kwame Appiah, "Cosmopolitan patriots," in Peng Cheah and Bruce Robbins (eds.), *Cosmopolitics: Thinking and Feeling Beyond the Nation* (University of Minnesota Press, 1998).
5. Homi Bhabha.
6. Motti Regev, "Cultural Uniqueness and Aesthetic Cosmopolitanism," *European Journal of Social Theory*, vol. 10, no. 1, 2007.
7. Peng Cheah and Bruce Robbins (eds), *Cosmopolitics: Thinking and Feeling Beyond the Nation* (University of Minnesota Press, 1998).
8. Steven Vertovec and Robin Cohen, "Conceiving cosmopolitanism," Introduction in Steven Vertovec and Robin Cohen (eds.), *Conceiving cosmopolitanism: theory, context and practice* (Oxford: Oxford University Press, 2002), pp. 1–22.
9. Motti Regev, ibid.
10. Introduction by Maria Rovisco and Magdalena Nowicka, *The Ashgate Research Companion to Cosmopolitanism* (Surrey, England: Ashgate, 2011), p. 3.
11. Nina Glick Schiller, Tsypylma Darieva and Sandra Gruner-Domic, "Defining cosmopolitan sociability. An introduction," *Ethnic and Racial Studies*, 2011, p. 400.
12. Kirsty Walker, "Intimate Interactions: Eurasian Family Histories in Colonial Penang," in Tim Harper and Sunil Amrith (eds.), *Sites of Asian Interaction: Ideas, Networks and Mobility* (Cambridge: Cambridge University Press, 2014), pp. 79-104
13. Ashis Nandy, "Defining a new cosmopolitanism: Towards a Dialogue of Asian Civilisations," http://vlal.bol.ucla.edu/multiversity/Nandy/Nandy_cosm.htm
14. Cheah and Robbins, *Cosmopolitics: Thinking and Feeling...* ; Sanjay Subrahmanyam, "Connected histories: notes towards the reconfiguration of early modern Eurasia," *Modern Asian Studies*, 31, 1997, pp. 735-62; and more in editorial by Sharmani P. Gabriel and Fernando Rosa, "Introduction: 'Lived cosmopolitanisms' in littoral Asia," *Cultural Dynamics*, 24 (2-3), 2012.
15. The ambiguities of the Migration Law of 2011 are several. The Kazakh Migration Law of August 2011 identified three key directions and objectives of migration. First, facilitating repatriation, settlement and integration of the oralman, denoting an ethno-national vision; second, maintenance of national security and prevention of illegal migration, reflecting a "securitisation" perspective; and third, management of internal migratory processes from rural to urban areas, particularly resettlement of citizens residing in ecologically depressed regions to other regions, which addresses issues of social welfare and equal distribution. The law also contains a quota for highly skilled foreign labour. The quota is miniscule. It was set at 66,300 in 2009 but then reduced to a third in 2011. The law is however silent about the status of CIS labour migrants who can enter the country legally under a visa free regime, indicating that the purpose of the visit is "personal" on the migration card. Such migrants are required to register within

five days, may only remain for the authorised period of stay and cannot work. An "illegal migrant," under Kazakh Migration Laws is simply defined as a person who has "violated the laws of the Republic of Kazakhstan pertaining to migration." A December 2013 law allows individual Kazakh citizens to hire foreign migrant workers with work permits. A complex web of personal connections, strategies and informal arrangements enable the migrants to acquire the relevant documentation to maintain their status as a "visitor" and keep their real status invisible to the law. Anita Sengupta, "The Migration State and Labour Migrants in Central Asia," *Interrogating Forced Migration*, CRG-MAKAIAS-ICSSR Workshop, March 16-21, 2015.

16. "Tsentr Evrazii," www.republika.kz, 5 Iuliya 2012 (July 5, 2012); "Astana. Retrospektiva," no. 73, *Subbota*, 26 Iuniya, 2010 goda (June 26, 2010). Astana has been promoted by the regime as the "geopolitical centre of Eurasia," an image that is inscribed in and through the city's symbolic and urban landscapes. Astana's geopolitical and nationalist rhetoric have been shaped by a number of factors: the environment, lived experience, the spectacle, the sport, the international presence and regional differentiation.

1. Competing Narratives

Multiple frames: Ethnicity and more

Kazakhstan defines itself simultaneously as *Kazakh*, i.e., the political entity of the Kazakh nation and its historical accomplishments, as *Kazakhstani*, i.e., as a multi-ethnic nation at the crossroads of the Eurasian continent and as *a transnational country* integrated into world trends. These transformations, though specific in each case, as Marlene Laruelle points out, also have shared trajectories.[1] In this patchwork, Kazakhstan is a unique case for various reasons: (a) it is the only Central Asian country to have the titular ethnic group, i.e., the Kazakhs, as a minority—a bare 39.7% of the total Kazakh population, while the rest of the population was distributed in disjointed clusters comprising the Russians (about 37%) and other European, Uzbek, Chinese, Dungan and Tatar minority nationalities; (b) its most sophisticated version of "friendship of peoples" or *Kazakhstani* nation that translated itself into the more popular Eurasian integration model; (c) its potential to "go global" and adapting to an architectural variety that is not only Asian but also typifies a modern international brand. It is the paradigm of Kazakhness that seems to be the most enduring and is evident through official declarations ever since the pronouncement of sovereignty (in 1990), independence (in 1991) and in President's Nazarbayev's speeches and books authored by him (*V potoke istorii,* in 1999).

What has been stressed repeatedly over time is the effort to legitimise Kazakhness by asserting the coexistence among representatives of the *ethnos* (a term that was in usage in the Soviet period). Kazakhness would be factored on both horizontal integration (among the entire ethnos) and vertical integration (between the state and its citizens). Symbolism was displayed through the state emblem that depicted the *shanyrak* (the circular opening at the top of the Kazakh *yurt* which is linked by the wooden poles or *uyuks* that in fact represent the nomadic Kazakhs whose home are the pristine, natural surroundings).[2] In official historiography, the Golden Man or the Scythian warrior has been cited frequently as a reminder of the country's heroic legacy. The ethno-national narrative in Kazakh cinema portrayed through films like *Nomad, Mustafa Shokai, Nebo Moevo Detsva* (*The Sky of My Childhood*), *Myn Bala* (*Warriors on the Steppe*) is dominant. Kazakhness is also displayed in the efforts to recreate the memory of *Bozok,* which according to archaeological data represents the old Kazakh nomad settlement on the outskirts of the new capital city Astana/Aqmola. Islamic motifs are blended into the new urban architecture. The *Bayterek*, situated on the left bank of the Ishim River, inspired by the country's folktale, symbolises the country's independence. Kazakhness of Kazakhstan is not a topic of the past. Rather it is about the country's visions for the future based on ideas of integration as intrinsic to Kazakh nomadic culture and tradition.

The Kazakh story revisited

What is also intrinsic to Kazakh tradition is steppe dynamics. In an earlier work of this author that dealt with "a Kazakh story,"[3] it was pointed out that research in the post-Soviet period reached out to new arenas of a steppe ecumene like environment and ecology. There was an attempt to combine the global discourse about nomadism with the Kazakhs' tribal culture. The use of the tribal discourse in scientific discourse, especially in natural sciences, has been a new aspect of the new historiography in Kazakhstan. Following their mentor Nurbulat Masanov, historians became exclusively concerned with the sphere of nomadic control, some also arguing about the satellite states that consolidated the *zhuz* structure.[4] Inherent to the steppe dynamics were not only nomadic traits of the Kazakhs, Kyrgyz and the Mongols inhabiting Semirechie region but also the mechanism of tribal order (a zhuz legacy), rejuvenation of nomad political organisation through judicial reforms during the regime of Tauke Khan (1689-1717), migratory patterns among Turkic groups after Mongol interference. How all that was affected by the imperial statutes of the nineteenth century was also considered. But primary attention was given to key issues of rupture—exercise of legality and control over collective rights (e.g., land) and individual rights (e.g., cattle). The diffused nature of the Kazakh voice became a key aspect of the new analysis. Dissent and rebellion in the nineteenth century and the revolts of 1916 after the "dramatic transformation" of the Kazakh economy as a cash belt, the genesis of a secular world view among educated Kazakhs, the origins of "imperial deputations" from Kazakhstan, the spread of alternative thinking among Kazakh Muslim intellectuals and the emergence of the movement for *Alash* (unity) and the significance of the Alash Orda movement (i.e., 1905-17) are some aspects of the new historical analysis.

Over time, research interest on other aspects of nomadic dispensation has unfolded though most of the discussions have primarily revolved round the aspect of political economy of nomadism. In the 1990s, a series of writings focused on other important aspects of steppe tradition. In 1998, *Nationalities Papers* published its special issue on Kazakhstan in which the Kazakh and non-Kazakh scholars shared their convictions about the khan's leadership qualities while participation in the will and the instruction of the *tengri* (sky) were important attributes of political authority. The wisdom of the *kagan* (khan), his ability to honour values gives him a special place in his tribe. The nomad leader is expected to be chivalrous, but more important is his political genius to perpetuate control of his tribe. Chingiz Khan was the trendsetter and the laws of succession and inheritance codified in his *yasa* (order) accounts for the durability of his regime. The power of union, demonstrated by the *qurultay* was another aspect of political tradition in the steppe. This also leads to introspection about other intricate patterns and inter-tribal relations, e.g., the Kazakhs' relations with members of a tribal confederation who inhabited the Dasht-i-Kipchak area. So, the Uzbek leanings of a Kazakh from Turkestan are as strong as the Uyghur or Usun legacy of a Kazakh residing in the Chinese borderland.[5] The rejuvenation of the three zhuzes and their tribal homes are other new aspects of the post-Soviet studies. Hilda Eitzen's study about the combination of genealogies among the Kazakhs with multiple affiliations to the Naiman, the Uzbek and the Nogai is an outstanding example of the new generation research. Another unique case study to prove this point is about the Nogai Horde lineage in western Kazakhstan, stretched between the rivers Emba and Yaik, which was conventionally regarded as Golden Horde territory.[6]

There were thus twists in tale and Soviet and post-Soviet Kazakh historiographies have dealt with episodic aspects of Kazakh history. There were different styles of writing and local histories of the region were interpreted differently. On the one hand there was a plethora of sentiments that merged on to a colonial setting. On the other hand, speculations about Kazakh-non-Kazakh (Chinese, Uyghurs, Mongols, Germans and Poles) relations have also grown over time. Relational patterns within the tribal structures were also discussed that gave a boost to the image of pastoral nomadism.

Nations and nationalities: Framed by ethnicity marker

Now such ideas of Kazakhness were completely overshadowed by genealogical claims of the great Kazakh nation. An ethnic state model suggests community of birth and native culture, associated with a form of biological or genealogical determinism. The Kazakh sociologist and historian Masanov used genealogy as a tool to describe Kazakh power structure. He "referred to a pervasive cult of seniority among the nomads, a cult that was produced by genealogical knowledge and memory (the ability to remember the *shezhire* [genealogy]) and revolved around demonstrating the position of one's segment in the historical chain of lineage in order to claim pre-eminence." Masanov's genealogical claims were reiterated by Hilda Eitzen who presents multiple registers of genealogy in Kazakh-Uzbek tribal confederation, some of which disappeared as the Kazakhs moved and migrated to new settlements since the fifteenth century.[7] The genealogies were fragile, some of them eclipsed but most of them were preserved because of the migration of the tribes. In assertions about Kazakhness, there is also reference to some of these tribal legacies reclaiming Turkic affiliations and identities that are common not only to Inner Asian tribal groups but extend up to the Near East and Europe. The ruptures within the tribal confederation did not signify an end to the tribal political tradition. Masanov's predecessor, S. E. Tolybekov, the dean of Soviet Union's Central Asian historiography, provided an insider's view of the development of Soviet sociology, taking immense pride in the effects of "modernisation" on Kazakh society and recounting milestones in the symbiotic relationship between a "semi-nomadic Kazakh society" and a "patriarchal settled one." Tolybekov noted that in the Kazakh nomadic system there was a combination of various traits. Every illiterate nomadic Kazakh, Tolybekov said, was, during the fifteenth–eighteenth centuries, simultaneously a shepherd and a soldier, an orator and a historian, a poet and a singer.[8]

Quite clearly, such fissures were not emphasised by the independent Kazakh state. Its singular focus was on the ethno-nationalist distinctiveness among the Kazakhs. This ethno-nationalist trajectory was established through symbolic events, public ceremonies and commemorations that openly celebrated "nation-ness." Now this brand of nationalism was more emphatic of an ethnic Kazakh identity rather than a more inclusive Kazakhstani identity. Billboards like "land of the Kazakhs" deified claims to primordial autochthony in the national territory of Kazakhstan in the post-independence period. Other ethnic groups were considered to be recipients of Kazakh hospitality. In post-independence Kazakhstan, this signalled ownership of the Land of the Kazakhs by the titular nationality, the Kazakhs that was reflected in the symbolism of the new state. Independence ushered in a period of Kazakisation including changes to street names, erection of new statues, a new flag, a new anthem, etc.

Now, this group mentality among ethnic groups due to privileging of one group over another has a negative implication. The argument against this ethnicity marker is that within Kazakhstan there are identities that are not bounded but are determined by heterogeneous affiliations. There could be an internal "Other" (like the *oralmans* who have been seeking repatriation ever since the Kazakh state announced return to Kazakh homeland for Kazakhs living abroad). All this has created reasoning about other identity markers like religiosity, adherence to linguistic orientations and cultural traditions. To overcome criticism of the Kazakisation drive, Nazarbayev emphasised a permissive environment, showcasing a sense of tolerance and endurance among the Kazakhs. The idea of repatriating *oralmany* (the 5 million odd Kazakh returnees spread over south Kazakhstan districts) and their integration based on Kazakh ethnicity has had a huge public mandate.

The fundamental concepts and terminology of ethnos, ethnicity, and ethnic relations took shape in Kazakhstan in the Soviet period on the basis of an all-Soviet Marxist-Leninist party ideology. According to the theoretical premises in Soviet historiography, there existed a strict arrangement of all ethnoses into nations, nationalities and so on, depending on the system of territorial-administrative order to which they belonged. What we have become aware of today is the Soviet imaginary of the state: the state was imagined to consist of many nations, which sometimes coincided with their national (titular) homeland. The Soviet state became operational through centrally-planned projects. Nations with fifteen titular nationalities possessed their own national-state formations: the so-called Union Republics. The majority of them gained union republic status in the 1920s and 1930s; the Baltic republics did so only in the pre-war period. Representatives of these fifteen nations on the territory within their state-administrative borders were designated titular nations. Besides union republics, there existed within their ranks autonomous republics, *krais, oblasts,* and *raions*. Representatives of ethnic groups, given the names of autonomous state formations, acquired the status of socialist nations. All other peoples who lacked statehood were usually termed "nationalities" (*narodnost*). The generic term "nation" referring to all ethnic groups having a union or autonomous republic signified all ethnic groups, rather than communities of citizens, as "nations."

There were different perceptions over the usage of the term "nationality." In the Soviet Union, "nationality" had two distinct meanings: one as a marker of citizenship (i.e., of an autonomous republic within the USSR) and another as a marker of ethnicity, which effectively became a "biological attribute" of an individual. These two meanings corresponded to a "dual conception" of national autonomy in the Soviet Union's 15 republics: (a) "belonging" to the titular nation and (b) as independent of territory.[9] The ordering of nationalities through the ethnic lens backfired in the aftermath of Soviet disintegration which let loose a series of "group identities." The group distinctiveness (as nomads and sedentary) hardly got the opportunity to project themselves at the "national" level (and the lapses are glaring in the entries in Soviet historiographies and encyclopaedias). The idea of linking an ethnic group to a territory was completely new to the entire Central Asian region—much of which was historically nomadic and forcibly settled by Russian imperial and Soviet regimes.

With the collapse of the Soviet Union, the "ideological" framing of categories of identity proved the futility of the ethnicity paradigm for describing the newly emerging geopolitical order.[10] While criticism about legitimisation of regimes through ethnic symbols is frequently noticed, it has to be acknowledged that an "over-ethnicised" reading of the collapse of the Soviet Union results in accepting the discourse of ethnopolitics at face value. Such a reading of the USSR's collapse also ignores the fact that there was very little popular mobilisation around ethnic/national identity in Central Asia. Actually, ethnic mobilisation was only pronounced in the Baltics and the Caucasus, but was relatively limited in Central Asia.

The ethnic paradox

In the first All Union Census of 1926 of the Soviet Union, ethnicity was singled out as a characteristic of self-identification which along with other criteria became entirely meaningless. The 1926 census recognised 194 nationalities, of which hardly 100 are remembered today. In the 1959 census documents, only 109 nationalities were recognised. Ethnologists questioned the arbitrary nature of the ethnic category.[11] As an ethnonym, the terms "Uzbek-Kazak" and "Kazak" were used interchangeably since the sixteenth century, roughly denoting not only the residual Uzbek settlements in Kazakh territory after a portion of Uzbek tribes, under Muhammad Shaibani Khan, relocated in Mawar al-Nahr but also a way of self-identification of the Kazakh people. Kasym Khan was considered to be the unifier of all Uzbek-Kazak tribes and historical sources have depicted the Kazakh way of life since his times: "We are inhabitants of the steppe; we have no rare or valuable possession or goods; our most valuable possession is our horses. Meat and the skin from it serve as our best food and clothing; our most enjoyable drink is their milk and what we prepare from it. We have no gardens or buildings on our land. Our place of recreation is the cattle pasture and the herding of horses. We go to the herds and take pleasure in the sight of horses." The Russian ethnologist N. A. Aristov noted that the Kazakhs "to a greater extent than all [other] Turkic nationalities preserved their cattle-raising and nomadic way of life ..." The basic means and mechanism of integration in the steppe region were through identification with the nomadic economy and the nomadic form of life. The first and most important question, therefore, that Kazakhs asked one another upon meeting is: "How is your herd doing?" So, what is being addressed more openly in the post-Soviet period is that the ethnic categorisation was superficial and arbitrary in nature. From the sixteenth century to the 1930s, Kazakhs never represented a consolidated ethnic group. This is plainly illustrated by a host of historical documents, which show that the Kazakhs were internally divided into different ethnic communities. The majority of the Kazakhs—the so-called *kara-siok* (black bone)—were members of a single, weakly integrated ethnic community, which cited its origins to the legendary hero Alash-khan. These were Kazakhs of the Elder, Middle, and Younger *zhuz*. Among the Kazakhs, the Alash ethnic community was most prominent but there were several less numerous, but much more influential non-ethnic groups: the Tore (descendants of Chingiz Khan), the *khozha* (descendants of Prophet Muhammad, his close associates, and other spiritual figures).

In the 1920s and 1930s, the economic and cultural term "Kazak" was gradually transformed into the ethnic category "Kazakh," i.e., a hypothetical category that never existed. When the Soviets constructed this homogenous ethnic category, the Kazakhs' group membership had a newer meaning—not defined exclusively by their nomadic activity, mode of enterprise or way of life, as it has been in the past, but in accordance with the official (Soviet) record provided in their passports, that had to be in agreement with their parents' ethnic affiliation. So, an arbitrary method of control and order was imposed and the ethnic identification through passport-control for the country's citizens, regardless of their own self-identification (*samoopredelenie*) or sense of identity (*samooshchushchenie*) became mandatory. The traditional principles of self-consciousness (*samosoznanie*) and self-identification (*samonazvanie*) were used interchangeably, and for the first time the terms denoted an ethnic category that was officially registered. So here was a system of obligatory categorisation enforced by passport norms that pitted individuals and groups against each other and that too in accordance with ethnic criteria and background. In Soviet times, ethnic affiliation was a convenient tool for determining an individual's success in life, prosperity, career advancement, etc. A hierarchical ordering of ethnic communities took place, based on territory and place of origin that essentially defined their rights, opportunities and authority enjoyed by their own representatives. Such positions of distinction created distinctive images in the public mind about the legitimate connection between an individual's success and his ethnic affiliation. By the same token, there existed a certain stereotypical image regarding the inappropriateness and illegitimacy of such claims if a person did not live in the territory of his titular ethnic group.

From the 1960s to the 1980s, there was this tendency in Kazakhstan towards the formation of a social stereotype that gave the Kazakhs a natural and legal right to have a social status in Kazakhstan: by having access to elite ranks and jobs as well as to higher education. The position of privilege also extended to their natural right for the advancement of values in the civil society and the right to defend their culture, language, tradition and historical lineage. So, the Soviet rhetoric of ethnic mobilisation allowed the ethnic Kazakhs to be masters in their own land—with a natural and privileged claim to self-identification or *samosoznanie* in Kazakhstan's territory.

In the 1990s, there has been a concerted effort of the Kazakh state to legitimise the notion of Kazakh rootedness through a policy called Kazakisation. The demographic variety of the Kazakh space and the diversity of nationalist groups necessitated serious rethinking. In order to address the perceived threat of controlling fractious groups and nationalities that itself became a liability in the early stages of the independence era. It became necessary to (a) homogenise or "Kazakhify" the country and (b) to try and negotiate with the "civic Kazakhstani identity" through a plethora of writings, the most prominent one being that of Eurasianism. Now, such a dual approach seemed rational and in the context of out-migration of ethnic Russians and

Germans as well as in-migration of Kazakh returnees from Mongolia and increasing tendency of mixed ethnicities to be identified as Kazakh. Now, the Kazakisation drive not only entailed the idealisation of the ideology of an ethnocratic state like Kazakhstan which adopted demagogic rhetoric about sovereignty, legislation regarding Kazakh as the state language, etc. A number of measures were taken to "nativise" governmental power structures, especially through measures that promoted the Kazakh language. Furthermore, the first article of the 1993 version of Kazakhstan's constitution declared that the state "is based on the 'the Kazakh people's statehood,' thus endorsing an ethnically based concept of the nation." The 1995 provisions signified that Kazakh patriotism was enshrined in the new constitution, but it also included a new formulation referring to Kazakhs as "the 'primordial' owners of their land."

All this had manifold impact on the demographic character of post-Soviet Kazakhstan as non-titular Kazakh minority nationalities either emigrated or immigrated in large numbers. The attraction of Kazakhstan was primarily for low-skilled workers from neighbouring countries while highly skilled persons tended to migrate to the Russian Federation or to countries outside the CIS. The main areas attracting foreign labour in Kazakhstan are: Almaty and Dzhambul regions (tobacco and vegetable plantations); South Kazakhstan (cotton and vegetables); Almaty, Astana and other major cities (construction, market and household workers); and West Kazakhstan (oil and gas, construction).[12] Evidence points to the presence of Uzbeks and Tajiks in construction work with Tajiks specifically seeking jobs in restaurant and catering business. The Chinese and the Kyrgyz migrants mostly indulge in small or part-time trade. Kyrgyz and Uzbeks are also active in cotton industry in the South of Kazakhstan. Nationals of CIS states, like all foreign citizens over the age of 16, must obtain a migration card at the border. Registration denoting places of residence must be completed within 5 days of arrival. They are entitled to visa-free entry to Kazakhstan and can reside, but not work, for up to six months. Coupled with the thriving informal economy in services, open air markets, farming and construction, this means that in practice CIS migrants have easy access to certain labour markets.

Work permits for foreign nationals are mandatory and the quotas of work permits tend to be illegible to the migrants. Citing Labour Codes (40 hours of work in a week) that were not strictly followed, respondents (mostly Uzbek) complained of exhaustion and overwork. While some employers were reported as being generous or fair with it, for others this was another means of profiting. These harsh conditions may have been impacting on health particularly among women. Such inappropriate work conditions lead to the obvious question—did the situation of migrants in Kazakhstan ever constitute "forced labour"? And does forced labour necessarily mean a measurement of severity of exploitation? The "exaction" of services seems to be a given premise of forced labour with factors that impinge on the independence of the worker concerned—with difficult conditions like "threats of penalty," "physical force" (like, abduction and physical confinement)—which happened mostly in the case of the Uzbeks. Besides physical coercion, the notion of consent becomes highly problematic. The workers often relented to difficult conditions—to serve the master till the end because of dearth of alternatives—such cases were quite common. "The universe of choices was extremely limited." Sometimes, the freedom of exit could not be judged in blanket terms—because there were subjective experiences of *unfreedom.*[13] Such trends were seen during the height of Kazakhstan's economic growth—i.e., during 2000-7—which attracted many migrants. Most of them were employed on the basis of informal networks—so the question of legality is involved here. The fact of the matter is that the Labour Code in Kazakhstan set a benchmark for migrants seeking work in Kazakhstan.

The role of the media in the re-ethnicisation drive ought to be mentioned here. Unofficial media reports about an ethnicised rubric were not few in number. Brawls and street fights in southern and southeastern Kazakhstan among Kazakhs and Kurds, Kazakhs and Uyghurs in 2006 and 2007 took ugly turns and newspapers like *Svoboda Slova* used provocative titles in their articles: "Uyghurs from Shelek: The Country is Yours, But the Land is Ours." Kazakhstan's media was the prime disseminator of interethnic issues in Kazakhstan. Studies point to reports in Kazakh newspapers and periodicals with ethnic content and assessments on ethnic lines.[14] Whether it is Kazakh newspapers, or Kazakh print media or Kazakh media outlets—all seem to promote Kazakh language publications. Minority status of ethnic groups depended on the use of the language: surveys of 2006 point to Kazakhs as passive Russian speakers—(but my own experience in Kazakhstan is that most Kazakhs spoke Russian very well). But it is the newsprint circulation that has made a marked difference: popular Kazakh-language newspapers like *Zhas alash, Zhas Qazaq, Ana Tili, Turkestan, Qazaqstan Zaman* have a wider circulation compared to *Vremya* (the Russian language newspaper).[15] The non-Kazakh discrimination was less in rural areas compared to urban areas. Uncertainties of employment have been reported in Ust Kamenogorsk while slackness in university admissions and promotions to prestigious positions were reported in areas like Uralsk, Kyzyl Orda and Karaganda.[16] Attitudinal problems marred relations in the oblasts of Atyrauskaia, Almatinskaia and Yuzhno-Kazakhstankaia. Intolerance towards labour migrants and out-migrants was also reported. Despite the large numbers of anecdotal reports, there is little data on the situation of migrant workers in Kazakhstan.

Kazakh Yeli: Re-ethnicisation

The discourse about re-ethnicization has opened up a can of worms. And this time the emphasis is on renaming the entire ethno-territorial unit called Kazakhstan. In an open decree, the President expressed his desire to rename his country *Kazak Yeli* (Kazakh People), dropping the "stan" suffix synonymous with obscurity, human rights abuses, post-Soviet corruption. His speech on the subject is described as an effort to erase bad memories of being bracketed with other "stan"-countries.

> In our country's name, there is this "stan" ending which other Central Asian nations have as well. But, for instance, foreigners show interest in Mongolia, whose population is just two million people, but whose name lacks the "stan" ending. Probably, we ought to consider with time the issue of adopting Kazak Yeli as the name of our country, but before that, we definitely need to discuss this with the people.[17]

Such random thoughts were baffling for both the older and younger generations of Kazakhs: they discussed alternative names in the public domain that further pointed to the lack of seriousness in the nationwide debate about *Kazakh Yeli*. These were *Kazakhapalooza*, *The United Federation of Kazakhs*, *The Wonderful Land of Kaz*, *Kazaguay*, *Kazachusetts* and the fantasised concept of a dream project: *Nursultopia*. The renaming issue became a joke:

> Where are you from?
>
> —From Kazak Yeli.
>
> Where is it???
>
> —In Kazakhstan.[18]

Humour aside, the renaming proposal witnessed mixed responses from the common man. In Radio Free Europe's programme on "public discussion" that was endorsed by Nazarbayev, people reacted by saying that there was every need to dump "stan" but did not think *Kazak Yeli* was the alternative to that. The objection of a Russian-speaking citizen to *Kazak Yeli* concept was that it tended to generate the feeling of hegemony of one nationality in this multinational Central Asian state.

A whole range of debates has emerged since the official pronouncement of renaming of an ethno-territorial unit called Kazakhstan. Mostly, support for the change has come from nationalists who see it as an opportunity of breaking free from Soviet memories. Others argue against the relevance of replacing the suffix "stan" with "yeli." From the point of view of semantics, the official discourse has been denounced by experts. For them, *el* is a stand-alone noun in modern Kazakh. *El* has changed meaning over time and certainly is, like -stan, a word that existed long before one could say that there were only Kazakhs in the land of the Kazakhs. *El* occurs in the Orkhon inscriptions—and the translation of that word has received scholarly attention and there seems to be a consensus, according to the *Encyclopaedia of Islam*, about the term as equivalent to the modern English variant of "empire." In that sense, people are assumed to be unified under the rule of a leader, in this case a *kagan*. However, there is also the sticky point that the same word also meant "peace," from which comes the word *ilchi*, or *elshi* in Kazakh—ambassador, in the sense of "bringer of peace," "peace-maker." It should be clear, then, that because the word has such a long history, its meaning has changed over time.

One can consider a larger issue here—the struggles of the people—for which the people need to be classified as a unified category: that is, as a nation, state, people, folk and country. Attempts to have one-to-one translations of these words in Kazakh would fail, partly because there is a serious amount of history involved in each of these terms. In the local usage, there are equivalent terms in Kazakh denoting an administrative system that was replaced in the nineteenth century by the Tsarist administrative system. Now, this erasure of Kazakh history has been continually criticised by Kazakh nationalist historians. This pre-colonial administrative apparatus of a *kagan* or a ruler, however incapable it may have been as a military force vis-à-vis the Cossacks, did preserve a certain way of life and also allowed a vast steppe territory to assert a certain degree of confederative status. That status was subordinated to the Russian colonial order. Perhaps even without this history of replacing one administrative set-up by another one, one would still find it difficult to differentiate Kazakh *khalk/khalyk* from *ult*, *el* from *ulus*. In southern Kazakhstan there were sarcastic comments among Kazakhs like "Which *el* are you from?" The answer to this is identification would be in accordance with the clan belonging—i.e., horde/orda signifying differences between different tribal orders: Orta Zhuz, Naiman and Sadyr.[19]

People reacting overly to the official pronouncement have tried to suggest that even though it is fair to argue that there is a problematic of the term "Kazakhstan" because it implies a homogenous Kazakh population, it does not seem fair and acceptable that *Kazakh Yeli* is an improvement on that. Neither can "Kazakh Nation" be a good translation of the term *Kazakh Yeli*.

One comment on the social networking site *Facebook* read as follows: "The situation of the people will not change for the better by renaming the state. *There are more important issues* to improve the welfare of the people and they must be addressed.[20] (Here, one might cite another unpleasant experience for the average Kazakhstani—i.e., devaluation of the *tenge* announced by the Central Bank on February 11 by 19%. This resulted in countrywide reaction out of fear of inflation and decline in standards of living in the country. People started withdrawing the money they had invested in the Bank. Small protests against the devaluation have resulted in arrests. The countrywide protests and demonstrations were of every hue and shade.)[21] Other social media users derided the idea by saying they were born in the Kazakh SSR and were now living in Kazakhstan and would die in a country called *Kazakh Yeli*.

Opinions soon turned in favour of the President's will. Dosym Satpayev, the political analyst associated with Risks' Group, said that this was a fair opinion given the fact that analysts abroad hardly take into consideration the political differences among the five "stans" of Central Asia. Moreover, the Kazakh Yeli proposal needs to be seen in the broader context of the variety of proposals about connecting people and spaces of Central Asia and South Asia. (The US Greater Central Asia initiative was as significant as the UNESCO projects about shared histories and shared cultures of Central Asia.) Distinct from these initiatives was the "the Kazakh way" or "the Nazarbayev Way" portrayed in the Kazakh official website *Ak Orda* as well as in the President's official biography. These paths or ways do speak a lot about the political and diplomatic intention behind such decisions. That the Kazakh path was unique would be reflected in the unique decision of renaming the country.[22]

But renaming the country would be a costly exercise and would involve a burden on the National Fund. The taxpayer's money will be at stake. Also, earlier decisions about making Kazakhstan an international brand will lack relevance henceforth—meaning the money that was spent then would now appear wasted. However, since public opinion is involved here, the realistic feeling is that regime will exercise caution and not hasten the process.

Also, some do not consider this to be a unique decree. The reason for this is that the renaming process has been going on for quite some time. Between 1991 and 2005, three oblasts, 12 cities, 53 districts and 957 small settlements in Kazakhstan were renamed.[23] For example, besides Alma Ata that was renamed as Almaty, Guriyev was renamed as Atyrau and Shevchenko was renamed as Aktau. Astana had name changes in the past as well as in the present: Akmolinsk and Tselinograd (during Soviet times) to be followed by Aqmola and Astana (after independence). Semipalatinsk had a shorter name Semei and Ust Kamenogorsk became Oskemen, Aktyubinsk became Aktobe. Spellings also differed in some "cases"—e.g., Kustanai became Kostanai. So, if random selection of Kazakh names is the argument of critics here, one could say that there have been precedents of rebranding and the *Kazakh Yeli* debate is just a continuation of that trend.

But in recent times, there has been a reversal in official pronouncements. For the first time the Presidency has acknowledged the challenges for which he counts on support for his pet projects *Mangilik Yel* (Eternal Nation) and *Nurly Kosh* (Sunny Path). In a novel attempt to restore the past, the *Mangilik Yel* tribal union of Uzbek Sultans Kerey and Zhanibek who walked out of Sultan Abul Khair Shaibanid's stronghold in the Dasht-i-Kipchak area during 1460s-1470s and rendered support to their "rebellious cousins" (the Kazakhs) is being recognised as a milestone event that united the fractured Kazakh family. On the eve of the 550th anniversary of Kazakh statehood, the Kazakh regime proudly declares an Uzbek-Kazakh tribal combination in the Kazakh family of nations. Talks are centred round Uzbek Naimans as "compatriots" which is a way of bridging differences among nomad cousins in the past.[24] The confidence of the government as a consistent and persistent player in the CIS region received a jolt for the first time due to the turn of events in Ukraine and its immediate impact on the partnership deals that Kazakhstan committed itself to. The tables are turning in favour of the Russian roulette, once again. Nazarbayev's Eurasianist ideal is losing popularity, and so is the Eurasian Economic Union. Speculations are gaining ground about the need to improve the mandate for governance through snap presidential polls that are scheduled for April 28, 2015. There are also fears of social rupture. The economy's failing strength (unlike the first 15 years of Nazarbayev's regime) is a source of worry both for the government and the people. The choice of the government to champion the cause of the Eurasian Economic Union has proved to be an economic curse as cheap Russian goods are putting the Kazakh domestic economy into stress. Appliances, electronics, automobiles are less costly in Russia and most Kazakhs have chosen the wiser option. The Kazakh *tenge* is more or less pegged to the Russian rouble. But the sudden devaluation in February 2014 by 19% has led to aftershocks which neither the Kazakh banks nor the people can handle. A year later, the Kazakh government has announced plans to "de-dollarise" the economy by urging citizens to convert dollars to *tenge* and to encourage holding savings in *tenge*.[25] Given the inconvertibility of the *tenge,* the people have to act rationally.

The Kazakh government is continuing to woo foreign investors, especially the western ones through "reforms." Astana has already dropped visa requirements for many foreign citizens doing business in Kazakhstan and drafted a programme to compensate foreign investors up to 30 per cent of their investment and up to 10 years in corporate tax breaks. More draft laws to attract investment include creating free economic zones, simplifying procedures for foreigners and repealing quotas on Kazakhs working on foreign projects.[26] Foreign observers are already calling this early poll to be one last chance for Nazarbayev.[27]

The other pole: Cosmopolitanism in Kazakhstan

Cosmopolitanism, extremely attractive to an international audience, is often posited as the opposite pole of ethno-nationalism in Kazakhstan. Cosmopolitanism is often labelled as "cosmopolitan consumerism," whereby the ability of Kazakhstan, with its large market potential, to influence people's attitudes and purchase behaviour also has an effect on consumer willingness to buy domestic and foreign goods in Kazakhstan and therefore also affects its integration into world economy.[28] States like Kazakhstan are being advertised as "brand states," the success of which depends to a large extent on trust and customer satisfaction. So, here we are talking about the state's personality and the preference is increasingly about Kazakhstan's global image as an oil-rich country which can easily counter other rising giants like China and Vietnam that have been looking for an entry into Kazakhstan's oilfields since the late 1990s. An unusual method of "joining hands" with Chinese technocrats has unleashed a series of collaborative oil projects in which both China and Kazakhstan nurture ambitions of development of resources. This brand named Kazakhstan has a completely different take on the management of her resources—and this makes her collaborative stance towards her eastern neighbours more appealing and attractive.

Some observers have made this point amply clear. Konstantin Syroezhkin, chief researcher at Kazakhstan Institute for Strategic Studies pointed out that the Chinese enterprises have supported the political establishment in Kazakhstan and elsewhere in Central Asia. To facilitate a dynamic regional economy, the only thing that Kazakhstan needs to do, according to him, is to guarantee that China's presence should be in favour of socio-economic development of Central Asia.[29] Several blog posts have asserted about China's money making the big difference in Central Asia. Grigori Marchenko, the head of Kazakhstan's Central Bank remarked that "Kazakhstan's economic elite increasingly looks to Beijing (and others in Asia) because, well, 'that's where the money is.'"[30]

Broadly speaking, the cosmopolitans are an internationalist group that comprises a wide spectrum of intellectuals in the political, cultural and economic spheres. Most of the cosmopolitans belong to what may be loosely called "the new sector" in Kazakhstan, and have carved a niche in the economy and politics of Kazakhstan. They fill up positions in the NGOs, research centres, private universities, opposition parties, local branches of international governmental and non-governmental organisations that have mushroomed in the cityscape of Kazakhstan. They act like local extensions of various international lobbies in Kazakhstan. Kazakhstan's internal policy brings tangible assets and advantages for its individuals while its external policy showcases an international image that brings pride to its citizens. Since its independence, Kazakhstan became the role model for the CIS by getting access into the WTO, obtaining chairmanship of OSCE, thriving on big business with the exponential increase of FDIs, showcasing the Bolashak educational programme and international scholarship of Nazarbayev University for training young professionals which promoted the brand name called Kazakhstan.

This brand of cosmopolitanism is rooted in the intellectual tradition in Kazakhstan that shared the Eurasianist ideology of cultural adaptation. In Kazakhstan, the creative intelligentsia spearheaded by the orientalist Chokan Valikhanov (1835-65) whose records of Kashgaria are legendary, Abay Kunanbaev (1845-1904), the founder of Kazakh literary language, poets Dzhambul Dzhabayev and Olzhas Suleimanov are considered to be the precursors of cosmopolitanism in Kazakhstan. Eurasia does not only designate a geographical area but also a cultural and civilisational entity and implies the coexistence of Slavic and Turkic communities. Historically speaking, the Kazakh steppe lies at the intersection of the moral and philosophical streams of European and Asian civilisations. In the Russian context, too, Eurasianism envisages a reaffirmation of Russia's Asiatic linkages. So, in multiple intellectual hypotheses, there seems to be a convergence of Kazakh and Russian ideals and interpretations of Eurasianism. In post-Soviet appraisals of Kazakh history,[31] attention is pivoted on independent thinking that flourished in Omsk and other parts of northern and western Kazakhstan, the aristocratic background and career-profile of ideologues and activists who were trained by the Russian government as educators or service personnel and worked within the tsarist apparatus. There are also reflections about an earlier generation of conscientious Kazakhs who because of a Russian environment in Omsk where they were trained as military officers were motivated to meet the challenges of a naturally Kazakh environment. The "unusual partnership" between the Ministry of Education represented by N. I. Ilminskii and the schools imparting exclusive Kazakh education also produced a generation of students who were receptive to instructions of their masters.[32] It is this relationship of accommodation between Russia and her imperial subjects that is the major theme of the discourse about integrative mechanisms in the educational centres. The Kazakh intellectual sphere opens with the life and times of the first modern Kazakh intellectual, Chokan Valikhanovich Valikhanov (Shoqan Walikhanov in Kazakh, 1835-65). He was a scholar-enlightener whose family background and military training (in the cadet corps of Omsk) brought him into close contact with notable orientalists like G. N. Potanin, outstanding Russian novelists like Dostoevsky (who encouraged him to write about the Kazakh people and interpret the steppe for Russia) and military personnel of the Siberian Line Cossack army that served the Western Siberian Governor Generalate which was responsible for organising scientific expeditions to regions that were opening up as sensitive hotspots of Chinese or Eastern Turkestan. In the course of a brief life span he rose to prominence from his Khan family[33] to the highest echelons of the Russian scholarly community. In the words of his biographer, Kermit McKenzie, Valikhanov believed that Russia was the most important conveyor of education and progress. Like Ibrahim Altynsaryn and Abay Kunanbaev, Valikhanov was an unwavering advocate of friendship between the Russian and Kazakh people. Valikhanov's training in Omsk was a unique experience not only for him but also for his mentors who were impressed by Valikhanov as "an interesting subject" with passionate interest in Kazakh folklore. Like European intellectuals of the early nineteenth century, prominent sections of the Kazakh elite became interested in a phenomenon of what is called "the discovery of the people." Omsk was a major centre of archival literature about the steppe. Valikhanov was sufficiently trained in the archives of the Siberian administration centred in Omsk and it was here that he deepened his knowledge about the farthest outposts of Central Asia in the east. His knowledge of the Chagatai language (spoken by Turkic business families) helped him in his imperial mission to Eastern Turkestan in the 1850s where he travelled as a Marghelani merchant. Valikhanov became the illustrious explorer in service of the frontier administration of the Tsarist government in western Siberia and the suburbs of Omsk. Valikhanov became a prominent name in the annals of Imperial Russian Geographical Society (IRGO).

Memories of Valikhanov as a scholar-enlightener continue to exist among the present generation of Kazakhs, the cosmopolitan elite in particular that perceives Russia as the harbinger of modernisation. Anatoly Fyodorovich, an old Party official in Kostanai and Pavlodar, in the course of a conversation with Bhavna Dave, recounts memories of such transformation:

> Urbanisation among the Kazakhs became tantamount to their Russification. The Kazakh and Kyrgyz steppe domain was overflowing with Russian settler towns from late eighteenth century onwards (*ukreplenye punkty* or fortresses), military outposts and administrative centres filled with Cossack military battalions and populated almost entirely by traders and civilians (as in Semey, Ust Kamenogorsk,/Oskemen, Vernyi/Alma Ata/Almaty)—some of which became transformed to *rabochie posel'ki*

> (workers' settlements) in the 1920s (with the loss of cities like Orenburg to Russia and Tashkent to Uzbekistan due to national territorial delimitation). Most of them (under the territorial rearrangements of 1924, 1925, 1927 and 1936) were inducted into the Kazakh ASSR and Kazakh Soviet Socialist Republic as major mining and industrial towns of Temirtau, Karaganda, Shevchenko/Aktau, Mangyshlak/Mangistau that became home to wartime settlements with *gulags* that rendered an image of isolation to a rapidly industrialised Soviet Kazakhstan. The First Five Year Plan and the Turksib railroad in 1928 was the beginning of the dramatic transformation of a nomadic space to an industrial environment. The virgin lands' campaign that was launched in 1954 transformed northern and eastern Kazakhstan (that were inundated with Russian workers from the European parts of the Soviet Union) into Russian-speaking settler regions (*pereselencheskii raiony*) that bore the names of Slavic cities, such as "Moskovskii," "Leningradskii," "Kievskii," "Minskii," "Simferopolskii," "Voronezhskii," "Dnepropetrovskii," "Yaroslavskii," in celebration of the spirit of internationalism related to Kazakhstan's development. European settlers were credited with the setting up all these industrial towns while local Kazakhs, as gracious hosts remained in the background.

Kazakh sociologist and historian Nurbulat Masanov, confirms such mentality of closeness in Kazakhstan—"Kazakhstan ne imeyet budutshego bez Rossii"—(Kazakhstan won't be able to do without Russia).[34]

The Russophone urban clusters in the dispersed Kazakh territories had little ethnic ties with the indigenous people of the neighbouring *auls*. In the late 1950s, Almaty was virtually a Russian city. The titular nationality, the Kazakhs, constituted only about 10 per cent of the total inhabitants. The old residents of Almaty described it as completely "European" in its architectural layout, ethnic composition, dress code and language repertoire—at least up to the 1990s. The sense of alienation was very much evident. As one informant said to Dave: "Almaty is the capital of the Kazakhs, home to the Russians, and a guesthouse for the Uyghurs. In Almaty, the migrants from the *auls* tended to congregate initially in the suburbs (*mikroraiony*), rather than in the city centre. While they intermingled with the Russophone urban milieu, the Kazakh migrants from the *aul* found it difficult to be *integrated* in those surroundings. In trying to migrate to the capital city, knowledge of Russian was essential." Dave's respondent Maira Sharipova, a resident of Zhambyl found it very difficult to socialise in a *kollektiv* that raised toast to friendship of the people of the Soviet Union/international friendship. Search of better conditions, material benefits were driving migrants from the auls to the cities in the 1960s. Many more Almaty narratives of the time recount this *mankurt* identity among the Kazakhs. In the 1990s, Maira, a 35-year biologist talks about her experience to Dave:

> I came to Almaty with my mother in 1957 from our native *aul* in Zhambyl. I was six and knew not a word of Russian. My mother was a single parent. Relatives helped us to move to Almaty, found a place for us to stay and used their connections to find her a job in order to get a *propiska* (residence permit). I was sent to a Russian school—there were no Kazakh schools in Almaty. I was the only Kazakh in a class of all Russians. I used to cry upon coming home because everyone in the class made fun of me … Today I speak as good Russian as any … but in the process was forced to *forget* my own language …[35]

Maira's story illustrates the experience of a young Kazakh who at the height of Soviet internationalism, adjusted in a Russophone urban milieu with the result that he forgot his mother tongue, i.e., Kazakh. This narrative might evoke sympathy to an outsider—but the fact of the matter is that fate has not been unkind to her because of the choice she or her family made—to migrate from the *aul* to the city. A Soviet misfortune was not the only story—there was also a lot of promise for Kazakh nomads—the bright future of Soviet socialism.

Dave experienced such polarised views in Almaty in the Kazakh Academy of Sciences in the early 1990s. Akseleu Seidembekov, the scholar whom Dave interviewed, spoke about *mankurtzitsiia* of nations—which was in stark contrast to the oft-repeated concept of Soviet community of nations. *Mankurt* is a widely used metaphor to convey loss of ethnic identity and one's own vernacular language—and the word has become synonymous with being Russified. It refers to a mythical character in a Chingiz Aitmatov novel—a character who could not remember his ancestry and preferred an isolated life devoid of painful memories of a past he did not wish to recollect. The scholar used the word to denote de-ethnicisation, cultural amnesia, the loss of group solidarity symbolised by the Kazakh *aul*, the demise of rich oral tradition of the nomads and above all, erasure of genealogy and memory which were so central to nomadic identity. Aitmatov, the celebrated writer of Soviet internationalism, regretted that his novel could incite such introvert views. The conflicting perspectives among the intelligentsia indicate the fallout of pervasive sovietisation of Kazakh social life. Urban Russian-speaking Kazakhs were part and parcel of this sovietisation process. The urbanising strata that had command over the Russian language which served as a means for survival and as a catalyst for personal and collective empowerment spoke at length about their experiences and expectations in that international environment.[36] The Russian presence in urban Kazakhstan—especially in North Kazakhstan is pretty obvious. In the early 1990s, the celebration of republicanism translated into Kazakh activism and there was a lot of open talk about forced settlement, collectivisation, purges of the Kazakh intelligentsia under Stalin, etc. Linguistic Russification of the Kazakhs was irreversible but the Kazakh academia sought to redeem the present by introducing certain norms that would restore Kazakhness to the society—by designating Kazakh as the state language, affirming titular nationality of the Kazakhs and so on. Such efforts brought to light "the lack of language environment"—and the mandate for Kazakh language was also voiced by new generation scholars like Anna Yessengalieva of Lev Gumilev Eurasian National University. The emphasis was on a concerted language policy. Language as a means of expression of ideas and the fact that there was a disparity in statistics regarding the national language speakers (i.e., Kazakh) and a linguistic nationality in Kazakhstan indicates that the time had come for a reassessment. An interethnic dialogue between Kazakh and Russian was welcomed, but that was for diplomatic exchanges and goodwill visits. What was needed was a language policy that would be sensitive to the Kazakh nationality that spoke the Kazakh language. And in nationality terms, the demography of Kazakh language was considered important. Scholars were aware of the insignificant volume of high school teaching in the Kazakh language. To redeem the situation, the renewed role of Kazakh language in such spheres as legislation, science, culture, mass media was emphasised.[37]

Therefore, there are different perceptions of ethnicity—as a trait and a marker of identity that integrates or ignores other ethnicities and non-titular nationalities. With transition, long-time fears and tensions among diverse ethnic groups in Kazakhstan, including the Russians have resurfaced. Handling such diverse sentiments was one of Nazarbayev's prime tasks in the first years of Kazakhstan's nationhood. His personal experience as a steelworker in Karaganda *magnitka* which was an environment of diverse ethnic groups and had yet shown tolerance to immigrant families like that of Nazarbayev's father had given him the ability to prioritise the Kazakh homeland over and above other priorities of radical ethno-nationalist or ultranationalist caucus groups. These caucus groups popularised blasphemous ideas as "the Russian lands in Northern Kazakhstan" (an idea aggressively pursued by Zhirinovsky) or the "creation of a new Soviet Union" with the amalgamation of Northern Kazakhstan along with parts of Russia, Ukraine and Belarus (a concept that was launched by Alexander Solzhenitsyn). Nazarbayev warded off "those pseudo-patriots" with his rebukes as "ethnic this" and "ethnic that"[38] and promoted his idea about Kazakhstan as one big family. His cautionary tale about a nomad family that wanted to protect its hearth reflects the sensibilities of a Kazakh leader who lived and was trained in the cosmopolitan milieu of his times.

Cosmopolitan debates: Capital transfer from Almaty to Astana

Capital shift from Almaty to Aqmola has been described as a phenomenon—ever since the dramatic announcement by President Nazarbayev on December 10, 1997 following a presidential decree he had signed in 1995. The move, according to observers, was nothing extraordinary because it seems to be a rational move in the context of nation building. "Each example has its own story, though none is mysterious and beyond persuasive interpretation."[39] For bystanders (especially western ones), there were pros and cons for the capital shift:

> For a bona fide, independent Kazakhstan (whose rich natural resources lie further westward), Alma Ata—quickly renamed Almaty in accordance with ethnic nationalist demands—proved to be in the wrong place. If the diverse ethnic population was to be ruled effectively, a capital had to be found closer to the economic and ethno-demographic centres of the Kazak state. With the choice of Aqmola (the former Tselinograd) a political statement was made by the President and those who supported the move. But what precisely was it? How should or can one interpret the decision to leave the relatively modern metropolis of Almaty for an obscure, backwater town? And, not incidentally, how was one to pay for its transformation into a functional modern capital, including an international airport?[40]

The capital change debate, promoted by political elites, creates an impression of the state as an authoritative actor. At the same time, citizens also participate in that discourse and, in so doing, confirm their role in the society. Kazakhstan's scheme of change of capital (which began as Nazarbayev's vision in 1994) is the major theme of debates centred round state-building in post-Soviet Kazakhstan and offers the ideal ground of discussions among bureaucrats and ordinary citizens. Relocating capitals—from the purely symbolic to the geostrategic—is not uncommon. Each example of capital shift has its own story. It seems to be a rational move in the context of nation building. That Kazakhstan joins the ranks of nations that have at one time or another relocated their capital should, therefore, be taken as an example that this was sought as a long-term opportunity by its authoritarian leader to assert power. As per official rhetoric, it was not helpful for independent Kazakhstan to govern from a regional capital, Alma Ata or Almaty that was situated in the southeastern-most corner of a vast territory like Kazakhstan. For independent Kazakhstan (whose rich natural resources lie further westward), Almaty was at a disadvantage. From the point of view of the diverse ethnic population of Kazakhstan, a capital with wider economic opportunities and closer to the ethno-demographic centres of Kazakhstan made practical sense. From that perspective, Aqmola (formerly Tselinograd and now Astana) was a better choice. But even then the question that arises here is how people who were identified with Vernyi/Alma Ata/Almaty over generations could think of leaving a metropolis with a rich history and intellectual heritage for an obscure, backwater town? Also, an inevitable question was the enormity of expenses for making a capital modern and functional. However, closer inspection reveals that there were several plausible reasons, both political and non-political, that justified the search for a new capital: Almaty has become overpopulated, with housing problems and almost no scope for demographic expansion on account of the narrow Ferghana Valley. The congested nature of the Ferghana valley in turn, has led to apathy regarding several environmental problems which have lessened Almaty's attraction as a city. So, due to the sheer requirement of living space, a capital shift was considered to be potentially useful. Aqmola, because of its unlimited steppe land, despite its unfriendly climate was projected to have a better future, especially for the Kazakhs. According to the 1989 census, Aqmola's population comprised 60% ethnic Russians and 27% ethnic Kazakhs. With the out-migration of Russians, it was anticipated that Kazakhs will have an advantage in Aqmola's government structure. The reason for this was the demographic ratio: the zero growth of Russian aging population vis-à-vis the larger fertility rate of much younger Kazakhs increased hopes about Aqmola's small but growing Kazakh majority—which in a decade will be true for the rest of Kazakhstan. So, here was the new opportunity for the Kazakh state—to bring the Kazakh population closer to the Russian-population centre signified closer ties with Russians (who were on the lookout for economic opportunities in a resource-rich Kazakhstan than in a fractured Russian Federation. Experts thought that this was a master stroke of Nazarbayev to dilute a Russian breakaway faction (like the Cossack LAD). So, by making a public commitment to a multinational state, Nazarbayev was playing his cards safely. The capital shift would ensure an ethnic balance of power and the Kazakhs empowered with more and more measures like the language law that gave Kazakh speakers a clear edge over Russian-speakers. Priorities of oil route and gas route gave the Kazakhs a global vision—that made the knowledge of Russian less important than the knowledge of English. The Kazakh authorities saw the opportunity of making Aqmola the new regional centre and the showpiece of what turns out to be a power game. The selection of Aqmola is a calculated move with a desire for positive results for the ruling elite.

The question that is often asked—why was the decision to replace Almaty as capital with Astana? Lovelier of the two, Almaty's residents felt the choice was unfair. But the Soviet city Tselinograd was the chosen one to become Aqmola and subsequently the new capital Astana because it seemed to be best suited for all architectural designs and innovations given the vast expanse of the steppe. Verniy renamed as Alma Ata and subsequently Almaty continued to be the choice among residents who belonged to various nationalities and having lived over generations gave the place its composite character. Also, Almaty's financial status was safe by Central Asian and CIS standards. But the idea of the government was to compete and reach higher standards. Kazakhstan was aspiring for an international status and Astana seems to have generated a lot of hope among the noveau riche and the business community. The 1997 Master Plan of the Japanese architect Kurokawa was approved as the blueprint for the city's development as the new capital.

There may have been other issues that worked in favour of the new location—was it not because of the desire to overcome the fringe status of the Kazakh capital and also to revive the steppe profile of Kazakhstan focusing on provincial centres in the north that were also close to Russian provincial hubs like Omsk and Orenburg? Another implication was that the new capital would symbolise a departure from Soviet legacy—and the city would have a new urban look and would become the face of the new government of the republic of Kazakhstan. The government used the Soviet rhetoric of raising a garden-city (*gorod sad*) in the midst of the steppe—but it was soon realised that in a post-Soviet set-up, it would be a futile exercise. The lavishness of the project was criticised—but the goal was to build an "exemplary centre" and give the citizens a feel of social change, order and rebuild on motivation of development and progress. A newly built Astana, according to Kurokawa's plan, was to incorporate into itself nature, history and even the region's national nomadic traditions. A symbiosis could be created between city and nature, tradition and modernity, and also between old city on the right bank of the Ishim River and the new city on the left bank of the river. The reconceptualisation of Astana as a river city was very appealing—because the river had been the centre of life in the town. There were parks, beaches, and public facilities on both sides of the river. There were precedents of development in the Soviet period—in the 1962 Soviet Master Plan of Tselinograd, the territory around the river was labelled as a recreation zone (*zona otdykha*) which amounted to an open space and natural park on the edge of the city separate from the residential zone. So, like all other socialist cities, Astana in its previous avatar had Ishim River at the centre and residential neighbourhoods all around—and large-scale development would cater to these neighbourhoods. A buffer green zone (an economic corridor) would be the source of sustenance for the city and water for the greenery around would be brought in by canals from the Ishim River—so a symbiosis between nature and development was also the essence of urban development of Nazarbayev's Astana. Like all socialist cities Tselinograd/Akmola had a centre with rings around it. The general tendency was to decentralise and move away from the central core city. The decentralisation of cities and spread of development into the urban periphery is a phenomenon seen across the world.[41]

For Astana, these city rings would actually become bigger and wider. Astana's old and new inhabitants were expected to instil life and make it a living city. But living in such a "Disneyesque" city must be a peculiar experience.[42] Such criticism is very common among visitors: "the images depict a Kazakh Disneyland, but what they fail to show is a sense of proportionality and good taste." In fact, megalomania is the name of the game in Astana. Local opposition press (*zonakz.net*) referred to the architecture in Astana as mindless borrowing from the west (Louvre in Paris) and also Turkey: "Where is the uniqueness … What is innovation in Astana?" And then the sarcastic conclusion: "It is all there … tinted glass windows, Turkish tiles and the blue domes of Samarkand"—referring to the dome of the Presidential Palace (*Ak Orda*). The Millennium Alley—the Nourzhoul Boulevard stretching from Ak Orda to Khan Shatyr Mega Shopping Complex and Entertainment Zone produces a sense of disorder that goes against Kazakhs' cultural sensibilities. Also, what was the need to have an egg-shaped National Archive? (also looking like an inverted submarine!). Where was the sense in having two glittering cylindrical buildings that house the government offices? The inappropriateness of Astana cityscape—spectacular but lacking taste is a criticism that is quite common among visitors. The expanse of the steppe stretching out in all directions is the logic behind megacity planning but the fact that the Ishim waterfront is shrinking in size or that the view of the steppe from the residential buildings has been blocked by the Presidential palace hardly makes the city useful for the public. The extreme weather conditions also reduce the attraction of the city after the first visit.[43]

However it is the construction narrative that survives the test of strength. The outcomes of the "breakthrough" brought about by capital relocation are repeatedly enforced on the people's minds. Nazarbayev was spreading the message about Astana as the heart of Eurasia:

> The capital relocation became a turning point … Nowadays Astana is becoming a symbol of the rise of the state … Ideas of patriotism and civic virtue (*grazhdanstvennost'*) receive their content precisely owing to the example of the construction of this city. Thousands of young boys and girls go to the capital in quest for opportunity … Citizens have developed faith in themselves and their strengths, as well as an awareness of the fact that the future … can and must be built with one's own hands …[44]

Cities: Different frames

(a) Astana-the global modern

What is worth explaining is not the "degrees" of what is modern and what is not, but the actual bordering process—how and by whom some people and objects are classified as modern. What—and where—is the "other" that Astana's architects and residents seek to exclude? In fact, there are many "others"—but most notably Astana is not Soviet and Astana is not the village. I will consider some of these bordering practices in more detail, tracing how an ever-shifting "modern/backward" binary is spatialised in Astana itself. "What" is the other that Astana's city architects and residents seek to exclude? In fact, there are many others that Astana is not interested in—but Astana is definitely non-Soviet and Astana is no longer a village as sociologists would have us believe. The Astana project was designed for elites to spatially distance themselves from a Soviet past that was associated with Tselinograd which was a Soviet city. Consequently, various neighbourhoods which were part of the original Tselinograd city, have been deemed unworthy of preservation by city planners.

And yet, the influence of a *Soviet-era* "city" had not gone—in terms of both its function and its symbolism. The planners were not new to the socialising aspect of the city. Magnitogorsk, the showpiece of Soviet urban development projects, long served as "the quintessential emblem of the grand transformation."[45] But Soviet discourses were also about producing new urban citizens, who were expected to enact "a specifically Soviet way of life: a new economy, society, politics—in short, a new culture, broadly conceived." Although discourses about the "modernity" of Astana are juxtaposed to the "other"—i.e., the Soviet past—these imaginaries are nonetheless underpinned by thoroughly Soviet conceptions about the relationship between the urban and rural, the modern and the traditional.

Talking about Astana, attention tends to converge on the physical appearance of the new capital which has the look of a dream city. But this transformation was restricted only to the Left Bank of the River Ishim while the Right Bank was where overcrowded micro-regions of the Soviet era still survive and where most of the migrants' housing districts are located. So the new idea was not to continue Khrushchev's policy of industrialisation for which Tselinograd earned its name (literally meaning virgin land city) but by bringing in a new element—that of restoration of steppe settlements of the medieval period like *Bozok* (of the Kipchak Khanate). With the transfer of capital, Tselinograd/Aqmola was renamed Astana. With this, the moment of choice for the Kazakhs, i.e., the right to choose their own history—had appeared.

Astana has become Nazarbayev regime's favourite site for an endless parade of international conferences, national celebrations and concerts, sporting events, and sensational new architecture. Official reports are filled with Kazakhstan's resource generation mechanisms like export earnings which have attracted an increasing number of foreign direct investments (FDIs). Unfortunately, the country's population may not have been able to enjoy the full benefits of resource exploitation because of the political and economic challenges created by the resource revenue. The maximum negative effect was reflected in the Kazakh currency, the *tenge,* which depreciated in a major way in comparison to the Russian rouble in the past 7-8 months.

Discussions principally revolve round the physical appearance of Nazarbayev's Astana. There have been talks of absolute population growth that radically altered the ethnic and socio-economic character of the city. Mateusz Laszczkowski, a social anthropologist has researched extensively on the cityscape of Astana. He describes Astana as the "city of the future." The futuristic project corresponds to the "radiant future" discourse of the Kazakhstani state. By raising the standards of this "utopian capital," the regime aims to create an icon of a futuristic society. It is like a "Disneyesque" city where politics, pragmatics and aesthetics are combined together to give it the image of a living city. Transition implies a future-oriented process, so in that sense Astana is a city that represents transition. In the regime's de-historicised visions of the future, there is quite clearly a tension between the past and the present.[46]

The impact of these transformations reaches far beyond the municipal boundaries of Astana. Astana's development is linked to various imaginaries about the country's domestic geography (e.g., a north/south divide, and an urban/rural divide), but also to broader geopolitical imaginaries about Kazakhstan's place in the world. In particular, Astana has been promoted by the regime as the "geopolitical centre of Eurasia," an image that is inscribed in and through the city's symbolic and urban landscapes: Astana's geopolitical and nationalist rhetoric have been shaped by a number of factors: the environment, lived experience, the spectacle, the sport, the international presence and regional differentiation.

Domestically, the target audience of the Astana development project is not just Astana's residents, but the country's population at large, since the image of the city is projected around the country in various visual media, such as photographs, television clips, and billboards, as well as the spectacles surrounding Astana Day. It is also projected to an international audience, as part of what has been called the country's *imidzh proyekt* ("image project"), i.e., the elite project to improve Kazakhstan's prestige and name recognition internationally.

While some people may not accept the rationalisation that the development of Astana is "for the people," the fact remains that the city has undergone a dramatic transformation as the result of real material exchanges. Nazarbayev's aim was to showcase Astana as one of the largest "economic megapolises in Eurasia." The very success of the project lies in providing a rationale for progress and comfort for the citizens. In Kazakhstan, like the Gulf states, state authority has been achieved through a close relationship with the command and control over natural resources, that are invested in various development projects. Like the spectacular urban development schemes in the Gulf, Astana has become Nazarbayev regime's favourite site for an endless parade of international conferences, national celebrations and concerts, sporting events, and sensational new architecture. These urban-based projects are frequently framed as being representative of development that trickles down to the hinterland. But development projects are also symptomatic of power and ego. Most Kazakhstanis and especially the urban people have experienced dramatic improvements in their quality of life over the past 10 years. For them, the woes of the rural poor, such as the oil workers, are difficult to imagine. For example, when Sting, the singer-performer cancelled his Astana Day performance after receiving an Amnesty International advisory about the protest situation in western Kazakhstan, Astana residents were outraged. This was not because of the injustice exercised towards fellow citizens, but that Sting should cancel his concert over such a "trivial" issue and for people so unworthy as oil workers (the implication being that they are the last ones who should be complaining about their pay, because it is assumed that they have well-paying jobs), when they had paid good money for their concert tickets. Popular attitudes in Central Asia are characterised by what Anna Matveeva has termed, "a certain hierarchy of regional disasters, making people think that 'here it is still not as bad as elsewhere.'" Among Kazakhstanis, this has more or less ossified into a "don't rock the boat" ethos since the early 2000s.

(b) Almaty-the charming city

Almaty is represented as a city that has experienced the maximum negative effect in terms of relational shifts among Kazakhs and Russians, Kazakhs and several minority nationalities. Rural to urban migration started in the

Soviet period and this was due to spread of education and vertical social advancement—and it was a gradual and controlled process.[47] Rural Kazakhs, who live in close-knit *aul* communities, have preserved a patriarchal and authoritarian set-up. The dissolution of the Soviet Union is associated with a massive influx of rural Kazakhs into cities. These newly urbanised Kazakhs familiarised the cities with their way of life—it is a kind of a cultural artefact which the contemporary Kazakh government has tried to preserve as a way of legitimising its existence as an alliance between marginalised Kazakh ethno-nationalists and the Soviet era *nomenklatura.*

In the immediate aftermath of Soviet disintegration the Soviet urban set-up was fractured in which the titular nationality, the Kazakhs, shared urban space with the Russians and several minority nationalities. Officials are keen to identify themselves with the Almaty mentality, which has been vibrant and living since the Soviet days. In the late Soviet period, Almaty was inundated with more and more Kazakh settlers coming from small towns who became increasingly aware of their privileged status as members of the titular nationality and also being inducted into administrative elite. This group faced competition of the rural impoverished Kazakhs who after 1991, settled in the free land around the city (*raiony*) and became the source of dispute with their Kazakh brethren or had trouble with the local authorities. The constant penetration of this section of rural Kazakhs who posed themselves as the upholders of Kazakh tradition, representatives of the concept of "being Kazakh," created a rupture in the Soviet fabric. So, here was a distinct perception of "belonging" which was legitimised through symbols and which created fissures in the society as urban Kazakhs were distanced from the rural ones. The emerging fault line lies not so much between ethnic groups but between urbanised, modern Russian-speakers and the marginalised Kazakh-speaking population.

The ambience in Almaty is attractive with numerous options as housing, investment, education, lifestyle and living, fairs and exhibitions, media opportunities, etc.[48] Individual accounts of transformation of the urban space of Kazakhstan are interesting. In her posts for the website "One steppe at a time," Catherine Alexander points to her fond reminiscences of the Soviet period.

> What I love second-most about working in Almaty's libraries and archives are the old Soviet books. First, there is the feel and look of the books. Like everything else, paper was scarce throughout the USSR, and no one had

> much spare money with which to buy books anyway. Therefore, books had to be made as cheap as possible by printing in small fonts, reducing the margins to all but nothing and using thin, poor-quality paper. Today, these books feel so light and so dry in my hands; if I turn a page too quickly, I'm libel to rip it; and in many books there is an overwhelming volume of teeny-tiny language squeezed onto each page.[49]

Almaty has always been an attractive city, even though less stylish. Today, the makeover of the city through show and grandeur is least appealing:

> The skyscrapers that greeted me in Almaty were scraping against the memories of a city I held dear. When I lived here for two months in 2005, I thought of this city in southern Kazakhstan as a charming Soviet leftover, full of dusty streets and pleasant parks. The tallest building was the Hotel Kazakhstan, a Soviet behemoth on the corner near the language school where I studied Russian and Kazakh. Now, as I drove into Almaty from Bishkek, the horizon was blotted with modern pillars of glass, testaments to the power of oil. Back then, they certainly knew about the oil in the Kazakh slice of the Caspian, but Chevron's money hadn't yet trickled down. Now, it was everywhere. The streets were all black and fresh, new underpasses built to streamline the sudden influx of Mercedes and Land Cruisers. A subway system would open next year. Al-Farabi street was lined with buildings that were humorously large, boastful symbols of a new Eurasian power. I desperately looked for something familiar, but found nothing. It felt odd, a familiar place stamped over with the new.[50]

Almaty is a popular case study among urban geographers who have keenly followed a historical timeline to explain the city's transition from a colonial capital to a post-Soviet city rehabilitating its past but also trying to keep pace with globalisation. Almaty in the imperial era was a walled city and was surrounded by Cossack garrisons. It became a Russified centre that was well connected by road and railways that facilitated in-migration of Russians. It was transformed into the seat of the Kazakh revolutionary government of Alash Orda (1917-20) and with a two-stage territorial delimitation it became the locus of Soviet authority and national sovereignty. Till the 1990s, the Kazakhs became aware and developed pride about national sovereignty centred round Almaty. Almaty, till independence, became firmly entrenched in the imagination of the Kazakh people. In fact, Almaty, though located down south, earned its reputation as the seat of government and the Nazarbayev government, like its Soviet predecessors, devoted considerable time and energy and resources in grooming this capital. Almaty still remains the imagined centre of economic and cultural life in Kazakhstan, though Astana is becoming a "seductive career option" for many Kazakhs belonging to the twenty-first century mindset.[51] The wider cosmopolitan milieu of Almaty saw the Russians developing both formal and informal connections with state offices. Kazakhness in Almaty was hardly noticeable, and was a very loose term with Russians having a lot of cultural influence but very little command in state offices. Elite Russians of Almaty were not happy to be segregated from those networks due to sheer geographical distance of the new capital, Astana. Even if there was an economic rationale for shift of capital, Almaty's Russians were not to be influenced by the ambitions and expectations that were being offered by Astana. So relocation of capital to Astana mentally segregated people who lived in Almaty across generations.

The iconic capitals vis-à-vis others

The rent drawn from the sale of oil and gas is massive. This naturally created a loss of faith among the people who did not reap the benefits of a state aspiring to global standards. Atyrau is one such playing field of competition. The regional administration (*akimat*) there has a fairly strong voice. As one *akim* boldly proclaimed, "if it were up to me, of course, I would keep all the revenue here ... But we are forced to share (it). So, I say, let Astana come and get it." Such statements reflect the strong sentiments revolving round oil resources in the Caspian region. In terms of revenue collection through oil enterprises that has brought western deals to the region, Atyrau has a strong bargaining power vis-à-vis the central government.

Assertions about both de facto and de jure economic decentralisation in "the donor regions" of Atyrau, Mangistau, Pavlodar, Karaganda and Almaty are very strong, and the central government seems to be responding directly to demands from administrative heads (*akims*) in these regions for an increase in official levers of control over the economies within their jurisdiction. De jure decentralisation is a conscious attempt to officially recognise the demands of the wealthier regions for more autonomy. This is the fact of the matter as leaders of these regions have been actively demanding greater autonomy in both the economic and political spheres. The same sentiment is seen among people who are directly involved in the international companies like Tengiz Chevroil and have got access to wealth and have not shared it evenly with other partners of these contracting companies. Such issues of decentralisation that have turned the spotlight on the western regions have been discussed more often in the context of the expansion project of the Caspian Pipeline Consortium that was formed in 2001 and became operational through its pipeline route that extended beyond Atyrau into the Russian Federation oblasts of Astrakhan and up to the Black Sea. Nine years after its formation, i.e., in 2010, the CPC pipeline from Tengiz Oilfield to Novorissisyk, a Russian port on the Black Sea, became operational. Oil started flowing towards markets in the Mediterranean and Western Europe. This pipeline was considered to be a major breakthrough for Tengiz Chevroil. Before the pipeline was built, the only ways to ship bulk oil exports from Kazakhstan to recipient nations were by the railways or by boat or ferries across the Caspian to Azerbaijan. That was an extremely costly and time-consuming affair. The pipeline on the other hand was a big cost-saver and also raised the image of Kazakhstan as the real giver to the world's oil economy. With its expansion plans, Tengiz Chevroil was rated high because of its engineering skills. Kazakhstan's economic growth since the collapse of the Soviet Union is undoubtedly impressive, but it has not translated into a better socio-economic situation for citizens outside Almaty and Astana.

The country still has "have" and "have-not" regions. The "haves" include Almaty, Astana and the oil-producing western regions like Atyrau while the "have-not" regions include the old industrial belts in the north, the desert regions in the west and the centre and the agricultural regions in the south. While the government has visions and long-term plans for economic revitalisation, most of these plans seem to be caught in the web of oblast-level obligations. People's protests were due to expectations raised by the oil boom during 2005-11 in various nerve centres of oil and gas, mostly in Atyrau and Mangistau. The most frightening challenge however would be the southern regions where most of the Kazakhs (42.6%) are employed in agricultural activities. Any discontent there would lead to a slump in grain productivity (as Kazakhstan is still the largest grain grower in the CIS region) which would endanger food security. While there is a risk of employment in such cases, the fact of the matter is that Kazakhs as self-reliant nomads would hardly wish to undertake any menial job. Reforms undertaken to match Eurasian or at least South Asian levels have not produced desired results.

Notes

1. Marlene Laruelle, "The Three Discursive Paradigms of State Identity in Kazakhstan," in Mariya Omelicheva (ed.), *Nationalism and Identity Construction in Central Asia: Dimensions, Dynamics and Directions* (London: Lexington Books, 2015), p. 1.
2. "The Shanyrak Crystallises Kazakh Culture and History," [As eloquently described by the Embassy of the Republic of Kazakhstan to Canada], *KazakhWorld,* http://kazakhworld.com/the-shanyrak-crystallizes-kazakh-culture-and-history/
3. Suchandana Chatterjee, *The Steppe in History: Essays on a Eurasian Fringe* (Delhi: Manohar, 2010). (A publication of MAKAIAS.)
4. Chatterjee, "The Kazakh Story" in *The Steppe in History...*, chapter 2.
5. Hilda Eitzen, "Refiguring ethnicity through conflicting genealogies," *Nationalities Papers,* 26 (3), 1998, pp. 435-38.
6. Vadim Trepavlov, "Altytuly: ostatki Nogaiskoi ordy v kazakhskikh stepyakh," *Viestnikh Evrazii*, no. 2 (13), 2001, pp. 33-44.
7. Hilda Eitzen, "Refiguring ethnicity..."
8. S. E. Tolybekov, *Kochevoe Obshchestvo kazakov v XVII-nachale XX veka: politiko-ekonomicheskii analiz* (Alma Ata: Izdatel'stvo Nauka, Kazakhskoi SSR, 1971).
9. Rogers Brubaker, "Nationalising states revisited: projects and processes of nationalisation in post-Soviet states," *Ethnic and Racial Studies,* 2011.
10. In his description of the varieties of nationhood in "new Europe" and Central Asia, Rogers Brubaker points to competing positions and competing stances of ethnocultural groups which then become the "core" of nationalising states. Rogers Brubaker, *Nationalism Reframed: Nationhood and the national question in New Europe* (Cambridge University Press, 1996).
11. Nurbulat Masanov, "Perceptions of Ethnic and all-national identity in Kazakhstan," Institute of Developing Economies, Chiba, Japan, 2002.
12. Elena Sadovskaya, *Migratsionnaia Situatsiya v Respublike Kazakhstan v 2005 g., Analiticheskii obzor i rekomendatsii*, Report commissioned by ILO, 2005; Meiram Baigazin, "The Migration Situation in Kazakhstan," *Central Asia and the Caucasus*, no. 5 (29), 2004.
13. Bridget Anderson and Blanca Hancilova, *Migrant Labour in Kazakhstan: A Case for Concern?* Working Paper no. 69, University of Oxford, 2009.
14. Dinara Tussupova, "Mass Media and Ethnic Relations in Kazakhstan," *Problems of Communism*, November/December 2010, p. 33.
15. Tussupova, "Mass Media and Ethnic Relations ...," p. 35.
16. Tussupova, p. 36.
17. http://registan.net/2014/02/10/nazarbaev-and-kazakh-yeli/
18. "The President who could not stand his Stan," *Global Voices,* February 19, 2014.
19. Michael Hancock Parmer, "Nazarbaev and Kazakh Eli," October 2, 2014, http://registan.net/2014/02/10/nazarbaev-and-kazakh-yeli/
20. Baur Sekenov, *Facebook*, February 6, 2014.
21. For instance, a few protestors started brandishing lacy underwear (in protest against a rule regulating synthetic fabric as per treaty laws of the New Customs Union between Russia, Belarus and Kazakhstan). The protests reflect that the President's will to trade with partners has involved the complete neglect of people's freedom and most importantly indicating the inherent absurdity of what such protestors consider to be a Kazakh dream. The flight of currency from the market reflects an all-round failure—of

investment. Trade follies of partners like Russia and Kazakhstan were unacceptable. The devaluation of the Russian Rouble also mirrored the devaluation of the *tenge*. "Anger at devaluation hints at a broader malaise," *The Economist,* February 22, 2014.

22. Birgit Brauer, "Rebranding Kazakhstan by Changing Its Name," The Jamestown Foundation in *Eurasia Daily Monitor*, vol. 11, issue 30, February 14, 2014, available at http://www.refworld.org/docid/5301c7814.html (accessed March 6, 2014).
23. Total.kz, October 30, 2012.
24. Editorial, "Why Celebrate 550 Years of Kazakh Statehood?" *The Astana Times,* February 28, 2015; E. Assanov, "Uzbekskoe Plemya Naiman," (Section Compatriots. Frontier), *Mangilik El*, June 3, 2014.
25. Jax Jacobsen, "Kazakhstan Braces for 2015 Elections," *Silk Road Reporters*, February 17, 2015.
26. "Kazakh Elections Raise the Spectre of Unrest," *Stratfor Global Intelligence*, February 25, 2015.
27. "Kazakhstan: One Last Time for Nazarbayev," *The Diplomat*, March 16, 2015.
28. Liza Rybina et al., "Patriotism, cosmopolitanism, consumer ethnocentrism and purchase behaviour in Kazakhstan," *Organisations and Markets in Emerging Economies*, vol. 1, no. 2, 2010.
29. Zhao Shengan Ciu Jia, "Oil and money: a match made in Kazakhstan," *China Daily (European Weekly Edition)*, September 12, 2011.
30. Evan A. Feigenbaum, *Asia Unbound,* November 15, 2010.
31. Zifa Alua Auezova, "Conceiving a People's History: The 1920-1936 discourse on the Kazakh past," https://www.academia.edu/6873274/4_Conceiving_a_peoples_history_The_1920_1936_discourse_on_the_Kazakh_past. Scholars who have been trained in that academic circle have recounted the tradition of Oriental studies in the Soviet Union. Introduction by Alfrid K. Bustanov, *Soviet Orientalism and the Creation of Central Asian Nations* (London: Routledge, 2015).
32. Isabelle Kreindler, "Ibrahim Altynsaryn, Nikolai Ilminskii and the Kazakh national awakening," *Central Asian Survey,* 2 (3), 1983, p. 100.
33. He was the great grandson of Ablai Khan of the eighteenth century.
34. N. Amerkulov and N. Masanov, "Kazakhstan ne imeyet budutshego bez Rossii," *Caravan*, February 4, 1994, in A. Sarsanbayev, "Imagined Communities: Kazakh Nationalism and Kazakification in the 1990s," *Central Asian Survey*, 18/3, 1999, pp. 319-46.
35. Bhavna Dave,"Becoming *mankurts*? The hegemony of Russian." in *Kazakhstan: Ethnicity, language and power* (London: Routledge, 2007), p. 62.
36. Bhavna Dave, "Becoming *mankurts?....* pp. 51-52.
37. Anna Yessengalieva, "The Role of Language in Forming Modern Society in Kazakhstan,"in Anita Sengupta and Suchandana Chatterjee (eds.), *Eurasian Perspectives: In Search of Alternatives* (a MAKAIAS publication), Kolkata: Shipra Publications, 2010, p. 178.
38. Jonathan Aitken, *Nazarbayev and the Making of Kazakhstan: from Communism to Capitalism* (London: Bloomsbury Academic), p. 120.
39. Henry R. Huttenbach, "Whither Kazakhstan? Changing capitals: From Almaty to Aqmola/Astana," vol. 26, no. 3, 1998, p. 582.
40. Huttenbach, ibid.
41. As with other planners of the period, Soviet urban planners were enamoured with Ebenezer Howard's Garden City principles (Miliyutin, 1974; Talfuri, 1987). Howard

called for the creation of autonomous new settlements far from the metropolitan area to increase the amount of green space, decrease the distance from home to work, reduce crowding in the inner city, and bring urban amenities to the countryside. The Soviets were particularly interested in Howard's idea that the Garden City was to be a small, communal place, where the municipality would collectively own property. The Garden City, an idea that flourished in the West, could also be interpreted as a starting point for an ideal Soviet suburb. One can see the Garden City concept in early Soviet plans. W. M. Stephen Scott, "The Ideal Soviet Suburb: Social Change Through Urban Design," *Panorama*, 2009.

42. Mateusz Laszczkowski, "City of the Future—the politics, pragmatics and aesthetics of the future in Astana, Kazakhstan," http://www.ucl.ac.uk/mariecuriesocanth/
43. Sheila Fitzpatrick, "Kazakhstan's City of Gold: All that Glitters," http://www.themonthly.com.au/issue/2013/october/1380549600/sheila-fitzpatrick/kazakhstan-s-city-gold
44. Nazarbayev in his book *The Kazakhstan Way,* Stacey International, 2008; Mateusz Laszczkowski, "State Buildings: Built Forms, Materiality and the State in Astana," in Madeleine Reeves, Johan Rasanayagam and Judith Beyer, (eds.), *Ethnographies of the State in Central Asia: Performing Politics* (Bloomington: University of Indiana Press, 2014).
45. Stephen Kotkin, *Magnetic Mountain: Stalinism as a Civilisation (*University of California Press, 1997).
46. Mateusz Laszczkowski, "City of the Future—politics, pragmatics and aesthetics of the future in Astana, Kazakhstan." Poster, available at http://www.ucl.ac.uk/mariecuriesocanth/
47. J. B. Abilhojin, *Ocherki Sotsal'no Ekonomicheskoi Istorii Kazakhstana-, XX Vek* (Almaty: Universitet Turan, 1997).
48. Aleksandra Babkina, "Kazakhstan to modernise housing and public utilities—country drawing on Europe's experience," *Central Asia Online,* January 17, 2012; Alima Bissenova, *Post-socialist dreamworlds: Housing Boom and urban development in Kazakhstan*, Cornell University Doctoral Research, 2010.
49. https://onesteppeatatime.wordpress.com/category/almaty/page/2/
50. "A City of Change," November 10, 2010.

51 Shonin Anacker, "Geographies of Power in Nazarbayev's Astana," *Eurasian Geography and Economics*, 45, no. 7, 2004, p. 527. In *Nezavisimaya Gazeta* (April 28, 1998), observers have expressed concern that the regime has been only *too* eager to seduce people to move to Astana.

2. Relational Shifts: From Soviet to Post-Soviet Times

The new ambience in post-Soviet Kazakhstan was attractive despite the ambiguities in interethnic behaviour and the delicate political balance between the two communities, Russian and Kazakh. The relationship was sometimes interpreted as a fragile harmony that was common to the whole of Central Asia.[1] Sometimes, there were unprovoked expressions of pent-up ethnic acrimony. Here is a visitor's experience in 1993 in a flight that had Uzbeks and Russians as co-passengers. The Uzbek's joke irritated his Russian fellow passengers whose home was Almaty. Referring to the mass exodus of Russians from Uzbekistan, a middle-age woman retorted: "No, it's you who are making the Russians leave."[2] Despite such reactions, the absence of ethnic strife in Kazakhstan for two decades (not since the Zheltoqsan uprising in 1986) was a positive trend.

Nevertheless, the exchange between the Uzbek woman and her Russian co-passenger underscores the ethnic tensions that have taken root in this part of the world. In 1991, young Russians had expressed negative feelings about the nationalities question. They said it was not a great moment to them. Two years later, Kazakhstan was busy testing the mood of its people to determine whether ethnic issues have taken the lead. The "nationality" criterion is still vital for all internal passport holders. Ethnic groups—such as Russian, Ukrainian, German, Korean and Jew—are all listed as nationalities. Nationality plays a major role for admission in educational institutions, for job prospects, for career advancement and access to privileges. The ethnic question, synonymous with the nationality question, pervades business relations in Central Asia. Kazakhs living in Russia (about 750,000) decided to come home to Kazakhstan with the clarion call for Kazakisation. The question before Kazakh returnees was—would their return lead to the creation of the Kazakh nation to the effect that it would exclude other ethnic groups? Or, would it be the Kazakhstani nation, an inclusive home to many people?

Such questions have been addressed in several ways, and sometimes very carefully by scholars referring to the "return to homeland" as the clarion call that attracted Kazakhs worldwide. What impact that would naturally have on non-titular nationalities is anybody's guess. But, implicit in the rhetoric was the conscious attempt to make a fine distinction between ethnic and civic elements of nation-building. Isik Kuscu argues: "He (Nazarbayev) thus distanced himself from nationalist depictions of Kazakhstan's Russian citizens as remnants of the old colonial power. Nazarbayev's caution here reflects his broader rhetoric in which he is careful not to upset the Russians and other minorities in Kazakhstan. The elite groups in Kazakhstan frequently used similar discourse recalling distressing events of the past, particularly the Russian Civil War (1918–21), and the subsequent period of collectivisation and forced sedentarisation in the 1930s. Such discourse appears to constitute an attempt to legitimise ethnic Kazakh migration from a demographic perspective as well. Traumatic events reduced the number of ethnic Kazakhs to a great extent. From the point of view of cultural elites, the in-migration of Diaspora Kazakhs can be justified as a means of asserting the heritage of unity and oneness and the renewal of national culture and tradition.[3] This was a rather lenient view about Kazakh ethnic nationalism and was soon opposed by a faction in the Qurultay. It was realised that the government was not being able to handle immigration effectively.

Only a few scholars seem to be aware of a pragmatic approach that accounted for policy revisions. In fact, President Nazarbayev was extremely cautious of Russian sentiments during the initial years of independence. Kazakhstan's dependence on Russia was magnified by the lack of adequate pipeline infrastructure to generate sufficient oil revenues to boost its economic recovery. Therefore, Kazakhstan had to export its oil through Russian territory via Russian-controlled pipelines, argues Martha Brill Olcott—one of the leading analysts who has researched on Kazakhstan's changing fortunes:

> Kazakhstan knows perfectly well that, at least in its own case, there is no realistic way that Russia can be cut out of the Caspian oil profits, because it is too easy for an excluded Russia to ensure that no one else can have the oil, either pipeline or no pipeline.[4]

The new language law and various decrees were perceived as a harsh measure by the Russians. Russians responded with sharp remarks: "all the factories are run by Russians ... they (the Kazakhs) wanted sovereignty ... let them live in yurts ..." A more specific answer was: "I am leaving just as soon as I can ..." The choice of leaving was felt mainly among young Russians who had relatives in Russia. Some say that in Kazakhstan, Russians are of "a second sort," i.e., reduced to second-class citizens. A Russian child studying in a primary school has to learn Kazakh because language-learning is mandatory in order "to know the country." For the child's mother, it was not needed for her daughter to learn Kazakh—more important for her would be to leave the country. The Kazakh Parliament's seats mostly went to the Kazakhs (about 75% of Deputies were Kazakhs). Even with a better representation in post-1994 elections by Russians and other non-titular nationalities, the desire for leaving did not go down. Russians perceived that their opportunities (not jobs) were limited. Their delegation visits were limited, Kazakh universities were abundant but the percentage of Russians working full-time there was limited. Russian families in Kazakhstan often had to go through a long waiting process to be united with their extended families who wanted to join them in Kazakhstan. Newspaper reports about steady streams of Russians leaving Kazakhstan in 1993 are in plenty.

But a large-scale migration from Kazakhstan has not happened, compared to other Central Asian republics. There are 2.3 times as many Russians as Kazakhs in industry. And vice versa, there are three times as many Kazakhs as Russians in agriculture. Businessmen, entrepreneurs, corporate people of small companies are heavily reliant on Russian supplies (literally from nails to cars—every component of metal which cannot be sourced locally).[5] Like many Kazakhstanis, Mantai Tulegenev, managing director of a construction company in Almaty, refers to Kazakhstan as a former colony of Russia.

> Because our republic was, to put it mildly, a colony of Russia, that is Moscow, only the extraction and refining industry developed in the republic. We have virtually no machine-building. For us, all of the final manufacturing of products is done in Russia, and therefore the economy of Kazakhstan is closely connected with the Russian economy. At the present time we have become a politically free republic, but economically we cannot say that, because our economy without the economy of Russia

> cannot move. Therefore, we are always looking at the political stability of Russia. If everything is fine in Russia, then our economy will develop normally.[6]

So, economic prosperity took top priority in post-Soviet Kazakhstan. The expectation was about "We-Kazakhstani" as the mantra, irrespective of nationality, that will help improve the economy. In the initial years since independence, the reliance was on Russia and the rouble zone. Till 1993, such loyalty was total. But with creeping dissent in the Russian Federation and lurking fears of a cracking Kazakh economy, Kazakh authorities sought to boost up strategies for a robust economic policy irrespective of Russian support. The prominence of a parliamentary faction within Russia stressing on the protection of Russians everywhere made Kazakisation sound more realistic. There were also fears of being trapped in a rouble economy which led to the introduction of an independent currency, the *tenge*.

The Kazakhs' ambiguous relationship with Russia has been discussed quite often. The Kalmyk threat of the 1720s led to clan leaders of the Small Horde to seek Russian protection. In 1731, Russian protectorate status over Small Horde territory ended its independent existence. Throughout the eighteenth century, Kazakhs of the Middle Horde also received Russian patronage. By the nineteenth century, the Kazakh lands were integrated into Tsarist Russian territory. So, a Kazakh-Russian accord can be traced back to 1731—since then the Kazakh fate was entwined with that of Russia's. Memories of a historical alliance are brought back in contemporary discussions about Kazakh-Russian relations. Not only is there a suggestion of a tacit alliance between Golden Horde clans of Nazarbayev and Middle Horde clans to defuse Russian and Cossack separatist movements in Middle Horde territory but also to keep in check Lesser Horde elite's aspirations in western Kazakhstan (especially Mangyshlak Peninsula) where there were large deposits of oil, gas and mineral wealth.[7] It seems that Kazakh clans in power have been trying to utilise historical alliances and networks with Russians in order to curb dissent in the north and the west.

But there have been cracks in this relationship of trust. This is particularly true in the case of the diaspora groups and non-titular nationalities of Kazakhstan, some of whom share the traumatic experience as being dispossessed or displaced during the Stalinist era. Scholarship on the subject of Stalinist deportation of minority nationalities has increased ever since the accessibility of the NKVD-MVD (Internal Affairs Ministry) archives in the Russian Federation. Scholars have also pointed out that a unidirectional movement of people cannot be considered the beginning and end of existence for a minority community. The extent, scale, distance and trauma of deportation cannot be treated as a singular trend in migration flows and patterns. Population shifts took place over the entire Soviet era, from the 1920s to the 1950s. Therefore, it is also important to consider other factors like social ties, community bonding over generations which often tend to have a lasting impact on the migrant's mind. This is particularly the case of Germans in Kazakhstan and Siberia who have an enduring relationship with their Slavic partners which is why, despite their shrinking numbers in Central Asia (2.4% in 2009), they have a significant role to play in Central Asian affairs as a revitalised diasporic community. The Cambridge school of historians feels that the Soviet socialist experiments during the Stalin period were industrial achievements (outstanding examples being the metal cities of Magnitogorsk and Kuznetstroi). But such dramatic changes during the 1920s-1940s affected human lives in the most serious manner. Since the 1980s, the strongest criticism was voiced against (a) collectivisation of farms and dekulakisation that disrupted the lifestyle of indigenous communities in the grain-producing regions like Kazakhstan and (b) deportation of non-titular nationalities like the Koreans, Volga Germans, Ukrainians, Poles, Crimean Tatars, Uzbeks and Meshketian Turks who felt dislocated and exiled. Their style of questioning was not related to the man and his methods, i.e., Stalinist terror, but about an entire process, a Soviet mechanism that combines economic policies with political methods. Also, Khrushchev's reforms were no less questionable. The reforms did not ease the condition of the agricultural people of Kazakhstan, and the fact that the Virgin Lands' campaign was not an episode in the entire process of a voluntary agricultural policy as some Sovietologists have suggested. In the 1990s, the issue of mixed successes of the Virgin Lands (*tselina*) episode was addressed, with a pointer to the heavy price that the Kazakhs had to pay due to the incoming groups of Slavic settlers (about two million) in the Kazakh steppe.

The fact remains that the legacy of Soviet collectivisation lives as a memory of violence. Now, even this aspect of violence is not the only story because the victims of violence (the peasants mostly) often retaliated. This story of retaliation often goes unnoticed in the saga of post-revolutionary political and administrative experiments that affected not only the *inorodetsy* (foreigners) but also the *inovertsev* (people belonging to different faiths). Such depictions not only bring back memories of repressive acts and punitive measures against the ethnic groups who were targeted as enemies during the Second World War, namely the Poles, the Germans and the Koreans, but also bring out the resilience of a silent group of individuals and groups—those who are indigenous communities and belonged to the neglected corners of the USSR like the Meshketian Turks, Karachays, Ingush, Balkars, Crimean Tatars and the Kalmyks. The next section deals not only with the adverse conditions of the dispossessed nomads and dispersed nationalities but also with their resilience and survival methods that they narrated to their kith and kin.

Dekulakisation and deportation

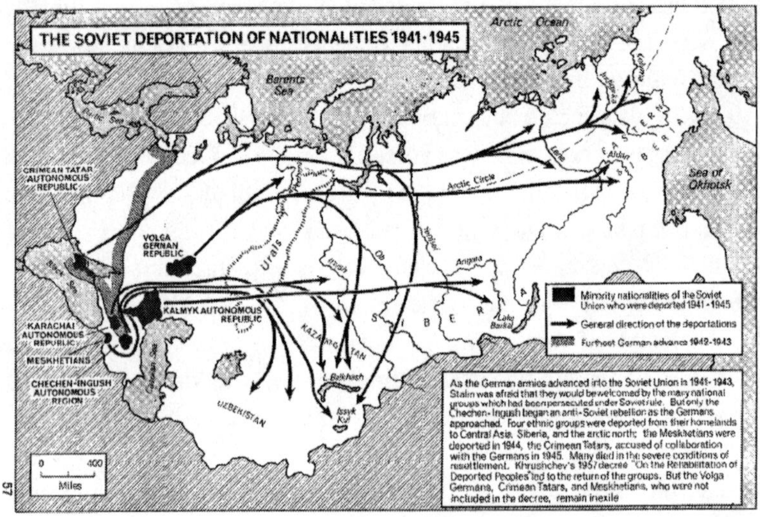

Kazakhstan has been traditionally reliant on livestock economy and seasonal agricultural farming. But the Soviet authorities as part of the collectivisation project decided that settling the nomads was the only way to achieve quick agricultural production. Scholars who have identified patterns of state violence in the early years of Soviet power have argued that the process began since the First Five Year Plan (1928-1932) when pressures on the wealthy peasants increased with punitive taxes. Archival research points to Stalin's closeness with advocates of collectivisation at a fast pace, that would help the provinces to push the campaign to and beyond the limits. There have been disastrous consequences of forced settlement of nomads—perishing of almost 90% of the cattle and an ensuing famine which resulted in loss of human lives. Stalin's speech to the Conference of Marxist Agronomists on December 27, 1929 called for the "liquidation of the kulaks as a class." The process was stepped up once again during the Second World War when the regime's control mechanism reached out beyond the borders of the Union and touched nationalities like the Germans and the Poles. Case studies point to the excesses of the Stalinist regime and its notorious dekulakisation and deportation campaigns.

The Volga Germans were historically perceived as privileged subjects of the imperial regime and the collectivisation and dekulakisation programmes resulted in the perception of Volga Germans as affluent peasants and therefore class enemies. Anti-German sentiments increased during the First Five Year Plan and the Soviet Germans were disproportionately victimised during the dekulakisation campaign throughout the collectivisation period. The German-Polish Non-Aggression Pact of 1934 was viewed with apathy for it endangered Soviet international image. Ethnic Germans and Poles were collectively branded by the Soviet regime as the enemy of the people. Hitler's rise to power and the suppression of the German Communist Party escalated the Soviet Union's concerns. NKVD's Order Number 00439 specifically targeted ethnic Germans for repression. By 1939, all German territories outside the Volga German Republic were liquidated followed by indigenisation of Germans (*korenizatsiia)* within the Soviet system. Following Nazi invasion of 1941, about 400,000 Volga Germans were forcibly deported to Kazakhstan and Siberia and the Volga Republic was formally abolished.

The Kazakhs of Polish ancestry and Kazakhs of Polish descent, originating from the western part of the Ukrainian Republic of USSR and deported to Kazakhstan during the Second World War were repatriated during 1944-48. The Polish government's resolution of repatriation has theoretically allowed these people to settle in Poland. But in reality, having been brought up in the Soviet system and in Central Asia, the younger generations had no connect with their ethnic homeland in Poland. The deportees were divided into two groups. Members of the first group were luckier—they were dispersed in groups along the railway line. The others were settled down in the distant steppe, hundreds of kilometres away from the railway. At first the colonies created in this way did not even have a name. The authorities simply referred to them as batches (first consignment, second consignment, etc.) or as points on the railway line.

The period of the Second World War was the next tragic period in the history of Polish settlement in Kazakhstan. After September 17, 1939, the day the Red Army invaded Poland, the Soviet authorities started to deport the population of the Eastern Polish territories they had occupied. This time deportation did not embrace entire families, but a part of them which had a deeper effect. Exile affected mostly women and children of Polish origin. Many Polish men were either absent due to army service or they were murdered on the spot by the NKVD. According to an estimate, during the Second World War about 150,000 Poles were deported to Kazakhstan. After the Second World War, during 1944-48, the repatriation of Poles from Western Belarus, Western Ukraine, Southern Lithuania and other territories of the ex-USSR took place. The condition of repatriation was, only War-affected Poles could claim repatriation. After the War the number of Poles moving to Kazakhstan in order to settle there significantly diminished. Settlement in Kazakhstan became voluntary and took place as a component of internal Soviet population movement. It seems impossible to determine the precise number of Kazakhs of Polish ancestry living at present in Kazakhstan. Soviet census figures show that largest concentrations of Polish minorities were noticeable in Kokeshetau, Karaganda and Akmolinsk.

The official cause of deporting the Koreans was the same as in the case of the Volga Germans, that is, espionage. On August 21, 1937 the order was given to deport all Koreans living in Vladivostok Oblast (region) and several adjacent territories of the Far East (the Far-Eastern Krai included Khabarovsk, Amur, Nizhne Amurskaia, Ussuri, Primorskaia, and Jewish Autonomous oblasts). Koreans were also deported from the Buriat-Mongol Krai and Chita Oblast. At least 175,000 Koreans (37,000 families) were deported, like some other "unreliable" Russians and Ukrainians. There may have been sporadic resistance, for observers recorded the arrest of 2,500 Koreans (a 1938 NKVD communiqué spoke of their "aggressive acts"). The Far East NKVD chief Genrikh Liushkov reported in 1938 the arrest of 9,000 party workers and military men for participation in "illegal groups" suspected of connections across the border. Scholars who argue in favour of the conspiracy plot have highlighted such numbers and phased deportation of the Koreans from the Far East to Central Asia. By the mid-1930s, the Soviet authorities were gravely concerned by Soviet Koreans crossing the border on various grounds: hunting, visiting relatives, smuggling, or simply making excuses to run away to Korea or Japan (with Koreans among the Border Police trying to help them out). The overall concern was about the Japanese presence in Manchuria and Korea.

Local authors are emphatic about other reasons of deportation. The discriminatory measures of local Soviets against Korean kolkhozes such as land allotment, and heavy taxes on Korean farmers in collective farms fuelled discontent. Another cause for deportation was the need for reclamation of the wastelands of Kazakhstan that lay deserted after the famine and epidemic that broke out in the aftermath of forced collectivisation. The Soviet authorities relied on Korean labour from the Far East. Another reason for deportation was the Soviet attempt to silence the Korean demand for establishment of a Korean autonomous region in the Far East. The challenges of deportation confronted the Koreans who had, over generations, settled in Russian Far East, having enjoyed the patronage of Russian governors who had allowed them to set up Korean colonies in Western Siberia near Omsk, Tobolsk and Tyumen. Due to antagonism towards Japanese imperialism, some Russian officials saw the Koreans as their natural allies. By 1910 more than 50,000 Koreans inhabited over a hundred villages, popularising the practice of rice culture and silk-farming in the Russian Far East. The past faded into memory as deportation of Koreans into Central Asia was carried out in a phased way: all Koreans spread over 23 districts of the Far East were expelled to the vicinity of the Aral Sea and Lake Balkhash in southern Kazakhstan and to the Uzbek SSR. Destinations of Korean deportees were Tashkent, Kyzyl Orda, Ushtobe, Alma Ata (Almaty), Frunze (Bishkek), Samarkand, Bukhara, Urgench, Ashkabad, Taganrog.

Tales of dispossession

In heart-rending tales about their experiences during dekulakisation campaign in the 1930s, survivors have narrated how these communities were forced to send off young and old members of their families to their kith and kin staying in borderland regions of, say, China, to escape the after-effects of collectivisation of agriculture. From the account of Mukhamat Shayakhmetov, a Kazakh nomad (born in 1922) under Stalin, we get an idea of how the nomadic people were dislocated from their habitat stretching from the eastern shores of the Caspian to the Tien Shan range which has the Altai range in the north that constitutes the frontier of Kazakh territory and is also a borderland region of Kazakhstan and China. The account recounts the horrors of the collectivisation drive which empowered the police and party officials to confiscate the property and livestock of individuals who were branded as *kulaks,* arrested them and their families and exiled them to penal colonies (in Siberia, Central Asia, northern Russia) or executed them as class enemies. Death by starvation and execution followed immediately after the Stalinist order that deported 1.8 million peasants (about 400,000 households) as class enemies who even dared to resist collectivisation. Many of them were dispossessed and resettled into special farms in their home districts. Some even died due to harsh conditions even before they reached their places of exile. So, by sheer force, the authorities had managed to drive 60 per cent of peasant households to join collective farms, while about 40 per cent had actually resisted the state campaign, and continued to exist legally by paying huge tax and agreeing to comply with procurement policies. The relaxation of taxes resulted in peasants streaming out of collectives—a process that was stopped after the authorities persuaded the peasants to stay in the collectives by owning their own livestock and farm their own plots of land. With these measures, there was an increase and decrease in the collectivisation ratio: 83% in 1935 and 63% in 1940.

For the mountainous people of Kazakhstan who were accustomed to periodic migration in search of summer pastures (usually in the month of July), short movements by foot (called *zhayau kosh*) when the weather became cooler in September or October, settlement in winter dwellings from November to March that would mark the end of one migration cycle, the misery began with the dispossession of peasant holdings and confiscation of livestock, the sole property of the nomads. The families were then relocated to remote regions in the southern Altai and the upper reaches of the Irtysh—a process that lasted for an entire year, 1928-29. The wealthy peasants tried to save themselves by crossing the Chinese border where the government allowed them to settle but offered them exemption from tax for three years. Others tried to evade the authorities but were caught and arrested. Such was the case of Toimbai, the survivor's uncle.

> On May 1, 1929, the farm belonging to my Uncle Toimbai (who, according to official calculations, was the most comfortably well off among us) consisted of 350 heads of sheep, three geldings, one stallion, two mares

with their offspring from the past two years, five dairy cows, one working ox, four large-horned bullocks and four camels; he had sown no crops.

As an immediate way of eliminating kulak holdings, the authorities devised new taxes and obligatory in-kind deliveries of grain or livestock. The taxes were expressly exorbitant and unrealisable—in many cases they were several times higher than the total harvest or head of livestock on the holding. What is more, the time allowed for delivering the grain and livestock and paying off the tax was impossible to keep to. Failure to pay these taxes on time then resulted in the farmer being convicted of opposing Soviet policy, with draconian consequences.

Well-off nomadic Kazakh farmers who never went in for arable farming were expected to pay tax in the form of grain deliveries to the State, and so were forced to buy in grain from other farms. This meant having cash to pay for it, which was something nomadic farmers never had, since they were used to paying in kind; they were therefore forced to sell off their livestock as quickly as possible to get the cash to purchase the grain with. But inevitably, an increase in the amount of animals for sale caused their value to plummet; and since any livestock belonging to private individuals was being put in collective farms, very few people were interested in buying it.

Even if the livestock was successfully sold off or bartered, it took quite some time to amass sufficient grain to pay off the tax. Delays would occur and the deadline would pass; even if a farmer did manage to meet it, he was then presented with yet more demands, so that in the end some decided that they would never be able to pay everything they owed and simply stopped handing over their grain and livestock to the State. The authorities would respond by instigating criminal proceedings against them. Whether they refused or were simply unable to pay, their actions were categorised as anti-Soviet. Eventually the matter was solved in court. [8]

Justice was meted out to the "defaulters" in court and through outside-court arrangements. Unaccustomed to living in closed spaces, the steppe nomad sought routes of escape.

The convicted were escorted from the "courtroom" under guard and shortly afterwards their families had all their livestock and domestic property, right down to cups and cutlery, confiscated. Within two days twenty class enemies and exploiters from the various *auls* had been sent under escort to be imprisoned in the town of Ust-Kamenogorsk (now Oskemen), 250 kilometres away.

Accustomed since time immemorial to a life of freedom and to the fresh air of the vast open spaces, the people of the steppe found it hard enough during the winter months when they were confined to their huts … It was only natural for them to seek ways and means of escaping.

The method chosen by the authorities for transferring the prisoners to Ust-Kamenogorsk made it easy for them. As they had no organised means of transport at their disposal, the court officials decided to send the group under escort on their own horses. And so, loaded with provisions, the men set off on horseback accompanied by two militia guards. After travelling some 25 or 30 kilometres, the group set up camp for the first night in the *aul* of Kayinda and was warmly welcomed by the local residents, many of whom were acquaintances and even relatives. The arrested men were put up in small groups in their friends' homes. The people of Kayinda offered them traditional hospitality as well as heartfelt sympathy for their situation.[9]

The fugitive experiences are varied:

Some (fugitives) collected their families and fled across the border to safety in China, but these were a small minority … Among these fugitives were Toimbai-ata and one of our cousins, Muksiin Nurmukhametov. That night the two of them crossed over to the left bank of the River Irtysh, and found temporary shelter at the home of some distant relatives. They were convinced they had travelled far enough not to be recognised by any locals, whereas in actual fact they were only about thirty kilometres away from where they had escaped their guards, and seventy to eighty kilometres from their *aul* and families.

Their hope lay in the covert sympathy and support they were shown by ordinary people. It was no secret that most peasants did not support

> the Soviet authorities' policy of setting the poor against the well-off. The persecution of the kulaks and the coercion used to turn farms into collectives gave rise to deep discontent and this led to people to harbour fugitives as a form of protest. Nevertheless, within a short time most of the fugitives were recaptured. By staying on the run for a year before the night he reappeared at our *aul*, Uncle Toimbai-ata proved himself to be much the most resourceful ...
>
> But after he had been with us for a month, his grey horse was spotted standing by the water hole with the communal herd and seized by local activists; and though no one came looking for him in the days that followed, Toimbai-ata—discouraged by his loss and convinced of the futility of life as a fugitive—finally decided to give himself up to the authorities. They reaffirmed his sentence, and sent him to prison in the town of Zaisan.[10]

Friends and acquaintances of the fugitives and their families belonged to various clans (Karagerei, Naiman, Otei) and interacted fairly well, and discussed each other's travails. One of them was Yestayulet Yesberdinov, a guest in the author's family, who had stepped out at the age of 85 to escape to China.[11] There were different shades of this escape story. The fact of the matter is that most of these fugitives were *aul* members with solid experience of moving into China through secret routes. Some were Kazakhs with Chinese citizenship who had slipped over the border (taking advantage of the treaty between imperial powers) to lead their relatives out of USSR. There were others who had escaped to China on their own and were now returning for their families. People who did not wish to join the collective farms decided to pack their belongings and join the second group too. It so happened that local activists were called upon by the militia to catch hold of the migrants when they tried to cross the border. Beyond the Irtysh border, the experience was no less traumatic. The fugitive families faced the uncertainties of living when they were escorted to other distant prisons that were affiliated to the regional centres administered by the militia. The survivors who had to search grain for their living chose to send young children to mills (located about 25-30 kilometres). The author himself was only nine years old when his mother sent him with a horse to fetch the grain from the Karozek Valley that was situated between the southernmost spurs of the Altai range bordering the Zaisan Basin. Unlike his mother's convictions, the place (Karozek Valley) turned out to be deserted and the little boy had to depend on the help of a fellow traveller who introduced him to a Russian mill from where the grain was obtained. Here was a different picture: interaction among ethnic groups (the Kazakhs and the Russians) during times of trouble. This is an account that shows the excesses of regional officials. This has been corroborated in a review article about Siberian provinces. The major argument here is that vast spaces like Siberia have been either undergoverned or overgoverned during the Soviet period. So, whether we talk of the Kazakh grasslands or the south Siberian plains, it is the bureaucratic ways in which dekulakisation and collectivisation were carried out. The regional officials had specific instructions from the top. Local abuses often went unchecked.[12]

Tales of deportation

Several minority nationalities of the Kazakh republic share the traumatic experience as deported nationalities during the Stalinist regime. Personal narratives and reminiscences have depicted losses suffered by indigenous communities and have also expressed their feelings for interethnic bonding due to generations of living in the same space. Since the 1980s, the strongest criticism was voiced against (a) collectivisation of farms and dekulakisation that disrupted the lifestyle of indigenous communities in the grain-producing regions like Kazakhstan and (b) deportation of non-titular nationalities like the Koreans, Volga Germans, Ukrainians, Poles, Crimean Tatars, Uzbeks and Meshketian Turks who felt dislocated and exiled.

I. The Germans

Several writings, mostly in the form of reflections, portray the destroyed minds of German minorities who were forcibly displaced from the Russian borderlands (Ukraine) to Kazakhstan where they had to serve in labour camps organised by NKVD (the People's Commissariat of the Ministry of Internal Affairs) after the Second World War. The anti-German intent of Stalin has been severely criticised by German writers like Otto Pohl. His sole target of criticism was NKVD (Peoples Commissariat of Internal Affairs) that, he claims, to have used the measure of "ethnic cleansing" vis-à-vis the Germans as well as Muslim nationalities of the region. By 1939, all German territories outside the Volga German Republic were liquidated followed by limited process of accommodation/indigenisation of Germans (*korenizatsiia)* within the Soviet system. Between September 3, 1941 and January 1, 1942, the NKVD forcibly deported 799,459 ethnic Germans to confined areas of internal exile called special settlements. Some of these special settlements were located in Karaganda Oblast in Kazakhstan. In actuality, these were Soviet gulags or labour camps that were set up by the NKVD in 1931 in the North, the Urals, Far East and Central Asia. Most of these camps were theoretically set up to perform agricultural responsibilities. These were transformed into "colonies" of labour camps where more than 21 million people were either deported as prisoners or special settlers. In Kazakhstan's notorious gigantic labour camp, Karlag, there were settlers' points in New Karaganda (Maikuduk).[13]

Pohl's colleague Kristina Gray has written about Karlag, the labour camp complex that operated in Karaganda Oblast, Kazakhstan from 1931 to 1959. The Karlag prisoners engaged in a variety of economic activities including agriculture, coal mining, limestone quarrying, glass manufacturing and food processing. At the end of 1943, a contingent of Germans mobilised into the labour army arrived at Karlag. By January 1944 their number was 1,280 and there were 50,080 convicted prisoners. In January 1946, the NKVD demobilised the Russian-Germans working in the labour army at Karlag and reclassified them as special settlers. However, they remained legally obliged to remain working in other Karlag enterprises. The corrective labour camp complex in Karaganda Oblast continued to house prisoners for another thirteen years.

Criticism is mainly directed towards the labour army (*trudarmiia*). During the Second World War, the mass deportation of Germans from European Russia to labour detachments in Kazakhstan and Siberia which came to be known as the labour army or *trudarmiia* led to the recruitment of large sections of Germans in People's Commissariats of Coal, Oil and Munitions under direct supervision of the NKVD and later on the MVD. The MVD reclassified most labour army conscripts as special settlers in 1947-48 and did not release some of the mobilised Germans before 1957.

Special settlements were like prison houses. Not until January 8, 1945 in Order No. 35, "On Legal Regulations and Rights of Special Settlers" was there a proper codification of the position of special settlers. The settlers were given rights as USSR citizens but with limitations. Though not theoretically structured along ethnic lines, in practice, the settlements managed by the *komendatury* often ended up compartmentalising the largest batch of deportees, i.e., the Germans compared to the smaller groups (the Karachais) who were bundled up with other ethnic minorities during deportation and lived together during exile. Also, during each wave of deportation there was a resettlement and the groups were regrouped and resettled in different locations over different periods of time. Documents indicate that there was an undefined preference for Germans because of the optimism about their hard-working skills. The special settlements often turned out to be ethnic-dominant. The world of special settlers or special villages constituted the dark underside to what Stephen Kotkin praises as socialist desiderata. On paper, the special villages exhibited all the traits of "scientific planning" for everything from transport to village construction and house plans to epidemic diseases. Yet, the reality was the system of excessive control based on the recommendations of the functionaries of the OGPU (*Ob'edinnenoe Gosudarstvennoepoliticheskoe upravlenie* headed by G. Iagoda) and their fierce competition for institutional control vis-à-vis the NKVD which made people's life miserable. With the opening of the archives in the 1990s, an entire paper world of intricate plans was revealed. The omnipresent blueprints represented a vision of control and rational order projected by an authoritarian state to transform and control the peasant economy. In revisionists' writings, therefore, the Stalinist experiment represented a case of social engineering imposed on the subject population. Deportations of national minorities of 1936 and 1937 merged with mass repressions under Ezhov's infamous order numbered 00447—directed against collective farmers, state farmers, individual farmers and also former convicts, sectarians, and a host of marginal populations.

Eric Schmaltz points to the making and unmaking of the Volga German ASSR that constituted a strong support base for the Soviet authorities. In October 1918, the German Autonomous Workers' Commune was created and was subsequently (in 1923-24) transformed into a German Autonomous Soviet Socialist Republic (ASSR). In addition to incorporating the German nationality into the Soviet political system, the new Volga republic was intended to serve as an inspirational model for Moscow's international socialist revolution in politically unstable Weimar Republic. Soviet hopes to spread the revolution abroad in Germany were crushed due to Hitler's tactics. From August 1941, in a phased manner, NKVD officials ordered the deportation, resettlement, internment of all Volga Germans in the territory of the former USSR. The process continued till 1945 when a resolution of the Soviet People's Commissars announced the "legal status of the special resettlers assigned for special settlements" (*spetspolentsy*) that became the worst experience for all deportees. Following Nazi invasion of 1941, about 400,000 Volga Germans were forcibly deported to Kazakhstan and Siberia and the Volga Republic was formally abolished. Taking account of the historical timeline, Schmaltz not only assesses the scale of the deportation, but also re-examines a series of Soviet resolutions that went into the making and unmaking of a Volga German republic. According to him, the Volga German ASSR was clearly a political outgrowth of mid-1920s Soviet nationalities policies. It recognised three official languages—German, Ukrainian and Russian. It represented the most compact ethnic German settlement in the erstwhile Soviet Union. The community was widely dispersed over a vast geographical space of the USSR, with more than twelve German national districts located in Volynia, Ukraine, the Crimea, the Caucasus and Russian Siberia. The Soviet government formally liquidated the Volga German ASSR in September 1941. It is the memory of the Volga German Autonomous Republic that has ignited the minds of German activists like Schmaltz.

Narratives of belonging among Volga Germans indicate how the sense of rootedness differed from generation to generation. A grandmother's (Mathilda) experience of deportation from the Volga Republic to Siberia during the Second World War was reactivated during her emigration to Germany. Her daughter-in-law Tamara, born in 1959 in Siberia to a Christian family that was prime witness to internal dislocations due to the advent of the deportees of Mathilda's generation, conceptualises her belonging as member of a religious we-group; her granddaughter (Tamara Jr) sought to connect with her original homeland and peer groups. Mathilda's historical homeland was the Volga region because Catherine the Great, a Prussian princess issued a manifesto in 1763 calling all Germans to inhabit Russia's Volga region—which in due course of time developed as a German settlement. Subsequently, Germans inhabited Kazakh and Siberian lands and the German population in the Soviet Union during the First World War reached up to 2.4 million. Mathilda was born in 1928 in the Volga SSR and faced the trauma of being segregated from her family members during dekulakisation and forced conscription into labour army. She herself was deported to Siberia. Siberia, where she married a Volga German Catholic, is her place of exile. The Volga republic today is a symbol of her homeland, her property, her education. She abandoned her 50 years of living experience in Siberia to migrate to Germany in 1990. So, she has lived in three different worlds—while the Volga region is a paradise-like childhood memory, Siberia has instilled survival instincts in her mind and as she goes to her new home in Germany when she is pretty old, she gets nostalgic about her deportation years when she moved from the Volga to Siberia. Her deportee status is more vivid in her memory—being deported from the Volga and being deported to Siberia. Her new home in Germany cannot displace her sentiments about the Volga republic—it is deeply embedded into her psyche. In the early 1990s, the return law of Germany announced repatriation which along with the Kazakisation drive resulted in large-scale emigration of Kazakh Germans.[14] But emigration to Germany (by Germans along with their Slavic relatives settled in northern parts of Kazakhstan) was accompanied by certain problems. Another twist to the story is Russia seems to be the new emigration destination for the German Kazakhs.

II. The Koreans

The official cause of deporting the Koreans was the same as in the case of the Volga Germans, that is, espionage. In 1937, Stalin, Molotov and Ezhov—heads, respectively, of the party, state and security police—undertook the first full-blown ethnic deportation, that of the Far-Eastern Koreans. The past faded into memory as deportation of Koreans into Central Asia was carried out in a phased way: all Koreans spread over 23 districts of the Far East were expelled to the vicinity of the Aral Sea and Lake Balkhash in southern Kazakhstan and to the Uzbek SSR. Destinations of Korean deportees were Tashkent, Kyzyl Orda, Ushtobe, Alma Ata (Almaty), Frunze (Bishkek), Samarkand, Bukhara, Urgench, Ashkabad, Taganrog.[15] Koreans were packed into crowded cattle cars to make the 3,700-mile journey to Kazakhstan and Uzbekistan. This well organised, month-long deportation is vividly brought to life through the first-hand memories of survivors. About 98,000 Koreans were brought into Kazakhstan and dispersed throughout the country to establish collective farms. In the first years, many Koreans were relocated to uninhabited lands without any housing. At a small village named Ushtobe, 34,000 Koreans were brought and thousands lived out in the open steppe, digging holes in the ground for shelter. Others were sent far away to live among nomadic Kazakh herders making their homes in yurts. Native Kazakhs welcomed these Koreans and often assisted them as they settled into their new lives in these remote lands. The film *Koryo Saram* tells the saga of survival in the open steppe country and the sweep of Soviet history through the eyes of these deported Koreans, who were designated by Stalin as an “unreliable people” and enemies of the state. The film follows the deportees’ history of integrating into the Soviet system while working under extreme weather conditions in Kazakhstan, a country which became a concentration camp of exiled people from throughout the Soviet Union.

In their reflections on the purge period, the Korean Kazakhs have expressed their grievances as Communist workers in the Far East who were completely dislocated from their locales in the Stalinist period due to allegations of espionage activities in collusion with the Japanese. In the case of the Koreans in Kazakhstan, it has been pointed out that ethnic cleansing was not the only reason for deportation. One cannot ignore ethnic conflicts over land issues and collectivisation—discriminatory measures against Korean kolkhozes and privileges (like agricultural machinery, credits) doled out to Russian kolkhozes started the conflict. Korean elite members refused to participate in collective farming and preferred farming on leased land. Disgruntled Korean collective farmers took the lead in anti-collectivisation drives in the Vladivostok region which made Soviet authorities even more suspicious about counter-revolutionary activities among the Koreans. Added to this was the desire to use the Korean labour force to cultivate the vast steppe land of Kazakhstan which was depopulated due to famine, epidemics and agricultural collectivisation. NKVD documents indicate that Korean residents from 23 districts of the Soviet Far East were to be expelled to destinations in the region round Lake Balkhash and the Aral Sea. The official Korean theatre, originally established in the Far East but moved to Ushtobe, was under state control and only staged Soviet plays in Russian. Traditional styles of performing arts, for example, *samul nori* (percussion folk music) and *phansori* performances (traditional song, recital and dance) virtually disappeared among the *Koryo Saram*, as did traditional Korean calligraphy and painting which were replaced by socialist style of art. The *Koryo Saram* became an alienated community in the Stalinist period, to be revived to a certain extent in the Nikita Khrushchev regime. The film *Koryo Saram* tells the saga of survival in the open steppe country and the sweep of Soviet history through the eyes of these deported Koreans, who were designated by Stalin as an “unreliable people” and enemies of the state. The film follows the deportees’ history of integrating into the Soviet system while working under extreme weather conditions in Kazakhstan, a country which became a concentration camp of exiled people from throughout the Soviet Union.

What was lacking for the Korean deportees was their participation in Soviet life. The success stories in Soviet sport did not certainly take into account the contribution of Korean sportsmen. The latter were not encouraged to play in competitive sports that would have improved the sports image of the Soviet Union. They were simply labelled as Soviet men who created model kolkhozes throughout Central Asia. One notices the frustration due to failed opportunities in the account of Manghym Hvan, chairman of Kolkhoz Politodel. The Politodel was like an extensive sports complex and it began as a Korean kolkhoz which also included Uzbeks, Kazakhs, Tatars, Russians, Ukrainians and other Soviet nationalities. Due to their productivity and special talents (like football), the Politodel earned enough revenue and aspired to transform into miniature cities with paved roads, street lights, playgrounds, community centres, hospitals and sports stadiums. The Kolkhoz chairmen brought trainers who graduated from Soviet Physical Culture Institutes to train children in boxing and track and field meets. The Politodel became the powerhouse of Soviet Korean sport and that too because of its chairman Manghym Hvan. The expectations of the Koreans in Central Asia increased because of such management skills in sports. To be devoid of national support in the 1950s and 1960s was not a very happy experience for many Korean footballers. The kolkhoz teams were unable to have the best exposure because of their status as deportees.[16] This was a unique experience of marginalisation.

With land shortage in the Far Eastern border the Primorskii Koreans were forced to move to the steppe regions of Central Asia. Here was a case of social exclusion—a prominent Korean social group in the Russian Far East, i.e., the New Korean Village with centres in Vladivostok, Kraskino and Ussuri and Korean nationalist activist groups that moved to Siberian autonomy hubs like Irkutsk, Chita, Blagoveshchensk, Svobodny Gorod and Khavarovsk were exposed to power rivalry between Russia, Japan and Manchuria in the early twentieth century and were dislocated from these places to Central Asian locations. In the post-Soviet period, the *Goryeoin*, the immigrant Koreans to the Central Asian republics are seeking Kazakh state's patronage to reintegrate ethnic groups and restoring their national identity as the subject nationals. Goryeoin, who have adapted to the Soviet regime more quickly than other ethnic groups and have Soviet vestiges till date, are now adapting to the newborn republics' process of state formation. The social position of the ethnic Goryeoins in Kazakhstan would depend on the Kazakh's process of reintegrating their diverse minority groups.

Juxtaposed to this narrative of deportation is the narrative of adaptation. Among the most prominent Korean Kazakhs are the government official Georgy Kim, who attained one of the highest levels of any non-Russian in the former Soviet Foreign Ministry and serves as Minister of Justice in the Republic of Kazakhstan, the writer Anatoly Kim and the scholar German Kim. Until the age of eight, Anatoly Kim spoke only Korean. Then he learned Russian and unlearned his native language forever. Studying painting and later literature in Moscow, Kim's short-stories and novellas have as varied geographical backgrounds as his own life. In some narratives, Kim alluded to the Korean community on Sakhalin or in Kazakhstan, but he never told of the sad events of 1937. And only when he was in his fifties—after the Soviet Union crumbled—could he visit Korea for the first time. Kim was able to fathom the worth of that travel and stay there when he wrote that his voyage was actually a search for a continent with many histories that were completely forgotten by the Korean people. The real Korea was the land to which he belonged. According to German Kim, such nostalgic feelings of a Korean were quite dissimilar to the business mentality of South Koreans who were in Kazakhstan either for business or for "mission work." They were at first welcomed with open arms by local Koreans, but gradually, these outsiders were perceived as arrogant and condescending as they started considering themselves as the flag-bearers of Korean culture. In such cases, ethnicity becomes "fictionalised"—as is the case of Anatoly Kim's story, "A Cry About a Mother in Seoul." The story and the film express these two contradictory feelings—one about a true Korean who wants to connect with his roots and the other about a Korean-Kazakh who has been in Soviet Kazakhstan for a long time and whose successors sadly do not connect with their homeland Korea. To these Koreans, they were in Soviet land, and now in Kazakh land, they tend to be pragmatic and are adaptive to new situations like religious awakening. To them, religious awakening may or may not solve ethnic dilemmas of the Korean community which has lived in Kazakhstan for 70 years.

In the film based on Anatoly Kim's story, death (projected as ultimate displacement) provokes the narrator's sense of alienation, which is exacerbated further when he visits his historic "motherland," where he cannot stop thinking about his deceased mother. His unstated dilemma is because he is sad about his displacement and also because of his saintly mother's death for which he blames Providence. The sense of loss increases at the funeral scene when the deceased mother is all alone in a sea of Russian names while there is a mound of snow which may be of reference to traditional Korean graves. Critics' reviews of this film point to vague promises as Providence which appears to be too exotic. It is interesting how the mother does not at all raise the point of ethnic alienation. It is the narrator who emphasises the ethnic link and it is too simplistic to argue that the Koreans feel alienated in Kazakhstan.

III. The Poles of Kazakhstan

Kazakhs of Polish ancestry and Kazakhs of Polish descent, originating from the western part of the Ukrainian Republic of USSR[17] were deported to Kazakhstan during Second World War and were repatriated during 1944-48. The Polish government's resolution of repatriation has theoretically allowed these people to settle in Poland. But in reality, having been brought up in the Soviet system and in Central Asia, the younger generations had no connect with their ethnic homeland in Poland. After deportation, the Soviet authorities disbanded these autonomous regions and deported the Poles. The place they were deported to was Kazakhstan—some dispersed in groups along the railway line and others were settled down in the distant steppe, hundreds of kilometres away from the railway. Soviet census figures show that largest concentrations of Polish minorities were in Kokeshetau, Karaganda and Akmolinsk.

IV. The Crimean Tatars

Similar tales of dislocation due to deportation come across accounts of Crimean Tatars who were exiled by the NKVD to Uzbekistan and Kazakhstan during the Second World War. Like the Volga Germans, these groups underwent an intensive process of ethnic consolidation in the Soviet period with the creation of Crimean Autonomous Soviet Socialist Republic in 1921. In the 1950s, there was an attempt to restore some of the surviving groups to their original homelands. As far as the Crimean Tatars were concerned, the luck came much later and at a heavier price. After 1989, a significant number of Crimean Tatars could return to their ancestral homeland. Between 1989 and 1994, about a million Crimean Tatars migrated from Uzbekistan to the Crimean Peninsula. Their return was considered to be a symbolic victory ever since their deportation to Uzbekistan during the Second World War. A report indicates the difficulties Crimean Tatars faced when they tried to migrate back to their home country:

> "House for Sale," "House for Sale." The backstreets of Yangiyul, a Tashkent suburb, are covered with these home-made signs. Their message symbolises the tragedy of Central Asia's remaining Crimean Tatars, a nation charged en masse of Nazi collaboration during World War II and brutally deported by Stalin from their homeland in Ukraine's Crimea.
>
> On May 18, hundreds of Crimean Tatars gathered in Yangiyul and other locations across Uzbekistan to commemorate the 60th anniversary of their exile. Their meetings followed instructions from the Uzbek Ministry of Internal Affairs not to stage the large-scale commemorations in Tashkent typical of previous years. For a government easily worried by mass meetings, it presented an undesirable risk. For this Diaspora, it was yet another setback as they struggle with bureaucracy, depressed housing prices and minimal official help to realise their dream of returning home.
>
> Almost 100,000 Crimean Tatars are said to live in Uzbekistan today, the survivors and offspring of more than 150,000 people deported here during the lightning-strike deportations of May 1944. Deported without warning and in appalling conditions, the entire Crimean Tatar nation ended up in "special settlements" in Central Asia and Russia. Crimean Tatars estimate that 46 per cent of their people died during deportation, resettlement and the hard labour that followed. Only well after Stalin's death were they allowed to leave the cramped and frugal settlements and begin building a life for themselves. Not until 23 years after they were deported, in 1967, were the Tatars exonerated of blame for mass treason. Only in 1989 were they officially permitted to begin repatriation to the Crimea. It is a problematic process that has left many still in exile.
>
> For those still in Uzbekistan, one of the biggest difficulties is finding the money for the move. Many are forced to wait to sell their houses before leaving, a process which can seem interminable. In the late 1950s, many

Crimean Tatars were given land in Uzbekistan by their employers. Yet these plots were generally in the least attractive parts of towns, usually in suburbs that few Uzbeks found desirable. Today, as these Tatars try to sell their homes, that fact is hard to escape.

Fatima Abibulla was six when the deportations took place. By the time she arrived in the settlements, she was an orphan. In the late 1950s, her husband, Asim, and she were given a plot "beyond the river" in Yangiyul, in a part of town where nobody else wanted to live. They built their two-storey house by hand and carted all the materials across the river and up the bank on foot. Now, they will be lucky if they get $4,000 for the residence.

Their eldest children have already left for the Crimea and have pleaded with Fatima and Asim to join them there. But Fatima cannot leave her house. She is insulted by how little the residence, with its large, well-tended vegetable garden, would fetch. With eight dependants besides themselves to transport to the Crimea, Fatima and Asim face travel costs of $2,000, plus $500 for the container to transport their small load of belongings. With annual incomes in Uzbekistan averaging $1,700, it is an astronomical amount of money, and one that would leave Fatima and her family only a pittance with which to create a new life in the Crimea. Yet all she and her husband want to do is to return to their homeland—and to die on its soil.

The sun beats down mercilessly on the Muslim graveyard in Yangiyul. Here, many of those who did not make it back to the Crimea to die are buried alongside their Uzbek neighbours. The shared world of Islam helped make integration a little easier. It meant common religious rituals, dress codes, traditions and festivals. The Tatars are unfailingly grateful to their Uzbek friends. But in the graveyard there is a stark difference between the graves. The Tatars have been buried as people from the Crimea. Steadfast in their desire to return to an almost mythical homeland, their relatives have inscribed Crimean place names beneath the dates of their births and deaths. (These place names often no longer exist in the Crimea thanks to a de-Tatarisation campaign that followed the Tatars' removal.) While nearby Uzbek graves bear elaborate eulogies to the deceased, Crimean Tatar graves are inscribed with simple tributes to their lost home.

For Ali Hanzim, the Central Asian representative of the Crimean Tatar Mejlis, or governing council, these graves represent years of resistance to the Soviet state. Ali Hanzim works tirelessly to improve the rights of Tatars in Central Asia. He is a passionate example of the peaceful activism for which the Crimeans have gained renown, must notably, under Mustafa Dzhemilev, a leader of the Crimean Tatars who spent much time in jail and labour camps during the Soviet period for spearheading a non-violent campaign for repatriation and improved national rights (a cause which attracted the support of such Soviet-era dissidents as Andrei Sakharov, Pyotr Grigorenko and Alexander Solzhenitsyn).

But Ali Hanzim is quick to point out that the Crimean Tatar national movement is not only represented by Mustafa Dzhemilev and his like. "The movement," he says, "is the people." Over the years, thousands of Tatars have helped campaign for resettlement, whether through collecting signatures for petitions to Moscow or fund-raising.

Ali Hanzim's 23-year-old son Sherket, who helps his mother to make and sell salads at the local bazaar, puts it succinctly. "The Crimea is our home. We are only guests here whether we're here for 50 years or 100. If we earn any money here we don't spend it. We save it to spend there—in our homeland."

His grandmother, Mergube Mamutova, 66, was a young girl at the time of the deportations, and her eyes still well with tears at the mention of them. She watches quietly as her nine-year-old granddaughter, Alime, leaves for school. The Crimean language and history have no place there. In depriving them of a homeland, the deportations also deprived the Crimean Tatars of their national rights and much of their culture. While Mergube and her generation offer a bridge to that culture, it will only remain secure if they can return.

Yet, despite a 1992 agreement for countries involved in the Crimean Tatars' deportation to help fund the costs of their resettlement, so far, only Ukraine has contributed any money towards this goal. No help has been forthcoming from the Uzbek government towards the actual cost of return and house prices in Uzbekistan have been depressed by the country's dire economic situation. In addition, despite a 1998 agreement between Ukraine and Uzbekistan to facilitate the transfer of citizenship, it can still take up to a year to receive a Ukrainian passport, and the fees for renouncing Uzbek citizenship remain high.

Nor are the problems entirely financial or bureaucratic. Bekir Ganiev, 30, has already received his Ukrainian passport. He, like his compatriots, wants to live in the Crimea. But Bekir can see for himself the unsatisfactory conditions in which those Tatars who have returned to the Crimea exist. The majority live in cramped conditions in villages with limited housing, water, electricity, roads and other amenities, while over 60 per cent of the Tatar population in the Crimea are unemployed. They still have only limited rights. Worse still, ethnic conflict prevails. Revered sites such as the grave of the nineteenth century Crimean Tatar national hero Ismail Bey Gasprinskii has recently been defaced by Slavic skinhead gangs. Faced with such prospects, Bekir, a successful businessman with a modern flat in Tashkent, says he will not return.

By all accounts, nostalgia for Central Asia runs high in the Crimea. Alie Akimova, who lives in Tashkent, tells how in 1990 her parents returned home. She speaks sadly of her father's death after only two years, how he lived alone with his wife in a tiny house without a courtyard or garden and no relatives to visit him. In Uzbekistan, she said, deportees used to meet and ask, "'Where are you from?' The answer would be Alushta, Kerch, Bahcesaray, Simferopol and other towns and regions of the Crimea. And now, back in the Crimea, they ask each other the same question. And in reply they say nostalgically 'Andizhan, Fergana, Shakhrisabz, Tashkent ...'"

While much of the nostalgia can be attributed to a general longing for the lost security of the Soviet Union, in Uzbekistan the homing instinct lives on. "Many of our friends have returned," said Suzanna Hanzima, Ali's wife. "Yes, it's hard, but they have worked so hard to get back there. Despite all the problems, they say it's wonderful finally to be home."[18]

Such historical memories were transmitted across time and space to new generations of Crimean Tatars. The new generations have assimilated these narratives and have constructed a paradigm based on people's sufferings and longing to return to their homeland, a homeland which many of them have never practically seen but could relate to.[19] New generations of Crimean Tatars grew up with such stories.

IV. The Kazakhs

Tales of deportation of Kazakh leaders resonate in the ALZHIR memorial complex. The complex is the recreated version (in 2007) of Akmola Deportation Camp for Wives of Traitors of the Revolution (*Akmolinskii Lager'Zhen Izmennykov Rodiny*). It was a Stalinist deportation camp within the gulag system and had several high profile prisoners (mostly wives and families of Alash Party leaders), artists and actresses. Most of them were women of aristocratic backgrounds who were interned as traitors or were wives and companions of activists branded as "enemies" of the Revolution. Situated in Malininka village about 40 kilometres west of Astana, the Memorial complex bears testimony to broken families and sorrows of women and children of Kazakh, Uzbek, Azeri, Polish, German, Korean backgrounds who were forced into a life of seclusion in this camp in the Kazakh steppe in the 1930s. The camp was in operation from the 1930s through to the early 1950s (more precise figures claim from 1937 to 1946) and was one of the most notorious camps in central Kazakhstan—not just because of its special role as a women's camp within the gulag system, but also because it had several high-profile prisoners, including artistes and actresses. Living conditions were just as harsh as in any gulag. Hardest for most, however, was the fact that they had been separated from their loved ones—not only husbands (who were considered the actual traitors and often sent to other gulags as far away as eastern Siberia, never to return) but also from their children. The documentary film shown to visitors at the museum makes the claim that Kazakhstan is the only country in the Soviet territory where deportation sites have survived. The historical role assigned to Kazakhstan in order to come to terms with its gulag history seems to be an over-enthusiastic enterprise. The official tendency is to project a single narrative about "a people's history," depicting various forms of Kazakh activism. The idea is to combine resistance movements of different genres into a single category. The present regime attempts to idealise the anti-colonial movement, be it the peasant resistance movements against Stolypin's reforms in 1905 or the Alash Orda movement of educated Kazakh intellectuals who had demanded land rights of the Kazakhs. Interestingly, whoever backed or voiced such demands, like the acclaimed Kazakh writer Saken Seifullin or Ahmet Baitursunov who was the People's Commissar for Education of the Kazakh Soviet Socialist Republic, became outcast during the Stalinist period. These leaders opposed the collectivisation campaign and the confiscation of property by the regime. Discontent against the laws of the land was met with harsh punishment, and the harshest of all was the isolation of the leaders from their families. Often referred to as "dark tourism" in the popular websites,[20] ALZHIR memorial museum is an effort on the part of the Kazakh state to bring out archival details about the deportation programme and the social layers that survived or perished during the 1930s.

The museum complexes in ALZHIR and Karaganda bear testimony to the repression of Kazakh people by their Soviet masters. The official new history of Kazakhstan[21] portrays the NKVD directives related to collectivisation and dekulakisation that restricted the supply of grain for the families and fodder for cattle. The sufferings of the deported families in the biting cold of the steppe region have been depicted in graphic detail in these memorial complexes. Such documents uphold the value of regional archives in Akmolinsk oblast. A lot of information drawn from private collections and memoirs of that period that provide interesting information about Kazakh stories of deportation have also been recorded here.

Narratives about the margins: Diaspora groups in Kazakhstan

Narratives about the margins[22] indicate borderlands as prime sites of social and cultural change.[23] In fact, the view that ethnic minorities within a nation-state are marginalised does understate the symbiotic relationship with ethnic majorities. As anthropological and ethnographic research show, these borderlands are also the agents of social change.[24] Borderlands research reflects a rich matrix of identities in motion. The focus is on diversity and mobility that create awareness about "bounded collectivities" and diasporas in the region. Diasporas refer to the group identities belonging to ethnic, confessional and economic groups that were constructed out of multiple loyalties in a colonial or post-colonial space. The new attention to diasporas highlight the importance given to the intellectual and cultural communities who, at different points of time, were exiled or displaced from their homelands, and have adopted meaningful roles as translators of their indigenous historical cultures in their newly adopted surroundings. It is because of these diaspora linkages that the world of Eurasia has been connected with the world outside it.

Despite these positive assessments, one can hardly undo the general impression about diaspora as signifying dispersal and displacement. Most of the early discussions about the diaspora were firmly rooted in a conceptual homeland and the paradigmatic notion revolved round specific cases. The term initially referred to the Jewish population or any other population that experienced traumatic history of dispersal, myths and memories of the homeland, alienation in the host country, desirous of eventual return to the ancestral homeland that is receptive to a collective identity. Subsequently, the studies branched out to other examples of "classical diasporas" and specific categories like "victim diaspora," "catastrophic diaspora," "trading diaspora," etc.[25] But today we have new and hybrid forms of diaspora with more emotional and social content. From the point of view of the homeland, emigrant groups have been classified as diasporas. Today, diaspora, which represents a critical interface between nation-states and globalisation, can be extended to many other ethnic groups whose diasporic existence goes beyond a unique experience of trauma as it reflects a sense of belonging to evolving transnational networks that involves bonding not only with land of birth, land of descent and with the society of residence but across the border of other nation-states.[26] Sometimes studies are not limited to country-specific diasporas but tend to extend to "putative diasporas."[27]

Diaspora studies have brought to the limelight a new dimension, i.e., transnationalism. The concept of transnationalism, an offshoot of the borderlands' debate, points to interpenetrations in a global society. Transnational social spaces have entered the domain of diaspora studies and the gamut of knowledge has expanded to include not only spatial identities but also relationships between space, place and identity. There seems to be a basic difference between the two concepts—diaspora refers to the group identities (ethnic, religious or otherwise) living outside the ancestral homeland, and transnationalism as cross-border community networks reflecting durable ties among communities across countries. Sometimes these two concepts are used interchangeably though each of them signifies different interpretative traditions. In public debates and policy analyses, the distinction between these two terms often goes unnoticed. Sometimes there are overlaps which are rarely noticed either.[28]

The revival of the diaspora and the advent of the transnational approaches can be used to study central questions about social change and political transformation. The multiple trajectories of people's movements across shared spaces in Eurasia and the relationship between place and identity have made Kazakhstan's borderlands an interesting case study. A handful of scholars (Alexander Diener, Cynthia Werner and Holly Barcus) have critiqued the *oralman* project of the Kazakh government from the point of view of Mongol Kazakhs whose preference lies with their host country (i.e., Mongolia) rather than the ethnic homeland which is Kazakhstan. Such questions tend to dispel myths not only about ethnicity but also about diaspora behaviour. Repatriation policies promoted the notion of "homeland" and President Nazarbayev enthusiastically welcomed "home," his "Kazakh kin," offering migration, employment, education, and financial incentives to ethnic Kazakhs living outside of the Kazakhstan territory.[29] Arguing from a state perspective, Kuscu explains that repatriation *successfully "returned" ethnic Kazakhs*, tipping the balance of ethnic groups to favour a Kazakh majority by the late 1990s. Such ethnically privileged migration flows are encouraged for the purpose of increasing ethnic status thereby encouraging "return" migration to the homeland. Kuscu voiced the state's rationale, while Diener argued why the Mongol Kazakhs decided to migrate. He argues that some of the early migrants were elites of Ulaanbaatar who wanted to raise their children in the Kazakh homeland. These migrants were followed by those searching for economic opportunities as conditions in Bayan Olgii quickly deteriorated. The third category included young generation of migrants who opted for Kazakhstan's modern lifestyle. So, in Diener's argument, the "pull factor" for migration was pretty strong, and the vision of Kazakhstan as an imagined homeland for the Mongolian Kazakhs was an immense attraction in favour of migration to the ethnic homeland—at least till the end of the 1990s.

But the reality of "return" is often fraught with disappointment. This is the counter argument of Cynthia Werner and Holly Barcus.[30] Their studies reveal that one-third of the repatriated people returned to Mongolia by 2008, completely disillusioned with the repatriation programme, encountering troubles as they were considered to be migrants belonging to both Kazakhstan and Mongolia. Diener reviewed his thesis in the 2000s. The main reason for this was the Migration Law of 2002 with annual quotas of migration which fluctuated from time to time.

This "selective treatment" reduced opportunities for migrants within Kazakhstan and also created uncertainties of living due to competition (which increased maximally among the Uzbeks—their arrival recorded as high as up to 60%) and corrupt practices. The next phases of migration were during 2003-8 when there was a circular migration—as Mongol Kazakhs returned to the Bayan Olgii province where conditions improved, opportunities of employment grew (with emphasis on eco-tourism bringing in tourists and investors who employed Mongol Kazakhs for their expertise in eagle-hunting, cycling up mountains, research on petroglyphs and information-gathering for research on nomads, herders and pastoral farming in Mongolia. So, at this stage, the attraction for moving to Kazakhstan was not for economic reasons but for social networks—sharing experiences of living in Kazakhstan—and that too on a daily basis (e.g., through texts via cellphones which had become very cheap). These scholars have explored further to analyse "migration streams" or "migration flows"—indicating that the new destinations of the migrants were no longer Kazakhstan but Turkey and China.

The oralman programme has raised other doubts: since ethnic Kazakhs from other countries have all been welcomed as returnees to the motherland as bonafide immigrants. None of them could be turned away at the border. Not being awarded *oralman* status, however, means that there is limited entitlement to *oralman* benefits. This in turn made the whole system prone to corruption "at every level."[31] Not only does the *oralman* programme create new problems for Kazakhstan as new arrivals struggle to gain a foothold economically and socially but also illustrates the disconnection between the legal infrastructure and the grand vision of Nazarbayev in showcasing Kazakhstan as a multi-ethnic nation. For immigrants from China and elsewhere, who come with the expectation of land and a revival of their herding activities, the economic stress (not enough grass to fatten the sheep at a good market value) was compounded by other concerns (e.g., no legal right to grazing land, to find employment in unfamiliar settings, etc.), as well as feeling humiliated by their surrendered position to governmental authorities. To rehabilitate the *oralman* programme, the Kazakh government launched a new initiative since 2009 which is called the *Nurly Kosh* (Blessed Migration) programme—focusing on places in North Kazakhstan (like Aqmola and Kostanay) where out-migration in the aftermath of Kazakisation had created a demographic imbalance.[32]

In the light of diverse migration trends and corresponding identities of place that have appeared in Kazakhstan and its borderlands in the last two decades, it would be appropriate to argue that neither ethnic polarisation nor common diaspora behaviour associated with homelessness is the reality in the case of the Kazakh migrants. Not only have the discussions moved to fluid contours of space, place and identity but also to varying degrees of attachment to different places of origin and places of living. So, there is an aspect of dynamism in diaspora Kazakhs staying immobile or rooted in western Mongolia rather than returning to their ethnic Kazakh homeland which is alien to them. In their assessments, scholars have suggested interactive behaviour in various landscapes and the ways in which the people relate to that particular landscape.[33]

I. Kazakhs of China

It would be prudent to also consider whether yearning for the Kazakh homeland determines the everyday choices of Chinese Kazakhs (Dungan or Uyghur) who number some 1.1 million people in the Xinjiang Uyghur Autonomous Region. This vast region located in the northwest of China, adjacent to Kazakhstan, Russia and Mongolia and having a strong identification with a nomadic past is considered to be the new home of the minority ethnic groups in China. In Xinjiang, Kazakhs live in Urumqi and other cities, and are found dispersed mainly across the northern prefectures of Yili, Tacheng and Altai. Seeking occupational and cultural rootedness, they have embraced the idea of immigrating to Kazakhstan as a way of securing their pastoral livelihood. China's Kazakhs are attracted to leaving for Kazakhstan, where they believe they will have the freedom to migrate with their livestock. Due to the early twentieth century territorial delimitation, the ethnic minorities (including nomadic populations) of the Soviet space were dispersed and their grazing lands and migration routes were bifurcated and altered to fit inside new nation-states. This dispersed the Kazakhs of Mongolia from their brethren in Russia, China and Kazakhstan. Throughout the twentieth century, nomadic Kazakhs, Mongolian and Kyrgyz herdsmen endured great changes in their environment and animal husbandry practices. The Soviets implemented rigorous sedentarisation since the 1930s, bringing many Kazakhs under the *sovkhoz* and *kolkhoz* model of production, while allowing a continuation of limited migration of livestock. In Kazakhstan, following dissolution of the Soviet Union, in the wake of societal changes, migration and displacement of nomadic population took place. Kazakhs in the Xinjiang Uyghur Autonomous Region who chose to herd sheep and maintain livestock, had to encounter several problems. They are subject to geographical enclosures at a macro and micro level. These enclosures first began in the 1950s, but have become more stringent in the recent decade, especially since 2005. Coupled with the increasingly severe degradation of the grazing lands in both winter and summer pastures of recent years, which itself had been exacerbated by locusts, rodents and unfavourable weather conditions, the quality of pasturage for the livestock has become a grave concern across districts and counties to Kazakh nomads, government officials and scientists alike. What is the most important factor to the success of nomadic activity—the widest possible flexibility of grazing options—has been restricted for the pastoral Kazakhs in Xinjiang.

Furthermore, this tightening of access to high quality and sufficient quantity grazing land directly affected the nomad families. Thinner sheep fetch lower prices, but the difference is made up by adding to the volume, even though this is not sustainable. As the cost of living in China has been going up rapidly, even in this remote western province, the cash income for herding families has decreased under the impact of market forces. In recent years, many families find themselves caught in a vicious cycle contributing to their own destitution. This has forced households and their extended families to employ new strategies for survival, seriously considering options like continue to go ahead with migrations and herding or stop altogether and sedentarise, or consider emigrating to Kazakhstan heeding to the oralman programme. A recent study takes a new course by looking at the oralman programme as a pull-factor for China's Kazakhs.[34] The choice was very difficult indeed. Although emigration to Kazakhstan is an opportunity for these Chinese Kazakhs especially because it gave the chance of choosing a sustainable future, it had the same level of risk as their life in China—and sometimes additional constraints.

Attracted by promises of free health and education services, the mirage of greener grass and plentiful land on which to graze their livestock, the Chinese Kazakhs have been opting for permanent migration for the first time since the short-lived exodus in the early 1960s. They believe that Kazakhstan is somewhat of a promised land, rescuing them from the exhausted environments of Chinese counties. This imagined reality is mostly anecdotally known to the families in China, usually by word of mouth from stories told by émigré family members back to visit, potentially supported by random media reports. Not only the oralman programme, but also the ideas and opportunities of immigration into Kazakhstan have captured the imagination of many Kazakhs living in Xinjiang. Seldom does one realise that the emigration opportunity does little to solve the ongoing problems ensuing from grassland degradation or the risk of poverty among livestock herding Kazakhs in both countries. For instance, there is little entitlement to oralman benefits. The oralman policy has spelt out a quota system (with housing benefits, employment, travel costs, educational support, etc.) which signifies a restrictive policy towards immigration. But in practice more families from China have immigrated than the quota of, say, 500 families from China for the year 2006. The consequence is direct: the majority of the returnees remained ineligible for full economic and educational opportunities. The policy and the quota system have been very popular, though there are many more returnees that fall outside the quota, and there have been no benefits paid out except within the quota. Some returnees even found themselves counted as stateless if they gave up their previous citizenship without being extended the Kazakhstani citizenship.

Also, Chinese policy of development of Xinjiang has also resulted in restrictive flows. But usually the attraction for immigration has been immense, especially from the point of view of successive generations. Another interesting development is the development of bilateral trade between China and Central Asia and the presence of Kazakhstan as a strong player in the Central Asian region which has urged families to look for better business opportunities in Kazakhstan. Elena Sadovskaya has researched on this aspect of Chinese labour migrants in Kazakhstan—those coming for long periods of residence as oralmans (a large section of them being students) and those coming as trade migrants (like Dungans, Uyghurs) or as workers. There seems to be a fairly distinctive character of Chinese workers employed in the regions. Sadovskaya gives us the statistics: "In the 1990s, the Chinese presence was largely confined to the city of Almaty and the Almaty and Ak Tobe regions in the south whereas in the 2000s, the west of the country (Ak Tobe, Atyrau and Mangystau regions) became a significant destination. Apart from trade, the main economic sectors currently employing a Han Chinese workforce are mining (oil and gas) and small industrial production and services (including banking, hotel, restaurant, medical services, etc)."[35]

Besides the factor of mobility which a nomad is used to, the factor of immobility also needs to be considered. The responses of Kazakh nomads in China about settling down in Kazakhstan have differed on a case-to-case basis. For instance, families living in winter homes would have middle-aged male members who would subscribe to the option of settling down permanently in Kazakhstan, have some land, and give children a steady life. The other factor is the herding profession—to continue that requires skill and will as well as wealth, all of which have slackened over the years. For those families living in summer homes (yurts), the response is completely different—they have no reason to emigrate and settle down. Some even want to try emigrating if they can combine all activities of nomadism and sedentarisation, i.e., herding, growing seeds, producing hay through division of labour among family members. Generally speaking, the idea of uniting with their brothers, i.e., the Kazakhs of Kazakhstan was extremely appealing. However, some families felt that it was far too expensive to migrate. The expectations were often in contrast to the oralman experience. The difficulties of livestock management were a major constraint that pulled them back. Reports on social integration of oralmans were also not appreciable.

This was reiterated by members of a French NGO that was comprised of oralmans originally from the Kazakh Ili prefecture in China, who were "resettled in Kazakhstan" but migrated to European cities in Holland and France. As one respondent Marip, 38 years old (in 2012) narrated his case:

> I'm a Kazakh, born in China, but my grandparents came to Gulja from Almaty region in the 1930s when Soviets forced them to accept the massive collectivisation. My grandfather was a cropper and owned many hectares of lands forcefully confiscated by the Soviet regime that killed his younger brother. My parents were born in China and dreamed all their life of coming back to their ancestral homeland. But, the political context of both countries, China and Kazakhstan, did not allow them to realise their dream until 1990 when the borders opened after the USSR's collapse. My father could not, he died in 1986. When I heard about the Oralman programme promoted by Kazakh government, with my mother we decided without hesitation to go to Almaty. We felt then something really magnificent like the wind of liberty; we believed that we could leave China and its communist regime and go to live freely in Kazakhstan. There were many

> Kazakhs from our region interested by this programme and wanted to get to the country where we could speak our mother tongue and practise our own traditions and customs. You know, we are not considered as people by the Chinese who work in administration and own all the great businesses in our region. We asked the Chinese local authorities; who of course agree with Kazakh government, for a permission of departure (validity 5 years) and rest of the procedure was effected by Kazakh consular offices in China. It did not take a lot of time. Indeed, we don't have relatives in Kazakhstan, because our grandparents had moved with all their families' members. It was just the Kazakh government generous invitation that motivated us to come and to consider all Kazakh citizens as our relatives. When we arrived in Kazakhstan, we were initially proud of being Oralmans but things, in reality, did not take place as we had foreseen and believed …

The estranged feeling is further expressed in another account of a migrant in Holland. Talmas, 43 years old, explained the reasons:

> As many compatriots, I arrived to Almaty from China through the Kazakh State programme for *Oralmans* (*sheteldegiqazaqtar*—Kazakhs from abroad—in Kazakh language). Initially, everything was fine; we had a house, work and an ambience quite international because there were many different neighbourhoods; Russian, Polish, Korean, Ukrainian, born in Kazakhstan. And we could send our children to the Kazakh school where they also learned Russian. We were happy to get all this opportunity that was offered to us by our historical homeland …. You know, we had left China because we were not considered there as the part of the Chinese nation, where corruption and injustice are omnipresent in political and economic life. And coming to Kazakhstan, we hoped to be finally proud of being Kazakh and of having the Kazakh language and culture transmitted to us from generation to generation. But, in reality our hopes were in vain; in Kazakhstan, despite the Kazakh language being the official language of State, you must speak Russian, you have to pay backhander to study, to get your diploma and to land a job. If you have money, you are able to do everything you want. The political and economic life in society is governed by corruption; the exact situation that we had faced in China. Instead of finding again our historical homeland, we felt as foreigners and undesirable in the eyes of

> the local population. The Kazakhs that we believed eager of their own language and culture are still ashamed to speak Kazakh and to show their origins. Because I lived in Almaty, I talk to you about Kazakhs from Almaty. They consider other Russian speaking minorities closer to them than us. And they treated us as enemies who would leave the homeland in a difficult situation. They don't like that we came back to Kazakhstan after independence and where the government offers us social and juridical aid. Moreover, we don't have close resemblances; our Kazakh is quite different from theirs which is mixed with Russian words as their culture was influenced by Russian culture. When I first arrived in Almaty, I felt as if I were in Europe. That's why we have difficulties integrating into Kazakh society, contrarily to other Oralmans from Uzbekistan and Turkmenistan who speak Russian and grew up with the Soviet education.[36]

The alienation of the third generation is mostly because of the differing environments: Most of the Chinese Kazakhs are used to Arabic script while the older generations were accustomed to the Romanised Kazakh alphabet. Kazakh language in Kazakhstan has Cyrillic script. Their conversational Kazakh is derogatorily termed "do revolutsionnoi yazyk" or "staryi yazyk." The language dilemma has hindered the process of social integration of the new immigrants.

But there is another aspect to this Uyghur story. Describing the "in-between-ness" of the Uyghurs, i.e., looking beyond the standard perception of the Uyghurs as a minority community inhabiting the Xinjiang Autonomous Region of the People's Republic of China but with a meaningful presence in the Central Asian region, some scholars have distinctly deviated from sinophobic notions of a Uyghur separatist movement transcending the geographical space of China's western dominions. In the 2000s, *Uyghurovedeniya* has taken a new direction with focus on the dialectics of the homeland issue. Contemporary Uyghur scholars tend to revive Soviet studies about early Uyghur states of Eastern Turkestan—for example, the old Uyghur kingdoms which were oases settlements of the Alta Shahr (Six Cities south of the Tian Shan Mountains) had a pivotal role in the making of the spatial category "Eastern Turkestan." In this revivalist literature, names as Yatta Shahr Uyghur State (*Uygurskoye Gosudarstvo Yettishahr)* have come up for discussion. A much more lively debate about the homeland is related to the Uyghur community of the Semirechie (Kazakh name *Zhetysu* or the Land of the Seven Rivers)—a region in southeastern Kazakhstan.[37]

Ablet Kamalov, a Uyghur historian based in Almaty describes the shared histories of the Uyghurs of Kazakhstan and China.[38] The Uyghur community's spatial identity, according to common knowledge, is Eastern Turkestan, a term used interchangeably with "Chinese Turkestan" and "Sinkiang" from where large number of internal migrations occurred during the Qing period (1644-1912). The migration history of the Uyghurs in Semirechie, argues Kamalov, indicates Tsarist Russia's hold on the frontier territory of the Qing Empire.[39] The Ili District of China was reconstituted as the province of Xinjiang in 1884 after it was returned to the Qing Empire. The transfer of power by the Treaty of St. Petersburg was followed by a mass movement of Uyghurs westward towards Semirechie. The Uyghur migrants were settled in several *qishlaqs* (villages) in the Russian portion of the Ili valley (i.e., Semirechie) in Yarkand while six *volosts* or administrative districts were established for the Uyghur migrants in Yarkand, Aksu, Charyn, Koram and Qara Su and four settlements in Verny. From this time onwards, the Uyghurs have been constituted as one of the three main ethnic groups in the Russian portion of the Ili valley along with the Russians and the Kazakhs. A smaller group of immigrants from southern part of Xinjiang, called *Kashgarliks*, proceeded in the direction of the Ferghana Valley. By the end of the nineteenth century, a small group of Uyghurs also moved towards the direction of Bairam Ali. After the Russian revolution of 1917, a large number of Uyghurs moved eastwards towards China to escape Soviet repression. This back and forth movement of the Uyghurs dating back to the Tsarist Russia's settlement policy establishes the Uyghurs' rootedness in the Semirechie. The Semirechie homeland theory among the Uyghurs and other aspects of Xinjiang's shared spaces has been researched upon recently.[40] There seem to be linguistic connections between the Uyghurs and the Altai branch of the Turkic language family which also creates a commonality of issues between the Uyghurs and the Kazakhs, Kyrgyz, Turkmen and Uzbeks of Central Asia and the people of Turkey. The homeland issue centred round the Uyghur kaganate in the Orkhon valley (in present-day Mongolia) that existed from AD 744-840. The homeland that came into existence with the foundations of the Uyghur kaganate was considered sacrosanct. This homeland was originally situated in eastern Siberia and Mongolia and thereafter included parts of Kazakhstan, Kyrgyzstan, Uzbekistan and Xinjiang. The centre of this early Uyghur state was in Beshbalyk, not Kashgar. All these factual details are supplementary evidence about the Uyghurs as indigenous settlers in the Semirechie region. Such subjects became popular in Soviet historiography during the 1950s-1970s. Since the late 1980s at the time of the growth of nationalism in Soviet Central Asia, the issue of rootedness of the Uyghurs in Semirechie was revived.[41]

Such nostalgic moments were captured in the Kazakh film *Zamanai* (1998). In the film, the journey of a grandmother and her grandson (Amanai) to their ancestral land in Kazakhstan (Semirechie) and the conversation between her and her dead son Zamanai is the scene of action. The conversation till the end of the journey depicts the contested notions of the Kazakh homeland. The mother-son imaginary conversation reveals the mother's longing of being united with her tribal home in Semirechie while the son is still loyal to the Soviet military service in which he was trained and which cost him his life. It reflects the nostalgia among the Kazakhs for Semirechie which was their ancestral homeland, the tension between Kazakhs of Kazakhstan and the migrants from China and the attachment for the new home in China.

> *Grandmother to Alima (mother of Amanai)*:
> I will show Amanai his father's land.
> That is what Zamanai would love.
> My grandson, Amanai stays with me.
> He will see the birthplace of his ancestors.
>
> *Alima*:
> Grandmother—do as you please.
> You can stay.
> Amanai is not staying.
> You keep saying "home country" but where is it?
> Neither you nor me have it.
> One's home is a place where one feels good.[42]

These tangled connections so far hardly got the attention they deserve. The Semirechie homeland issue is a muted affair while transnational Uyghur separatism has become an issue of global concern.

The 1990s and the 2000s offered a new window of opportunity for the Uyghurs of Central Asia. The Kazakh city of Almaty had become in many respects the centre of an evolving transnational Uyghur community by the mid-1990s. The city of Almaty was symbolically poised as a city with opportunities for the majority of the Turkic nationalities including the Uyghurs. Almaty, only a few hours distance by car from China, has been a city of cross-border interaction for the Uyghurs and they have found themselves in the city negotiating between divergent influences emanating from respective sides of the border for over a century. As a result, the Uyghurs of Almaty can be divided into several groups determined by their respective experiences on each side of the border. The varied experiences of each of these migrant groups are reflected in their different perceptions of what it means to be a Uyghur migrant from China and a Uyghur settled in Almaty. Sean Roberts has an extreme view about Uyghurs of Almaty trying to showcase cultural unity as their only chance to avoid total marginalisation. His stay in a Uyghur neighbourhood in Almaty, *Zarya Vostoka* (Dawn of the East) during his field visit in the 1990s demonstrated the following features: (a) a socialist legacy among the *yerlik* or the locals, (b) cultural discourse among the Uyghurs who migrated to USSR in the 1950s and 1960s, (c) a capitalist discourse among all groups. There is also an Islamist discourse that displays unity of ideas about rituals and religious practice. These discourses interact with each other in the production of a Uyghur identity in *Zarya Vostoka.* So what emerges here is a collective perception of what it means to be a Uyghur even though the lived-in experiences are different for each group.

The Uyghurs of Kazakhstan have different tales of belonging. Certain myths and phobias about Chinese presence do haunt the Central Asian region and sometimes there are attitudinal issues, despite the fact that attitudes towards Beijing are changing. Seldom do they feel alienated from their host country, Kazakhstan. Transnational sentiments are also evident because of shared historical memories. The Uyghurs and the Dungans are China's Central Asian minorities who have displayed their trading skills to a major extent but whose competitiveness in Kazakhstan remains modest. However, these cross-border minorities play a significant role in the development of Sino-Central Asian economic relations and in the cultural mediations between the two worlds. For some Kazakhs, China is just one of their neighbours, which in recent years has been active in Central Asia. Even at the expert level knowledge about contemporary Chinese issues and the specificities of Kazakh-Chinese relations have not surfaced yet.[43] So, what needs to be considered here is the fact that even if there is no definitive research data or foolproof evidence about apathy towards Chinese influence in Kazakhstan, there is a set of questions related to Chinese presence in the region. There is indeed some amount of information each group has at its disposal about these communities and also there is a level of communication that the Kazakhs have with them. Sometimes there are complicated and nuanced views among the general public. These go beyond the rubric of phobias regarding China that date back to the Dzhungar period. It so appears that the Kazakh public is often a little indifferent to Chinese migrants. The most tolerant attitude is demonstrated by Almaty residents as well as in the northern regions.

The Dungans' Chineseness is often viewed with scepticism—i.e., "as Chinese, but not quite"—and their ancestors, e.g., the Huis are considered to be "familiar strangers."[44] But it is interesting to observe various theories regarding the origin of the Dungans—besides a Chinese theory there is also a Russian theory as well as a theory describing Turkic descent of the Dungans settled in Xinjiang. Sometimes the blanket word Dungan refers to people of Hui ethnicity, i.e., the Uyghurs, the Kazakhs and the Kyrgyz who settled down and lived in the Xinjiang region since the 1760s. The Dungans of Central Asia (and Kazakhstan) call themselves *Huizu*. I sensed some of these distinctive approaches during my field trip to Astana and Almaty in August 2013. It is these perceptions that have imparted a dynamic profile to the Russo-Chinese borderlands that overlap with Kazakhstan and Ili prefecture of China.

II. Kazakhs of Western Mongolia

Talking about varying degrees of attachment to different places of origin and places of living, scholars have identified interactive behaviour in various landscapes and the ways in which the people relate to that particular landscape. Others have argued that in post-Soviet Eurasia, social tension brews at the ground level, arising out of intra-ethnic differentiation and contested identities. The debate therefore swings between two poles—from areas of interaction to areas of confrontation and competition, indicating contrasting claims about place and identity, questioning assumptions about reciprocity, community interaction, etc. In this subsection, I will try to explain how Kazakhs of western Mongolia nurture different perceptions of "home."

There are opinions that home and homelessness are polar opposites and that homelessness represents the absence of home. A homeless person can also "feel out of place." Since the aspect of human attachment is directly related to the live-in space, it would be logical to argue that there is a dynamic relationship between a person and his environment—therefore, home can be judged to be an experienced space—which is dynamic and not fixed. The ways in which people negotiate and adjust themselves within that space is part of their homely existence and therefore indicates a dynamic process. Adaptation to the endlessly changing conditions makes a diaspora's condition dynamic. Theorists have also linked these arguments to the larger debate about migration. Among nationalising states of Eurasia, concepts of the homeland and return migration are invariably linked with the integration of titular nationalities. Within such a framework, it is assumed that non-titular nationalities are marginalised. Now, one would expect that dispersed ethnic groups would consider themselves automatically bonded with the new nation-states or their ancestral homelands. But it so happens that there is a dual response among migrants within the same community and this is what makes the Mongolian Kazakhs so unique. Their case reflects what is more important in the homeland issue—i.e., not *who we are* but *where we feel we belong* or also *where we do not belong*. These feelings are not primordial dictates but are related to certain historical contexts and settings. These settings impact on the psyche of the return migrants to such an extent that many continue to have enduring ties with their host societies and fail to identify themselves with their co-ethnics in their ancestral land—a feature among the Mongolian Kazakhs.[45]

Scholars examining the issue of transnational migration in the case of Kazakhs of western Mongolia point out factors like macroeconomic forces and local economic trends and practices that led to this trend. Numbering over 100,000, the Kazakhs are the largest ethnic minority in Mongolia. The majority of Mongolian Kazakhs live in the Western *aimaq* (province) of Bayan-Ulgii, a region that is near Kazakhstan yet separated by small strips of territory that belongs to Russia and China.

The Study Area: Bayan-Ulgii in a World Context

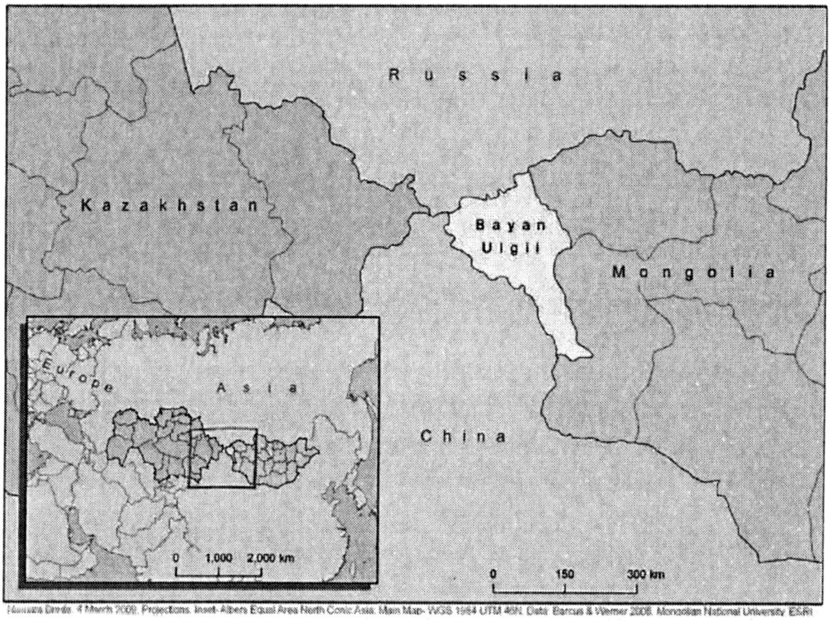

The majority of Mongolian Kazakhs, 78.4%, live in Bayan-Ulgii province (*aimaq*) in Western Mongolia. A significant number of Kazakhs also live in neighbouring Khovd province (*aimaq*) and the city of Ulaanbaatar. In Khovd province, the Kazakhs are a minority of the population but there are several sizable settlements in the city of Khovd and in a rural region (*sum*) named Khovd.

According to several sources, approximately 50,000–60,000 Mongolian Kazakhs emigrated in the 1990s, and possibly 10,000–20,000 returned to Mongolia by the early 2000s. Official statistics in Kazakhstan indicate that 71,507 Mongolian oralmandar and 22,117 Chinese oralmandar currently reside in Kazakhstan. Although Kazakhstan is physically close to Bayan-Ulgii aimaq, those choosing a land route travel approximately 900 kilometres through Russia to northern Kazakhstan because there is no direct road across the Altai Mountains. Alternatively, some migrants have travelled by air, using post-Soviet air routes from Ulgii, Mongolia to Ustkamenogorsk (Oskemen), Kazakhstan. Many but not all of the migrants have arrived by invitation of the Kazakhstani government, through an annual quota system for diaspora Kazakhs from outside of the former Soviet Union.

Similar to the perceptions of Chinese Kazakhs, the attractiveness of better life in Kazakhstan created an urge to immigrate to the ethnic homeland. Diener argues that some of the earliest migrants were Kazakh elites who lived in Ulaanbaatar and who believed it was important to raise their children in the Kazakh homeland. These migrants were followed by those searching for economic opportunities as conditions in Bayan-Ulgii quickly deteriorated in the early 1990s. Families, impoverished by economic crisis, chose to migrate. Young people opted against their herding lifestyle for a more "modern" lifestyle, and could now choose to migrate to either Kazakhstan or Ulaanbaatar. In the early 1990s, migration to Kazakhstan was idealised in Mongolian and Kazakhstani media for both cultural and economic reasons. Diener's suggestion is that Kazakhs are being "pulled" to Kazakhstan, not "pushed" out of Mongolia.

Policies on ethnic return were announced. The legitimising discourse on the part of Kazakhstani leadership was juxtaposed to the victimisation discourse about forced exodus of ethnic Kazakhs during collectivisation and forced sedentarisation in the 1930s. The repatriation policy was legitimised and there were expectations about an increase in the number of Kazakhs as the titular nationality. The policy was also justified from the point of view of a renewal of national culture and traditions in the ancestral homeland. The terms that were used to emphasise return migration reflected the governmental rhetoric. These were *atameken, atazhurt* (land of the forefathers), *otan* (homeland), *Tarikhi otan* (ancestral homeland). For diaspora Kazakhs, the following terms were used: *Shetel qazaqtari* (Kazakhs abroad), *shette zhurgen qandastar* (brothers living abroad). Subsequently, the relationship between place and identity became the dominant feature of the renewed vision about a civic nation and this change in stance is reflected in the recent usage of the word *otandash* which means the connection with land and its people rather than blood ties or genetic ties.[46] Ubiquitous trope of "hospitality" (*qonaqzhailylyq*), as a defining characteristic of "Kazakhness" (*Qazaqtyq*) and an essential part of Kazakh nomadic "heritage" was often used to explain the reason for harmonious interethnic relations in Kazakhstan.

The impact of this return migration has been tremendous, not only resulting in a quantum jump of immigrants from Mongolia (about 860,000 oralmandar) but also escalating social tension especially in western Kazakhstan where there has been exceeding pressure on housing which became scarce and expensive because Soviet-era buildings deteriorated and the new construction was inadequate to meet the growing demands. The pull factor often did not yield expected results beyond a certain stage (1991-1996). Kazakh-Mongolian tension seems to have prevailed in Bayan-Ulgii aimaq where the Kazakhs had actually strengthened their cultural and political autonomy since the mid-1950s. Ironically, the Mongolian Kazakhs have preserved Kazakh culture and language to a greater extent than many Kazakhstani Kazakhs whose first language is often Russian. It is not uncommon for Mongolian Kazakhs to be treated as outsiders by Kazakhstani Kazakhs. Unequal provision of housing and material support (social pensions, child allowances, free health care, and free education for children) and bureaucratic problems linked to the process of social integration and becoming naturalised citizens has disillusioned some migrants. This is why it is possible to explain why a significant number of the Mongolian Kazakhs chose to return to Mongolia after spending several years in Kazakhstan.

Also, the very notion that Kazakhstan is the historic homeland for all Kazakhs, an idea promoted by the Kazakhstani government, has been widely contested by many of the Mongolian Kazakhs who are not seeking to migrate. Special privileges (residence permits and voting rights) to all returnees on the basis of genealogy and kinship and announcements of "in-gathering" have created uneasiness among resident Kazakhs as the migrants from abroad got a new lease of life. There are critiques about this "recruitment of ethnic diaspora" as it beings the migrants into collusion with their kin state representatives.[47] As many as one-third of the migrants have returned to Mongolia disillusioned by their encounters with the homeland. Their experiences with co-ethnics have not been happy either. The stresses and strains of post-Soviet transition emanating from an urban-rural divide are reflected in the migrants' discourses about otherness. An Almaty-based analyst Naubet Bisenov remarked: "The main problem is with the acceptance of oralmandar as equals to local Kazakhs, because they think oralmandar are uneducated freeloaders. When they go for a job interview, people show genuine surprise that oralmandar can have a higher education and speak languages and be specialists in jobs that demand quite high qualifications."[48] But the pull factor often did not yield expected results beyond a certain stage (1991-1996). Kazakh-Mongolian tension seems to have prevailed in Bayan-Ulgii aimaq where the Kazakhs had actually strengthened their cultural and political autonomy since the mid-1950s. Ironically, the Mongolian

Kazakhs have preserved Kazakh culture and language to a greater extent than many Kazakhstani Kazakhs whose first language is often Russian. It is not uncommon for Mongolian Kazakhs to be treated as outsiders by Kazakhstani Kazakhs. Mongolian and Chinese Kazakhs, for example, are often referred to as "Mongolians" or "Chinese" respectively by Kazakhstani Kazakhs. Unequal provision of housing and material support (social pensions, child allowances, free health care, and free education for children) and bureaucratic problems linked to the process of social integration and becoming naturalised citizens has disillusioned some migrants. This is why it is possible to explain why a significant number of the Mongolian Kazakhs chose to return to Mongolia after spending several years in Kazakhstan. Also, the very notion that Kazakhstan is the historic homeland for all Kazakhs, an idea promoted by the Kazakhstani government, has been widely contested by many of the Mongolian Kazakhs who are not seeking to migrate.

However, such negativity has been replaced by positive assessments in the light of increased transborder trade and the development of telecommunications technology.[49] Cynthia Werner and her colleague Holly Barcus have analysed how the characteristics and directions of Mongolian Kazakh migration flows have altered in response to changing economic conditions in both the sending and receiving countries as well as changing incentives offered by the Kazakhstani government. The authors argue that familial conditions as well as economic conditions in local and regional contexts have influenced their decision to migrate. The "emotional pull" factor was fairly strong that brought Mongolian Kazakhs to Kazakhstan. In certain respects, repatriated Kazakhs received more assistance than citizens of Kazakhstan as they were also offered financial assistance, including lump sum payments for housing. A few respondents suggested that free livestock were also provided to some individuals. Economic conditions in Kazakhstan were also difficult in the early 1990s, and in practice, the government was not always able to provide everything promised.

One of the most striking characteristics of this initial migration phase is the fact that a large proportion of individuals moved as part of a large kin group. In other settings, it is not uncommon for families to migrate together. For example, individual accounts in Ulaanhus remember how 50 related households moved simultaneously to Kokshetau in northern Kazakhstan in the early 1990s. There were similar stories of how some of their relatives migrated with five, ten or twenty other households, all at the same time, to the same place. For many Kazakhs, one of the primary obstacles to migration is leaving behind one's loved ones and the social support that comes from living near relatives. By migrating in large kin groups, these problems were reduced. Several scholars have noted how oralmandar tend to cluster with large kin groups. Movement of many families to similar locations allowed for the development of large and extended family and friend networks in Kazakhstan. These networks, both spatially and socially diverse, facilitated, through the process of chain migration, the movement of additional Mongolian Kazakh families and individuals who had initially remained in Mongolia.

In Mongolia, the late 1990s and early 2000s witnessed increasing economic and political stability, albeit with continued hardships. The economic successes of the period however overshadowed social difficulties as unemployment skyrocketed to an estimated 19%. The economic hardships associated with the transition continued throughout the mid- to late-1990s, and were exacerbated between 2000 and 2002 when the region was hit by particularly harsh *dzud*. (*Dzud* is the description of an extremely cold, windy and dry winter in which livestock are unable to find sufficient pasture.) These two winters at the dawning of the new century proved devastating to many communities in Mongolia. At the national level, livestock numbers declined from approximately 33.5 million to 23.9 million between 1999 and 2002, resulting in impoverishment of families in the rural areas.

In 2000-2002, the situation improved and Bayan-Ulgii, the only province in Mongolia sharing two international borders, one with Russia and one with China, opened up to new opportunities as the borders became more open and created possibilities for small-scale trade and subsequently big business. But the situation again changed with discrepancies in the quota system and arrival of greater numbers of oralmans in 2002 from Uzbekistan (about 62%) compared to those from Mongolia (15%). The irregularities and failing quota policy resulted in return of migrants to Mongolia, only to return later. So, these people were "circular migrants" whose fortunes were restored during the next phase (2003-08) when economic growth in Bayan Ulgii was accompanied by expanding consumerism—a feature explained by Werner and Barcus. Tourism, especially eco-tourism, expanded in western Mongolia and it became the new destination along with Turkey and China for Kazakhs who were now spread evenly (along with their networks) in both Mongolia and Kazakhstan. A new Kazakh governmental programme entitled "Blessed Migration" was launched in 2009 to benefit Mongolian

Kazakhs who settled largely in northern Kazakhstan compared to oralmandar from Uzbekistan who settled in the south.

Further questions that need to be addressed

There are other factors that determine the diaspora's sense of belonging to the homeland. For instance, is religion or language an attractive force for diasporas wishing to come back to their ancestral homeland? Sometimes there are unspecified links that may or may not have been reflected in the standard literature on Eurasia's homelands, diasporas or transnational migrants. It would be interesting to find out about the Muslim Kazakhs in Iran[50] or the Christian Kazakhs in Russia, the Kazakhs in Turkey (actively propagating bilateral ties through Kazakh-Turkish Society in Istanbul) and the Uyghurs converted into Buddhists (despite the fact that their religion is Islam). There could be interesting comparisons with the South Asian diasporas, especially the diasporas of Indian origin (e.g., Patel migrants in Britain and Africa, the Chettinad diasporas in South East Asia), there is an intrinsic urge to identify diaspora as an imagined community that constantly reinvents and reinvigorates itself through cultural contact (language, food, art and religion). So, as debates and discussions about diaspora converge on to narratives of connectivity, there is an increasing need to revisit the diasporic concept. In fact the position of "going back home" needs to be reconsidered. With globalisation, there is no need of going back home again. There could be detour but no return.[51]

Notes

1. Keith Rosten, *Once in Kazakhstan: The Snow Leopard Emerges (*New York: iUniverse, 2005), p. 5.
2. Rosten, p. 6.
3. Kuscu in her research shows the Nazarbayev regime's "homeland stance." The first *Qurultay* (Assembly) not only declared independent Kazakhstan as the homeland for the diaspora but also announced the policy of ethnic return migration. This was reflected in the words of President Nazarbayev's speech at the first *Qurultay*: "For those who had to leave their homeland once and now wish to come back, the arms of independent Kazakhstan are wide open for you." Isik Kuscu Bonnenfant, "Constructing the homeland: Kazakhstan's discourse and policies surrounding its ethnic return-migration policy," *Central Asian Survey,* vol. 31, no. 1, March 2012; President Nazarbayev's speech at the First World Kazakhs' *Qurultay*, "Qushaghymyz Bauyrlargha Aiqara Ashyq," *Egemen Qazaqstan*, October 2, 1992.
4. Martha Brill Olcott, *Kazakhstan: Unfulfilled Promise*, Carnegie Endowment for International Peace, 2010.

5. Keith Rosten, *Once in Kazakhstan …*, pp. 22-23.
6. Rosten, in conversation with Tulegenev, ibid., p. 23.
7. Edward Schatz, *When Capital Cities Move: The Political Geography of Nation and State Building*, Working Paper no. 303, February 2003, p. 19.
8. Makhmud Shayakhmetov, *The Silent Steppe* (London: Stacey International, 2006), pp. 13-14.
9. Shayakhmetov, ibid., pp. 15-16.
10. Shayakhmetov, ibid., pp. 17-18.
11. Yestaulet's family was one of the many to head for the border (with China) … Within the great expanse of the steppe, it was easy to find new places in which (they wanted) to lead free and independent lives, and when people began being sentenced to prison and having their property confiscated, it was natural that they should react by fleeing en masse into China. This form of protest was widespread in Southern Altai, the upper reaches of the River Irtysh, the Zaisan, Tarbagatai and other regions of eastern Kazakhstan adjacent to the state border. Since the late nineteenth century, there have been three mass exoduses of Kazakhs to China. The first one took place in 1881-82, when the state border between China and Imperial Russia was finally established. It was voluntary in those days: people living along the border freely chose their citizenship and which side to settle on. Some crossed over to live in Russia, while others moved to China. The second mass exodus was organised in 1916, to protest against a decree conscripting young Kazakhs to the front to construct fortifications in World War I. The third and largest exodus took place in 1931. This last escape into China had begun in 1928-29 after the landowners' land had been confiscated: individual families crossed the border, taking a small number of relatives with them. Shayakhmetov, ibid., pp. 39-40.
12. Shayakhmetov, ibid., pp. 64-67.
13. "Politicheskie Repressii v Kazakhstane" in *Istoriya Kazakhstana*, vol. 4 (Almaty: Atamura, 2010).
14. The number of Kazakh Germans dropped to 2.4 per cent in 1999 while it was 7.1 per cent in 1959.
15. Lee Chai Mun, "The Lost Sheep: The Soviet Deportations of Ethnic Koreans and Volga Germans," *The Review of Korean Studies*, vol. 6, no. 1, 2003, p. 234.
16. Jon Chang and Jae Park, "Soviet Koreans: Redemption through Labour and Sport," *The Eurasia Studies Society Journal*, vol. 2, no. 3, April 2013.
17. Their origins date back to 1832—mostly in the form of an involuntary inflow. Those that arrived then belonged to secret organisations fighting against the Russian and Austro-Prussian empires in their resistance to the partitioning of Poland. There were soldiers and civilians who participated in the 1830-31 and 1863 uprisings. Those that arrived in the 1930s originated from the western part of the Ukrainian Republic (combination of Polish national regions of Marchlewski and Belarussian SSR).
18. Lucy Kelaart and Genya Vasyuta, "Crimean Tatars: Crimean Tatars struggle to leave Uzbekistan," EurasiaNet, June 26, 2004.
19. The homeland of the Crimean Tatar Turkic community was the Crimean peninsula that was inhabited by the Tatars, a heterogeneous community since the fourteenth and fifteenth centuries and was organised into a political community under the leadership of the Gerays, claiming descent from the Golden Horde of Chingiz Khan that also received support from the Ottoman Sultan. The Crimean Khanate was under Ottoman suzerainty till 1774 until the Russian invasion that marked the end of the Crimean khanate. The khanate experienced

further transformation after the Russian Revolution of 1917 and the Crimean Autonomous Republic that was formed in 1921. The Soviet deportations of 1944 decimated the prestige of the homeland and it was not until 1989 that they were given formal permission to return to their homeland. Ayşegül Aydıngün and Erdoğan Yıldırım, "Perception of Homeland among Crimean Tatars: Cases from Kazakhstan, Uzbekistan and Crimea," *Bilig*, no. 54, Summer 2010; Greta Lynn Uehling, *Beyond Memory: Crimean Tatars' Deportation and Return* (New York: Palgrave Macmillan, 2004).

20. www.dark-tourism.com/index.php/.../498-alzhir-memorial-kazakhstan
21. "Politicheskie Repressii v Kazakhstane," in *Istoriya Kazakhstana,* vol. 4 (Almaty: Atamura, 2010).
22. D. L. Wallace, "Alternative rhetoric and morality: writing from the margins," www.ncte.org/library/NCTEFiles/.../CCC0612Alternative.pdf, 2008; Barbara Estelle Verchot, "Creating marginality and reconstructing narrative: reconfiguring Karen Social and geopolitical alignment," MSc Thesis, Department of Interdisciplinary Studies, University of Central Florida, Spring Term, 2008.
23. Rainar Baubock and Thomas Faist (eds.), *Diaspora and Transnationalism—Concepts, theories and methods* (Amsterdam University Press, 2010).
24. By eschewing the view of the centre, van Schendel brings borderlands at the centre of the discussion and perceives them as active rather than passive agents of the nation-state. Michiel Baud and Willem van Schendel, "Towards a comparative history of Borderlands," *Journal of World History,* vol. 8, no. 2, 1997, pp. 211-42.
25. Rogers Brubaker, "The 'diaspora' diaspora," *Ethnic and Racial Studies,* vol. 28, no. 1, January 2005.
26. S. Vertovec, "Transnationalism and identity," *Journal of Ethnic and Migration Studies,* vol. 27, no. 4, 2001; S. Vertovec and S. Cohen (eds.), *Migration, Diasporas and Transnationalism* (Cheltenham, UK: Edward Elgar, 1999).
27. Brubaker, op.cit.
28. Baubock and Faist (eds.), *Diaspora and Transnationalism ...*
29. Isik Kuscu, "Constructing the homeland: Kazakhstan's discourse and policies surrounding its ethnic return-migration policies," *Central Asian Survey,* vol. 31, issue 1, 2013, pp. 31-44.
30. Holly Barcus and Cynthia Werner, "The Kazakhs of Western Mongolia: Transnational migration from 1990-2008," *Asian Ethnicity,* vol. 11, no. 2, June 2010.
31. Isik Kuscu, *Kazakhstan's Oralman Project: A Remedy for Ambiguous Identity?* ProQuest, 2008.
32. Gulmira Kamziyeva, "Astana Develops New Oralman Repatriation Programme," *Central Asia Online,* November 2, 2011; Joanna Lillis, "Kazakhstan: Aştana Lures Ethnic Kazakh Migrants with Financial Incentives," Eurasianet.org, February 26, 2009.
33. Multiple, overlapping and sometimes competing histories of forced and voluntary settlement and resettlement create images of "entangled landscapes." Madeleine Reeves, "Introduction: contested trajectories and a dynamic approach to place," *Central Asian Survey,* vol. 30, nos. 3-4, September-December 2011. In Central Asia, that landscape is mostly associated with tribalism and descent. But this association has also been recreated over time by the people who have carried out "acts of remembrance" and have perpetually engaged with that particular environment. Judith Beyer, "Settling descent: place making and genealogy in Talas, Kyrgyzstan," *Central Asian Survey,* nos. 3-4, September-December 2011.

34. Astrid Cerny, "Going where the grass is greener: China Kazaks and the *Oralman* immigration policy in Kazakhstan," *Pastoralism,* vol. 1 no. 2, July 2010.
35. Elena Sadovskaya, *Chinese Labour Migration to Kazakhstan at the beginning of the 21st century,* Norwegian Institute of International Affairs, 2012.
36. Ulugbek Badalov, *The Oralmans: Migration of Ethnic Kazakhs from China to Europe* [excerpts from PhD dissertation in political anthropology, School for Advanced Studies in Social Sciences (EHESS), Paris (2011)].
37. Natsuko Oka, "Transnationalism as a threat to state security? Case studies on Uighurs and Uzbeks of Kazakhstan," http://src-h.slav.hokudai.ac.jp/coe21/publish/no14_ses/14_oka.pdf
38. Ablet Kamalov, "The Uyghurs as part of Central Asian Commonality: Soviet Historiography on the Uyghurs," in Ildiko Beller Hann et al. (eds.), *Situating the Uyghurs Between China and Central Asia* (Surrey: Ashgate, 2007), pp. 31-48.
39. Ablet Kamalov, "Uighur community in 1990s Central Asia: Decade of change," in Touraj Atabaki and Sanjyot Mehendale (eds.), *Central Asia and the Caucasus: Transnationalism and diaspora* (London-New York: Routledge, 2005).
40. Sean R. Roberts, "Imagining Uyghurstan: Re-evaluating the birth of the modern Uyghur nation," *Central Asian Survey,* vol. 28, no. 4, 2009.
41. Kabirov, *Ocherki istorii uigurov Sovietskovo Kazakhstana* (1975) followed by *The Uighurs are autochthonous to Semirechie* (1988).
42. Film *Zamanai,* cited in Alexander C. Diener, *One Homeland or Two? The nationalisation and Transnationalisation of Mongolia's Kazakhs* (Woodrow Wilson Centre Press, 2009), pp. 275-78.
43. Konstantin Syroezhkin, "Social perceptions of China and the Chinese: A view from Kazakhstan," *China and Eurasia Forum Quarterly,* vol. 7, no. 1 (2009).
44. Kari Faugner, *Chinese Perspectives on the Dungan People and Language. A Critical Discourse Analysis on the Ambiguousness of Chinese Ethnicity,* Masters' Thesis in East Asian Linguistics, Department of Culture Studies and Oriental Languages, Spring 2012, p. 9. The author mentions the work of Jonathan N. Lipman, *Familiar Strangers: A History of Muslims in Northwest China* (Seattle and London: University of Washington Press, 1997).
45. This ambiguity is explained in the following literature: Alexander C. Diener, *One Homeland or Two?...* ; Diener, "Kazakhstan's Kin State Diaspora: Settlement Planning and the *Oralman* Dilemma," *Europe-Asia Studies,* vol. 57, no. 2, March 2005; Diener, "Problematic Integration of Mongolian-Kazakh Return Migrants in Kazakhstan," *Eurasian Geography and Economics,* vol. 46, no. 6, 2005; Sharad Soni, "Moving beyond nomadism: emerging equations in Kazakh-Mongol relations," in Anita Sengupta and Suchandana Chatterjee (eds.), *The state in Eurasia: performance in local and global arenas* (Delhi: Knowledge World). The discussion continues in this author's presentation, "Dilemmas of shared spaces among the Kazakhs and the Buryats" [Paper presented in IASFM 14—*The 14th Conference of the International Association for Studies in Forced Migration,* Kolkata, January 6-9, 2013], Paper published in Proceedings Volume of IASFM 14.
46. Isik Kuscu, *Kazakhstan's Oralman Project ...* , p. 34.
47. Tsypylma Darieva, "Recruiting for the Nation: Post-Soviet Transnational Migrants in Germany and Kazakhstan," Erich Kasten (ed.), *Rebuilding Identities: Pathways to reform in Post-Soviet Siberia* (Berlin: Dietrich Reimar Verlag, 2005).

48. "Kazakhstan: Astana Lures Ethnic Kazakh Migrants with Financial Incentives," Eurasianet.org, February 26, 2009.
49. Holly Barcus and Cynthia Werner, "The Kazakhs of Western Mongolia: transnational migration from 1990–2008" *Asian Ethnicity,* vol. 11, no. 2, June 2010.
50. The *Nurly Kosh* programme in the Iranian city of Gorgan is actively propagating the creative works of the Kazakh families who moved to Iran (compilation of the Kazakh-Persian dictionary, carpet weaving by Iranian Kazakh women, etc). *Caspionet,* March 24, 2012.
51. Roza Tsagarousianou, "Rethinking the concept of the diaspora: mobility, connectivity and communication in a globalised world," http://www.westminster.ac.uk/__data/assets/pdf_file/0014/20219/005WPCC-Vol1-No1-Roza_Tsagarousianou.pdf

3. Development Dynamics: The Big Picture and the Little Picture

Once in Kazakhstan, visitors became habituated to vague narratives of development which is portrayed as expressions of nationalism, revolving around symbols of the state (e.g., the flag or the state seal) and a Kazakhstan-2030 vision enumerating President Nazarbayev's (1997) vision of what Kazakhstan will look like in the year 2030. This development strategy provides the meta-narrative around which essentially all policy developments in the independent state are framed. Kazakhstan-2030 is formatted as a series of five-year plans and Nazarbayev's government is understood as a "developmental regime," i.e., one with the stated goal of "progress."

Official estimates say that Kazakhstan's natural resource abundance has generated massive export earnings, attracting an increasing number of foreign direct investments (FDIs). Unfortunately, the country's population may not have been able to enjoy the full benefits derived from natural resource exploitation because of the political and economic challenges created by the resource revenue. The maximum negative effect was reflected in the Kazakh currency, the *tenge,* which depreciated in a major way in comparison to the Russian rouble in the past 7-8 months. The rent drawn from the sale of oil and gas has not been comparable to the non-booming trade sector. This naturally created a loss of faith in the people who were not getting the benefits of a state aspiring for global outreach. Allegations of corruption at the highest level have been the most problematic issue for the business climate. Social and educational programmes have not been very promising despite the Bolashak exchange programme and Nazarbayev University's model of a westernised educational programme. These issues have had a large influence on the making and unmaking of the Kazakh mood.

Despite such mood swings, the attention is on Kazakhstan's manoeuvrings in the wider Eurasian space with focus on new trends in regional integration, some passé and some emergent; some static and some dynamic. Sometimes, these initiatives surfaced with a disclaimer: they were hardly regional with actors who were extra-regional. The inclusion of more and more global partners and different constellations with different sets of powers has led to new debates. Discussions prevail over whether the EU model of regional integration is effective for Central Asia and Eurasia, bearing in mind that Eurasia is not a homogenous unit and also the fact that economic imperatives are too overbearing to conceptualise any long-term engagement. Some Central Asian scholars are prone to believe that "regionalism from below" is mostly an illusion. In other words, they would rather prefer a combination of both—i.e., regional initiatives *for* integration, that can be directed from outside the CIS as well as from within the CIS. Externally, it could be the West or it could be the more dependable partners like Turkey and usual partners like Russia (especially in issues of security) or stronger partners like China (in East Asia) and diverse partners like Malaysia or Vietnam or Indonesia (in Southeast Asia).

The aspect of macroeconomic development was debated extensively, especially from the standpoint of too much dependence on oil and gas, creating an urge to look at possibilities of diversification of the economy. Resource abundance creates pressure on consumption abilities and retards the growth process. That disadvantage became the cause of major U-turns in assessments that have marred Kazakhstan's image of development in recent times. So, the new economic drive in Kazakhstan is explained by two features:

- Economic synergy focused on Astana as global capital with landmark events as the signing of the EEU which formalised the creation of a new economic union between Russia, Kazakhstan and Belarus, and also the new Partnership Agreement with the European Union (September 2014, as a follow up of the ten-year partnership treaty with the EU that was inked in 1999).
- Diversification involving sectors other than oil and gas.

The former was a direct diplomatic gesture to deepen relations with the CIS countries. The latter was inspired by examples of Southeast

Asia's expanding economies like Malaysia—whose economic success is supposed to be the result of prudent, strategic government planning and intervention. The Kazakh government has tried to promote diversification with an active industrial policy (instead concentrating solely on the institutional environment that would allow for a market-driven diversification process). This has led to a complex mix of liberal and interventionist economic policies. It remains to be seen if this strategy will enable Kazakhstan to sustain its growth and become the first "Asian Snow Leopard" as envisioned in President Nazarbayev's 1997 vision of "Kazakhstan 2030."

South Korean participation is considered to be an important factor for Kazakhstan's industrial development. After independence, Nazarbayev invoked South Korea as a potential model for Kazakhstan's development. The Republic of Korea's (ROK's) economic ties with Kazakhstan have steadily grown over the years. In 2008, South Korea's Kookmin Bank bought a 30 per cent stake in Kazakhstan's Centre Credit Bank for $634 million, its first major cross-border acquisition in nearly half a decade. Kookmin is South Korea's largest bank and has been trying to expand overseas and reduce its reliance on sluggish interest income at home. South Korean President Lee Myung-bak's trip to the region in 2011 spurred a fresh round of large-scale investment. LG Chem, South Korea's largest chemical firm, and the state-run Kazakhstan Petrochemical Industries will build a large-scale petrochemical complex in Atyrau on the northern banks of the Caspian Sea, and a 1,320 megawatt coal-powered plant in the southern city of Balkhash. When completed in 2016, the complex hopes to generate $1.4 billion in sales. In another thermal power plant project in Balkhash, KEPCO and Samsung C&T guarantees a 70 per cent stake in the project, which is expected to produce about seven per cent of Kazakhstan's total electricity. These projects make South Korea the top foreign investor in Kazakhstan's state-led industrial development. South Korea's engagement of the region poses less of a challenge to the West, especially the United States, compared to China or Russia.

Wish list: EEU

The idea of EEU as an economic lobby was not Putin's. The Kazakh President Nursultan Nazarbayev has lobbied hard to get the word "economic" in the title. Kazakhstan sees the creation of the EEU as a way to strengthen its position in an increasingly competitive global environment. The projection was that Kazakh business will have access to the EEU market, with a population of 170 million, and cross-border trade is to be increased with the 12 Russian regions bordering Kazakhstan, which have a population of 27 million. The idea was to make Kazakhstan also attractive to investors who want to operate in the Russian and Belarusian markets. Transport routes linking up European and Asian trade flows through Kazakhstan were given a serious thought and landlocked Kazakhstan's high transport costs would need to be lowered through equal access to the Russian and Belarusian railway networks. Kazakhstan's dream was a single economic space guaranteeing the free flow of capital, services, and labour, and a single financial market that would be fully functional by 2025. And Kazakhstan will gain access to energy infrastructure by 2025 on the basis of the EEU's single market for oil and gas.

But there will be real problems in achieving these official goals. It is impossible to create an equal union between strong and weak players. And it is even more difficult to create a working union between uncompetitive players if their economies are based primarily on the export of natural resources. All the members of the Customs Union have encountered corruption and state interference in the economy, with a lot of bureaucratic bungling and without potentials for market economy. It will also be interesting to find out whether authoritarian regimes are able to integrate in an effective way.

Sentiments in Kazakhstan

In Kazakhstan, EEU as an integrative mechanism has been interpreted as a decision made exclusively for the economic benefits of member countries. In reality, however, the Union undoubtedly caters to the geopolitical ambitions of Russia.

The Union offers a number of benefits as well as challenges for the economy. Since Kazakhstan is a landlocked country, the issue of economic integration is particularly important in improving the country's role in international trade. Joining the EAEU will grant more favourable conditions in terms of accessing the Russian and European transport infrastructure for Kazakhstani business, and thus will reduce the transport costs of foreign trade. Moreover, there are fair chances that Kazakhstan will be able to improve its image as a negotiator in the developing world market. Talks have already been conducted by the Customs Union with major economic blocs such as the European Union and the OECD. India and Vietnam are among those countries with a stable economic profile. Another expectation is that salary potential in Kazakhstan will grow at the same pace as Russia's and Belarus's.[1]

Nevertheless, the Customs Union and its transformation into the EEU caused divisions in Kazakh society. It is important to mention that in the first three years of the Customs Union (CU), Kazakhstan benefited less than both Belarus and Russia from membership. In early 2014, there were reactions to EEU as a threat to Kazakhstan's national sovereignty. In 2012, the opposition even proposed a referendum on Kazakhstan's membership of the precursors of the EEU, the Customs Union and the Single Economic Space. However, the influence of the opposition on domestic politics should not be overemphasised. The government needs to be cautious, because the EEU is becoming more and more unpopular among ethnic Kazakhs, including the influential Kazakh-speaking intelligentsia that is the main support base of the government. Moreover, the conflict in Ukraine and the West's sanctions on Russia raised speculation about whether Kazakhstan's union with Russia will create a dent in her international image. It is also unclear whether Kazakhstan and Belarus will remain members of the EEU after the regimes in both countries change. Russia made a tactical mistake and set a precedent when it declared that the change of regime in Kyiv meant that Russia did not have to recognise the Budapest Memorandum on Security Assurances for Ukraine. This leaves the door open to other countries in the future to leave the EEU if they consider that it is no longer in their interest.

Tajikistan, Armenia and Kyrgyzstan—The New Entrants

Tajikistan has perhaps the maximum advantage of joining the EEU because of its reliance on Russia in terms of remittances. According to the World Bank, remittances in 2014 equate to 48 per cent of the GDP of Tajikistan, making it the most remittance-dependent country in the world. The country's reliance on Russia entails that any legislative change restricting labour movement with countries beyond the EAEU may have significant negative consequences for Tajikistan's macroeconomic situation.[2]

Armenia's joining has raised a question about whether it is moving away from the West. By virtue of its "policy of complementarity," it has maintained mutually beneficial relations with both Russia and the EU. The drift was evident on September 3, 2013 when Armenia announced its reluctance to sign the Association Agreement with EU and showed preference to opt for the Eurasian Customs Union. Next month, in October 2013, President Sargsyan signed an agreement to join the EEU at the cost of suspending Associate Membership agreement with European Union (EU).[3] So, Russia's bargaining power vis-à-vis Armenia has increased. This was evident from Russian President Putin's optimistic comment: "All the participants of this integration process are already experiencing its real benefits ... We hope that in the first two years after Armenia's joining we will see a positive macroeconomic effect."

Customs controls at the border between Kazakhstan and Kyrgyzstan were formally eliminated in an August 12 ceremony that was held at the Kordai (Kazakhstan) and Ak-Zhol (Kyrgyzstan) customs posts. The ceremony was attended by the Presidents of both countries Nursultan Nazarbayev and Almazbek Atambayev. The ceremony legalised Kyrgyzstan's accession into the Eurasian Economic Union (EAEU). Joining the EAEU is considered to expand Kyrgyzstan's prospects for economic development by removing barriers to accessing external trade, services, capital and labour and opening up new investment opportunities and possibilities for launching large infrastructure projects. In addition, Kyrgyzstan's citizens are entitled to work in any country of the union under the same conditions as citizens of the state. The removal of customs control on the Kazakh-Kyrgyz border was an important move in the development dynamics of the region, especially in the context of Kazakhstan's investment in the southern industrial districts of Kyrgyzstan. The willingness to promote a beneficial environment through customs-free movement of goods, services and workforce was a positive trend. The expectation is that reforms in the border posts would be similar to those in a free trade zone, which is why distant countries like Vietnam and India too are interested to sign the Treaty of Accession. But there is one disclaimer: Kyrgyzstan's obligations to the World Trade Organisation (WTO) norms are not binding for the rest of the EAEU bloc.[4]

Integration as per EEU/EAEU norms may harm the emerging private sector and have a detrimental effect on the Kyrgyz economy. Considering the importance of the Chinese economy not only in terms of trade, but also in providing cheap products to Kyrgyzstani consumers, there are serious questions about the effectiveness of full EAEU membership for Kyrgyzstan. Kyrgyzstan functions as the biggest regional re-export hub for Chinese products heading to Kazakhstan and the Russian Federation. This hub located in Bishkek is a significant component of the GDP of Kyrgyzstan which provides 50,000 workplaces and contributes to the emerging garment industry which is source of employment to 1,50,000 workers among the total population of 5.8 million. Obviously, joining the union which hints at increase in tariffs and rising unemployment is going to be costly for Kyrgyzstan. The only advantage that Kyrgyzstan can think of is in terms of regulating issues related to migration, an important factor due to its significant dependence on remittances.

EEU's Uncertain Future?[25]

The EEU may develop in several different directions, depending on economic and geopolitical factors. In the ongoing trade dispute between Belarus and Russia, economic tensions between Moscow and Minsk have led to a public spat in spite of the supranational structures of the Eurasian Economic Commission and its Council (functioning since 2012), which is made up of the deputy prime ministers of the three member countries. These structures seem to be more of a show than of any practical use. Moscow accused Minsk of re-exporting banned goods to the Russian market. Moreover, Russia introduced limits on the transit of goods across its territory, including those destined for Kazakhstan. This was in violation of the basic principles of the Customs Union and Belarus retaliated by restoring its own customs controls. This means that as the EEU starts functioning in 2015, most of these internal tensions will come out in the open. The three current EEU members will likely retain their different views on the future of the project. This may lead to an increase in economic and political tension and to conflict within the organisation. Moreover, the EEU's enlargement to include underdeveloped and uncompetitive countries (Armenia, Kyrgyzstan and Tajikistan) may delay its progress because funding will be required to help their economies catch up. The EEU may take a backward turn as the post-Soviet space gets divided into pro-EEU and anti-EEU groupings: Russia and her allies like Kazakhstan, Belarus, Armenia, Kyrgyzstan, Tajikistan on the one hand and Azerbaijan,

Uzbekistan, Moldova, Ukraine, Georgia on the other. It is likely that Russia will continue to push for more political integration through the EEU, especially after the regime in Kazakhstan changes. This means that Kazakhstan's continued membership of the EAEU will undoubtedly carry serious political risks.

Although Putin is determined to push the EEU perimeter as far as possible, it is not yet clear what real economic benefit countries will gain from membership. In fact, Kazakhstan has strong reservations about the unified customs code that tend to have worked against the import of Kazakh goods and products. Kazakhstan seeks to work on its own terms and continues to chart its own plan of action through diplomatic overtures towards the European Union.

An asymmetrical situation has arisen due to Russia's overwhelming dominance compared to Kazakhstan and Belarus. Moreover, the functioning of the Eurasian Union is subject to Russian subsidies and coercion. Armenia and Kyrgyzstan have been coerced to join "in principle" while others like Ukraine have been coerced *not to join* the bloc. Russia's high-handedness was seen in the context of raised protection levels ever since the financial crisis and also regulating the Union by introducing occasional tariff controls (on milk products of Belarus, for example). Tighter border controls on non-union members have led to drastic reduction of imports on the part of Russia's neighbours. Trade growth within the customs union areas is almost nil and trade diversion has produced negative results for Kazakhstan. In Astana, people's buying power has increased and Kazakhstan is importing expensive but substandard Russian cars and adding more rents to Russia's automobile sector. The Swedish economist Anders Aslund reported that Kazakh consumers have already been hurt by tariff increases and are now buying substandard Russian cars rather than freely imported ones. The Belarusian President Aleksandr Lukashenka recently lashed out against her "eastern brother" (meaning Russia) for banning import of meat and milk from Belarus, which the Putin regime accused of purchasing EU food products and repackaging them for export to Russia. The Russian government has banned the import of EU foodstuffs as a response to Western sanctions.

Belarus, the prime signatory, is willing to be Russia's faithful partner and yet has no real voice in the Union. Most of the former Soviet states have stronger commercial links with either the EU or China than with Russia and this may weaken the Union. One is not certain how Central Asian partners like Kyrgyzstan, which is internally weak can be beneficial for the Union. Also, a mandate for a strong Turkey under Erdogan's new Presidential term is juxtaposed to Turkey's troubled Islamic neighbourhood. The single most concern today is that of Ukraine—and Kiev not being part of the Union due to Russian military intervention after the Maidan events was anybody's guess. But what it entails for the Eurasian Economic Union particularly in the context of EU's lobbies in the Union that are opposed to Russian military stance is something that creates a shadow of uncertainty.

Integration through EEU/EAEU is nevertheless necessary because of the nature of economic dependence and geopolitical configurations in the current era and may serve as the "legalisation" of economic dependence on Russia for other states of Central Asia such as Kyrgyzstan and Tajikistan.

EEU's Expansion: Mixed Feelings

What is intriguing is the erratic way in which the EEU has expanded, though the basic intention was to deepen its foundations. It began when the Customs Union was flagged off in 2006 as an initiative to "restart the Eurasian integration programme." At that time, there was little apprehension about whether this would differ from previous ineffective post-Soviet projects. The subject of economic integration was quickly introduced with the creation of a Single Economic Space (SES). The SES model ran into rough weather since 2012 when it sought to eliminate non-tariff barriers to trade as a Customs Code was being generated. All previous features like free movement of capital, development of technical standards were immensely appreciated. But it is the specific clause about removal of tariff barriers that practically exposed the domestic weaknesses of each state. The businesslike atmosphere and the streamlining of the reformed integration formula pointed to the persuasiveness of the actors in the business—i.e., the business community overshadowed the rest of the actors involved in governance. Now, each of the member states had its own style of functioning—a business-friendly regulatory atmosphere in Kazakhstan was more acceptable to the EU if not the EEU; Belarus was able to control low-level corruption and this hardly was a big thing. Belarus was also interested largely in Russia's energy diplomacy and therefore Russia had an advantage in its bargaining power with Belarus in this matter. Concessional treatment to Armenia has brought a conflict-ridden Caucasian belt within the Union. In doing so, Armenia has had to give no commitment—but its inclusion has given Russia a unique sense of moral triumph—of extending the EEU to its westernmost fringe. So, the regrouping was not on the basis of an economic rationale but on the basis of a geopolitical goal of building bridges through regional alliances with smaller partners that had nothing to promise in return. They were seekers of Russian concessions and had the least say in Union matters. Such was the case of Armenia and even the prime signatory Belarus—that were Russian dependencies rather than the Union's partners.

While there was no doubting the commitment of the Presidents of various states, the geopolitical considerations practically raised a finger at that specific clause: elimination of non-tariff barriers to trade. Yet the difference in this initiative soon became evident: not only institutional and legal factors but also Russia's ambitions for regional hegemony that became a constraint for the West. While Russia was looking for strengthening the parameters of the Union on its own terms and in so doing the signatories also saw tangible benefits and the world at large was extremely curious about this "opposite pole" and whether it would be viable as an alternative to the European Union in real terms.

The question that was pushed under the carpet was EEC's predecessor—the Eurasian Economic Community or EurAsEC. That organisation failed because of debate between Russia and Central Asian states (especially Kazakhstan) regarding reduction of non-tariff barriers and improving trade facilities. Russia too did not show great level of commitment at that stage. What has failed with EurAsEC might improve with EEC—this was the optimism in the initial years of formation of the organisation. The optimism was high on tariff schedule: all three countries of the Customs Union have agreed on common external tariff for the third party. Now, the reduced tariff that was spoken of was Russian tariff and this obviously resulted in the expansion of the market. Kazakhstan was outnumbered in the competition for low tariff to the extent that Russian sales went up in Kazakhstan. This meant an expansion of the Russian industry and therefore a net Russian gain. Trade was diverted—as economists said—from Kazakhstan to Russia.

Amidst speculations about EEU's prospects, the Ukraine crisis set the ball rolling and took its toll on the member countries' real objectives.

This is indicated in the recent remarks of the first Deputy Prime Minister of Kazakhstan: "We don't meddle into what Russia is doing politically, and they cannot tell us what foreign policy to pursue." "We lost someone along the way, I mean Ukraine," said Aleksandr Lukashenko, the President of Belarus. Belarus and Kazakhstan have often voiced their concern at the treatment meted out to Ukraine. They have worked to limit the political weight of the Union too. Both states demanded a high price—gas or cash—for joining.

Analysts are more direct in their observations about the Union: "Three weak economies getting together and integrating: How much good can come out of it?" said Nargis Kassenova, the Director of the Central Asian Studies Centre at Kimep University in Almaty, who is opposed to the Union. "Now, it is even worse because one is under sanctions and drifting away from the West," Kassenova added, referring to Western economic sanctions against Russia. Although the presidents of Armenia and Kyrgyzstan attended the signing ceremony and expressed an interest in joining, the missing guest at the party was Ukraine. The previous government in Kiev moved back and forth on whether it would join the European Union or the new Eurasian group, eventually choosing Mr. Putin's offer and igniting a public uprising that ended up bringing down the president in February. At the end of it, the Union appears to be Russia's diplomatic victory, while Kazakhstan is generating loyalty among its citizens by broaching the fact that it floated the idea of a Union 20 years ago—but exclusively forged on economic ties—nothing beyond that. In fact, Kazakhstan has tried to apply brakes on anything beyond economic ties. Belarus too is trying to maximise on the benefits it has reaped in recent times and not intending to go beyond that.

There are also speculations about how long the EEU will last. Since the first customs measures were introduced in 2010, only Belarus has benefited. The purpose of enlargement of the Union to include poorer states such as Armenia, Kyrgyzstan or Tajikistan would make the balance of the EEU even more precarious. But what counts for Putin is the image of Russia restored and the bolstered notion of a President lobbying for a conservative bulwark against the West. The signing of the Customs Union in 2010 and the Eurasian Economic Space (EES) in November 2011[6] by Belarus, Kazakhstan and Russia has not only brought Kazakhstan's "thinking space" into the limelight but has also revived a lot of thinking about the ever-expanding contours of a post-Soviet economic space.[7] The trajectory of an economic union, formulated in the early 1990s and transforming itself through various avatars, found a new meaning in this accord. As regional integration proceeds in much of the world (not just through the EU but also via NAFTA, ASEAN and Washington's proposed Trans-Pacific Partnership, among others), the post-Soviet space tends to remain largely on the sidelines. It is the desire to emerge from the shadows that have prompted the EES signatories to come together and clinch the deal. The deal draws a lot of attention due to its trade and tariff agenda. Putin's initiative about recreating a union of Soviet people is a major attraction for his chief partner, Kazakhstan, that aspires to have a WTO membership.

Kazakhstan's Eurasian policy has earned dividends in terms of new partnerships. On the one hand, the aim was to create a bulwark vis-à-vis a rising China. On the other, the aim is to transform Kazakhstan as a transit hub that integrates the West and the East. Beijing is increasingly involved in the construction of infrastructure projects that primarily provide transportation routes for natural resources and commodities. Pipelines from the Caspian Sea across Kazakhstan, a gas pipeline from Turkmenistan across Uzbekistan and Kazakhstan, and a highway leading to the Pakistani port of Gwadar—all are elements in an overall scheme conceived by China in which Kazakhstan's aspirations to become a transit hub between East and West is well met. According to Kazakhstan's President Nursultan Nazarbayev, the transportation grid between western China and West Europe should become an "artery (that is) due to turn Kazakhstan into a transit corridor between Europe and Asia."

The 1990s and the 2000s mark two diametrically opposite trends in Kazakh economy; a lean period followed by economic recovery. The recovery was mostly based on the growth of the energy sector and the country's oil output was the major revenue source. New pipelines reduced transport costs. The oil sector was the main reason for the country's growth performance in the 2000s. The establishment of economic order with integration as the motto created a sound policy environment and justified investment climate. This had a beneficial impact which was temporarily reduced during 2008-9 but then again turned positive in 2010-11. There were phases of exceptional highs in the mid-2000s. Kazakhstan's biggest achievement during this period was its ability to avoid a resource curse. Income levels increased substantially during these years and vision statements created an atmosphere for an increasingly urbanised knowledge-based society that inspired the country's youth. Robust optimism about Kazakhstan's oil fortunes also led to sunny assessments about Kazakhstan-China economic relations, though a lot of scepticism was generated about the environmental hazards of China's Big Push industrialisation. Nevertheless, China continued to be the main driver of economic growth as far as Kazakhstan was concerned. At the same time, its shuffling with regional models of economic management indicated the basic uncertainty about each model—none (East Asian, American, Nordic, German, Chinese or Indian) seemed to offer a long-term viable strategy for sustainable growth. Kazakhstan's reliance on rapid energy and resource intensive growth could not be sustained long—Vision 2050 was a way of showing Kazakhstan's inner strength. But in the context of global and regional uncertainties, whether this vision is destined to be a suitable pathway is something that cannot be said for sure. The will to adapt is Kazakhstan's plus point—the necessity would be to search for its own model of development rather than rely on international experience of what worked for some countries and what did not.[8]

China: Fatal Attraction

Generally speaking, in Kazakhstan China seems to be the major source of attraction. The bulk of Chinese investments in Central Asia are located in Kazakhstan. The China National Petroleum Corporation (CNPC) has an 82% stake in the "Aktobe Munai Gaz" Kazakh oil company. In 2005, CNPC signed a memorandum with Kazakhstan's KazMunaiGaz national oil and gas company for the development of the Darkhan oilfield on the Caspian shore. Bilateral cooperation between China and Kazakhstan is based on a number of mutual framework agreements between the two countries. As part of China's programme of industrialising its western regions, several joint Sino-Kazakh projects were introduced. One of them is the Khorgos border hub between the two countries. An Action Plan for Cooperation was signed in April 2008, which included 20 tangible development projects comprising agriculture, new technologies, cross-border trade, transportation, and communication. Kazakhstan's Aktau seaport is the head turner as it is armed with several projects—nuclear plants, Arcelor Mittal's oil pipe coating business that is thriving in the region, collaboration between Aktau

Seaport Special Economic Zone and Urumqi's Economic and Technological Zone, etc.

The Kazakh borderlands discourse has evolved as an interesting trajectory especially since China's entry as the new global partner in the Central Asian region. The pressure of neighbouring China as a demographic giant has been replaced by a new perception of China as an effective partner. This partnership has taken off in a major way since 2012 with the launching of China's New Eurasian Land Bridge through rail links via the border town of Khorgos. Earlier initiatives included the diversification of energy supplies that has resulted in oil and pipeline deals with Kazakhstan.[9]

The geographical proximity has enabled a strengthening of China-Kazakhstan linkages, exclusively based on inland transport. For example, the Eurasian Continental Bridge project, linking the port of Lianyungang on the Pacific coast to Western Europe via Lanzhou, Urumqi, Dostyk, and Russia over more than 10,000 km, including 3,200 km in Kazakhstan, has necessitated the upgrading of some sections of road. For instance, China is upgrading the section from Khorgos to Shymkent via Almaty. This sector of road development has been touted as the new Silk Road—an ambitious $7 billion project that will connect China and Western Europe along a 1,700-mile highway through the north of Kazakhstan. Prominent aid agencies like the ADB, World Bank, Islamic Development Bank, Japan International Cooperation Agency are expected to fund major sectors of this trade corridor, which, it is hoped, will upgrade the northern route of the Silk Road that will connect southern towns, like Kyzyl Orda and Shymkent, with northern towns, like Aralsk. This overland route is being resurrected as a passage for transporting a special item—i.e., several million laptop computers and accessories made each year in China and bound for customers in European cities like London, Paris, Berlin and Rome. Since 2011, Hewlett Packard, the Silicon Valley electronics company, has shipped laptops and accessories to stores in Europe via express trains across Central Asia. This route has become a major transportation route for freight trains, some of which also belong to the Chinese. The Kazakhstan rail initiative has spurred regional competition, especially from the Russian side. Russia is contemplating seriously to improve rail links to China, notably through improvements along the Trans-Siberian railroad. The railroad option is proving to be extremely beneficial for China and President Nazarbayev has also showcased this route as the new Silk Road. To the Western traveller, this is a twisting and threatening route on which the Baikonur space satellite zone is located. To the Kazakhs, this is a route of shining opportunities as the expectation is that job opportunities will increase with cafes and hotels built along the road.

The new description of the Silk Road is as follows:

> The new Silk Road is an ambitious $7 billion project to connect China with Western Europe along a 1,700-mile highway through Kazakhstan. Just as the ancient caravans transformed the world, bearing ideas and cultures along with their perfumes and spices, Kazakhstan is counting on the modern equivalent to stimulate economic growth that would have repercussions the world over, including in the United States.
>
> "It's not just pavement going from point A to B," said Juan Miranda, director general of the Asian Development Bank's Central and West Asia Department. "It's a Silk Road, leading to the creation of an economic corridor and stability, and I hope the road will benefit far more than Kazakhstan."

Completion of the links in the Kazakh sector signifies completion of the northern highway with interconnected networks that include existing or newly upgraded roads in China and Russia that are already linked to Western Europe. This northern highway network is reminiscent of the northern branches of the Silk Road that passed through Kazakhstan. There are practical concerns of establishing such links. Travel along that new route is arduous. The twisting route passes past Baikonur, the Russian-leased space centre. "The Western traveller along the road perceives bleakness but the Kazakhs see a lot of opportunity," said Abelgazy Husainov, who, until a recent reshuffling of the cabinet, was Kazakhstan's transportation minister. "It will have an enormous social effect, with cafes, hotels, businesses built along it. As cargo increases, new jobs will be created."

But it is the Chinese plan of linking the Central Asian countries with China's national railroad system that has been flaunted by development experts in both China and Kazakhstan. This is a mechanism that has stepped up other operations leading to new speculations about a "railroad war" in order to curb Russian influence.[10] The geopolitical influence of the new railroads will be far greater than the new pipelines. Now this policy of creating Eurasian landbridges dates back to the Soviet period. Dru Gladney points to the construction of a contemporary Uyghur transnational identity through the trans-Eurasian railroads.[11] A Sino-Eurasian railway that runs through Soviet and Chinese Central Asia dates back to the 1950s but was actually dismantled in 1962 following political purges of the Great Leap Forward resulting in the exodus of 60,000 Kazakhs and Uyghurs from the Ili area. The border was shut down shortly after this. In 1987, there were negotiations about rebuilding that railroad which was seen more as a southern link between Eastern Europe, Moscow and Beijing. The railway, rebuilt well ahead of schedule (in 1990 instead of 1992), stimulated Sino-Soviet trade but was considered to be of the least help for Central Asia. The border regions were fortified and the Military Corps are today partners of a border trade in an area that is functioning today as an area of international trade.

So, here we see a case of an internationalised boundary that besides being touted as a special case of renewed links across Sino-Soviet borders also represents a case of realignment of ethnic identities. It is these multiple images that current scholarship has been dealing with.[12] One description of the border town of Jimunai in the Ili River basin which was completely under-represented as the majority of attention had shifted to Khorgos, may be cited here:

> When I visited Jimunai in 2008, the trading area at the border was in the process of being relocated to the town itself, some 20 km away. On my way to the trading area at the border, I met a Kazakh man of Chinese nationality in his early twenties who was doing contract work for the government. Every morning he would travel twenty minutes to the border where he was helping to build a new road that led to the border itself. The man told me that he had already tried to make a life for himself in the coastal provinces of China. But before he even managed to leave Xinjiang, he got bogged down in the capital city Urumqi, where he drank all his money away. He then worked in Turpan for several months to make enough money to travel to eastern China. He finally made his way to the Chinese northeast (Dongbei) where he sold kebabs on the side of the road.
>
> This situation not being ideal, he had now returned to Jimunai, where he was working on his next project: to move to Kazakhstan to join relatives

> who had moved there in the 1990s. The young man informed me that they are now far more prosperous than his family in China. With government assistance they had started up a chicken farm and now had enough money to buy tractors. He had never been to Kazakhstan but it had now become his dream to go. He explained to me that it was his hope to raise enough money building the border road so that he could enrol in a Russian language programme in Urumqi. From there he would continue on to Kazakhstan where he would join his extended family.[13]

It was during the last two decades of the Soviet period when the reopening of the border between Xinjiang and Kazakhstan occurred that has resulted in renewed links across the borders. The significance of this area today lies in the fact that it shares the border with Xinjiang and is the area that the majority of the trade between Kazakhstan and China transits. From the outset of economic relations between the two countries, shuttle trade or "shop tourism" has developed, compensating partially for the collapse of the flow of goods from Moscow and enabling the professional redeployment of a whole class of engineers and service industry workers who had become unemployed with the dissolution of the Soviet Union. In 2002, shop tourism reportedly provided employment for nearly half a million Kazakhs, who are estimated to have spent more than $1 billion in Xinjiang between 1989 and 2003. These increasingly structured and organised shop tours (with specialised tourist agencies, Russian-Chinese translation services, hotels reserved for post-Soviet citizens, transport companies handling customs formalities, etc.) is now said to consume some $4 billion of goods per annum. China's "grand return" to the region started with the opening of the Urumqi trade fair in 1991. Economic relations between Kazakhstan and Xinjiang have evolved during the course of the decade. The export of standard consumer goods is no longer the main trade focus, and is now complemented by hydrocarbons. Kazakh companies have invested in Xinjiang in the transport, metals production, paper, and food production sectors. Kazakhstan has thus become the main foreign investor in Xinjiang, while Chinese investors from Xinjiang are concentrated in the Almaty region.

The shuttle trade has been strongly criticised by Kazakh experts, who blame it for the poor quality of Chinese goods bought at the lowest possible prices by Central Asian traders. Some of them are suspicious that Beijing is exploiting Kazakhstan's raw materials without enabling the country to acquire technological know-how. Others are also not very happy with the fact that the Kazakh national economy is relinquishing its raw material base and agricultural and food processing industries to Chinese companies. Strategic analysts are of the opinion that China's economic successes are at the expense of the socio-economic interests of the Central Asian region.[14] Too great a concentration of Kazakh trade with Xinjiang would therefore accentuate Astana's specialisation in raw materials and would prevent the development of trade relations with the eastern regions of China, particularly with the country's several special economic zones.

Sino-Kazakh economic relations are primarily seen through the lens of an exchange of raw materials and goods: China receives natural resources such as oil, gas and metals while sending consumer goods to Kazakhstan. This happens in the context of Kazakh-Chinese joint ventures for the large-scale and industrial trade sector, and small businesses and even individual traders for the consumer goods sector. Kazakhstan needs investments and buyers of its natural resources while China needs these resources to fuel its own economy and a buyer of the large amount of goods it produces. Currently, Kazakh-Chinese trade amounts to 70% of the Chinese-Central Asian trade.

Kazakhstani Uyghurs' economic involvement has been factored in the overall analysis of Kazakhstan-China trade relations. For them, the buying and selling of consumer goods offers a window of opportunity. Since the collapse of the Soviet Union, Kazakh-Chinese relations developed and the border became more open for trade. This allowed "shuttle traders" to buy goods in China and return to Kazakhstan on short business trips. The shuttle route trade takes place on the Khorgos road which runs right through the Uyghur district and the most direct route for shuttle traders to buy and sell goods, or by rail through the Alatau Pass and then on to Almaty or other parts of Kazakhstan. The Uyghurs were able to secure economic trade opportunities and flourish especially during the period immediately following the opening of the border. Generally, the Uyghurs are not involved in heavy industrial trade almost all of which is controlled by Kazakh or Chinese state-run enterprises.

With the increased trade between Xinjiang and Central Asia, Central Asian identities have become more relevant in defining Uyghur identities exposure to Central Asian culture has taken place in an extended way in

Xinjiang. The expansion of Xinjiang's economy and trade with Central Asia has brought new forms of cultural expression to the Uyghur middle class through consumer choice. Increased trade with neighbouring nations gives consumers more access to Central Asian, Russian and Turkish products than ever before.

The Grand Connector: One Road, One Belt

In dossiers of connectivity, the land element is most crucial. A One Belt, One Road Plan was proposed by China in September 2013. According to a document released by China's Ministry of Foreign Affairs, the Belt-and-Road will run through the continents of Asia, Europe and Africa, connecting East Asia at one end and developed European economies at the other, while encompassing countries along the route. Also diplomatically termed as twenty-first century Silk Road Economic Belt that will link China with the Persian Gulf and the Mediterranean through Central Asia and West Asia, and will also connect China with Southeast Asia, South Asia and the Indian Ocean, this project is not only the most recent but also the smartest that will give China a sweeping accessibility via land and via maritime connectors to South and Southeast Asia as well as West Asia and Europe. The possibility of a single window to Asia-Europe unit was conceived of in a unique way. One component was introducing reforms at border posts along the entire stretch. The added advantage was to expand its (China's) footprint in many of the strategic locations in Colombo, and a few ports in Africa.

Although the exact details of One Belt, One Road vary by map to map and proposal to proposal, generally, the overland belt, comprising roads, rail links, energy pipelines, and telecommunications ties, seeks to link China, Central Asia, the Middle East, Europe and Russia. The maritime "road" will sail from China's coasts through the South China Sea, the Indian Ocean, the Red Sea, the Mediterranean Sea (through the Suez Canal), with stops in Africa along the way. One Belt, One Road builds on earlier calls by Chinese academics to march west as a response to the United States' strategic pivot to Asia. The name of Beijing's programmes hark back to the ancient past—to the ancient Silk Road, recalling China's historical role in trade promotion between Asia and Europe. Interestingly, the belt project was announced in Kazakhstan and the road project was announced in Indonesia by the Chinese Premier. The prospects of development of China's western and southern regions were underlined. What was also noticeable was the effort to calm down ethnic unrest in the border regions. China hawks have tried to assess the outcome of the project:

> Translating the One Belt, One Road initiative from an ambitious cartographic formulation with a historical hook into a workable strategy for economic diplomacy and perhaps geopolitical influence will test China's capabilities across all aspects of foreign policy. The march westward could be a long one indeed.[15]

But there is a twist to the story too: Kazakhstan is the "buckle" of China's One Belt, One Road initiative.[16] Although there is a lot of expectation about a Kazakh hand in this Chinese gamble—whether through the Central Asia Regional Economic Cooperation (CAREC) and Corridor Investment programmes, or through multilateral institutions that channel funds into international corridor making that will connect China with Western Europe, or whether it is Kazakhstan's comfort zone with global banks like ADB or EBRD or World Bank and the new Asian Infrastructure Investment Bank (AIIB)—there seems to be lack of clarity about the real approach that Kazakhstan would be willing to take vis-à-vis its global partners: China, US and the West.

CIS: A Safe Gamble?

All eyes have turned to new development strategies within the CIS community. Russia is trying to play a more decisive role by extending its gaze beyond Central Asia and trying to enhance its position in the new security environment in the Far North, for example. For her, an institutionalised set-up is far more effective than dialogue partnerships. Hard talk about regional initiatives, especially linked to connectivity corridors is also the strategy of an oil-and-hydrocarbon resource based economy like Kazakhstan. In pursuance of her aims to diversify her economy, Kazakhstan has ventured into newer domains like East Asia and Southeast Asia. President Nazarbayev's fascination for successful Asian models was reflected in his much-publicised autobiography, *The Kazakhstan Way:* "My point is that the quest for the best model is still going on around the world. Here in Kazakhstan I'm trying to adopt the good experiences of other countries and get rid of the bad practices of the past." The Kazakhs are keeping all their options open: seeking a central role in the New Silk Road initiative of the US, permitting pervasive Chinese presence in their economy, promoting bilateral and institutional ties with the EU, becoming a member of the Eurasian Union and looking for alternatives in Southeast Asia. "Diversification" is the name of the new Kazakh game.

A substantial segment of Kazakhstan's robust economy is controlled by the Samruk-Kazyna national wealth fund, which was until December 2011 managed by Nazarbayev's son-in-law, Timur Kulibayev. It is now headed by former Deputy Prime Minister, Umirzak Shukeyev. Samruk-Kazyna's grip on the economy has substantially grown. Kazakhstan-watchers are aware that the President and his elite group have extraordinary influence over lucrative sectors of the Kazakh economy. For those who are able to navigate through this hierarchical system, the rewards can be great. For instance, China is doing very well in the energy sector and industry. Big players in the energy sector may be able to weather the uncertain conditions but smaller entities, typically those that could facilitate the Kazakh government's stated aim of diversifying the economy away from energy and mining, cannot afford the risk.

The expansion of Aktau Seaport Special Economic Zone (SEZ)[17] is primarily related to Kazakhstan's oil interests and the purpose is to widen the domain of services through the seaport. "The seaport should be used to transport goods produced in the SEZ to foreign markets via the Caspian Sea. We believe that we need to relaunch the SEZ, i.e., we need to move it away from general seaport functions and make it a zone specialised in oil and gas sector, including in export to the pre-Caspian countries."[18] By 2007, Kazakhstan plans to turn Aktau into a "special economic zone" so as to serve the so-called "North-South transport corridor." There is a strange premonition that the region would become the apple of Russia's eye in terms of a Eurasian alliance of gas producers. Russia's planned naval exercises in the region have been strongly countered by the Turkmenbashi, who is a prominent partner in such an alliance and without whom the gas deal cannot be clinched. Seeking a larger share of the Sea, Turkmenistan and Iran have disagreed with Russia's plan for splitting the Caspian bottom along a "modified median line" while keeping the waters in common. Kazakhstan agreed and clinched a separate deal with Russia last May, while Azerbaijan still mulls signing a similar agreement. In a closed sea, like the Caspian, major military exercises sound like a warning to disagreeing littoral nations who have fallen out of tune with Russia's "gunboat diplomacy."[19] The only exclusive partner of Russia here is Kazakhstan. The Kazakh navy is based in Aktau and Atyrau ports in the eastern and northern parts of the Caspian. Kazakh naval forces include some 3,000 personnel, and armed with 10 imported coastguard boats and five smaller vessels, built at the Zenith shipyard in Uralsk, in western Kazakhstan, as well as three Mil helicopters. Moreover, Kazakhstan recently launched its own Naval Academy in Aktau indicating that it was going to build up national navy. Kyrgyzstan too appeared to be a willing partner.

"Oil chronicles" in the Caspian and Black Seas involving Caspian littoral states like Azerbaijan and Iran and international partners like the EU have featured well in news reports ever since the opening of the Kazakh "west gate"—i.e., Aktau seaport in Mangystau region. Key industry events have been organised in the calendar year 2009. Besides oil processing and transportation and engineering companies, technological meets have been organised in the region by Mangistau region's Mayor-in-Council.[20]

Will This Gamble Last?

Two decades back, in a speech on March 29, 1994 at Lomonosov Moscow State University, President Nursultan Nazarbayev envisioned the future of the Eurasian space: "How do I see the future of that space that used to be one country? Nowadays, in the conditions of sovereignty, recognising equal rights for all, respecting the sovereignty and independence of each state, we could create a completely new unity. I would call it the Eurasian Union."[21] Two decades later, Nazarbayev's brand of a Eurasian Union has a new cover: that of Eurasian integration. But the idea was the same. Twenty years back, the idea was of no interest to his colleagues. But as his biographers have proclaimed, Nazarbayev was clearly ahead of his time. Even today, the EEU continues to be an economic project, without infringement on political sovereignty. As the leader proclaimed in his speech at Moscow State University on April 28, 2014, the aim was to boost economic competitiveness.

But some Eurasia watchers consider it to be a rickety Eurasian Union especially after the demise of the Soviet Union. Even though Nazarbayev's initial idea of the Eurasian Union as an economic lobby seems to have a lot of emotional appeal,[22] there was nothing in it that could be expected to last long. In Nazarbayev's opinion, it was caring for economy that mattered more than politics. Since that did not happen twenty years ago, the Union failed. To take the Union project to a new level requires a lot of effort even though conditions (like the will for energy and transport) are present. Kazakhstan's dream was a single economic space guaranteeing free flow of capital, services and labour and a single financial market that would be fully functional by 2025. Obviously Kazakhstan had her own aims in mind: to gain access to energy infrastructure by 2025 on the basis of the EEU's single market for oil and gas. Today, with the word economic being dropped from the Union, it rather appears to be a less cohesive unit, trying to expand its perimeter to what is called the *Russki Mir* or Russian world, denoting allegiance of the satellite states of Russia—e.g., Kyrgyzstan, and more recently Armenia. The constant striving on the part of the hostile partners as well as lesser allies to be either on the side of the European Union or China (or both) or Russia has created a dent in the Union. The presence of three distinct lobbies—the pro-Russian lobby, the anti-Russian lobby and the stand-alone lobby—the last two lobbies having partnership deals of various forms with the European Union and China—tends to make the EEU's future uncertain.

The fate of the Eurasian Union seems to be rather precariously (and peculiarly) balanced ever since President Putin has expressed his vested interest in pulling the reins of the EEU. For most analysts in the West, the EEU today appears to be degraded and also morphed—because President Putin is trying to lock states into some kind of Union. Since the signing of the agreement between the three states—Russia, Kazakhstan and Belarus—on November 18, 2011, the EEU has become the most cited diplomatic affair not only in terms of post-Soviet multilateral engagements that are relying more and more on regional partnerships but also in terms of Europe's Eastern partnership programme emanating from its very own neighbourhood policy that tends to divide partners rather than uniting them. Observers have noticed a strain in Kazakhstan's voices about the new integration strategy that is hurting Kazakhstan business interests most. Also, the Union seems to have lost its steam mainly because of the gaming intentions of the CIS states. Take the case of Georgia for instance. Around October 2013 Georgia expressed its willingness to join the Customs Union but soon backtracked on its decision. The main reason why it chose not to join is because of the common external tariff which will be higher than the present rate. This means that Georgia's imports from other countries will decrease. This means a trade diversion which the political opposition is unwilling to accept. Also, the WTO regulations are binding on Georgia. And to allow its competitor Armenia in the same bloc was unacceptable to the regime's opponents. There was a new twist to Georgia-Armenia economic relations with the dawn of 2015. Georgia shifted its course completely and joined the Association Agreement with the European Union. In 2015, as both Armenia and Georgia made their final choices by opting for two differing Unions—the Eurasian Union and the European Union respectively—the regional divergence among the CIS bloc came out in the open. Georgia's initial tricks were a clear case of "the cat coming out of the bag."[23] Armenia is invariably going to face a diminishing market but its only advantage is Russian subsidy—at least as it hopes will be the case by joining the Eurasian Union. Given Russia's "crawling" expansion, most of the bilateral trade relations in the CIS (as in the case of Armenia-Georgia) will be hugely hit.[24]

Attempts to reinvigorate the post-Soviet space are not new.[25] Observers have commented on the reintegration efforts that have proliferated among countries belonging to the Commonwealth of Independent States (CIS). In the past, the CIS organisations and platforms that were created with partly overlapping memberships and different integration objectives mostly showed allegiance to the European Union (EU). These pro-EU groupings include CSTO, GUUAM and Black Sea Economic Cooperation Organisation. In recent times, there seems to be a lot of expectation about maximum gains for members of the Eurasian Economic Union that is expected to be fully functional from 2015.[26] The Customs Union and the Common Economic Space (CES) between Russia, Kazakhstan and Belarus represent two components of this ambitious regional project that was envisioned by President Nursultan Nazarbayev in 1994. Today, the Union has a new mentor—Russian President Vladimir Putin. His vision for the Eurasian Union was not just to foster a new round of post-Soviet reintegration, but to turn it into one major block that would counter the European Union. And the Putinian formula of "building blocks" are being compared to the already existing European and Asian ones—the EU, the NAFTA, APEC and the ASEAN—rhetorically for global economic development but actually for reviving national prestige in a manner that was not approved by Putin's own partners—Nazarbayev and Lukashenko. Russia finds herself in a geopolitical mess in which only some post-Soviet states seemed to be interested or are coerced to join. Whether Putin's dream of a Eurasian Union (to revive Russia) will evolve out of this geopolitical bloc is still open to question.

A Drop in the Ocean: Experimenting with Decentralisation

Assertions about both de facto and de jure economic decentralisation in "the donor regions" of Atyrau, Mangistau, Pavlodar, Karaganda and Almaty are very strong, and the central government seems to be responding directly to demands from administrative heads (*akims*) in these regions for an increase in official levers of control over the economies within their jurisdiction. De jure decentralisation is a conscious attempt to officially recognise the demands of the wealthier regions for more autonomy. This is the fact of the matter as leaders of these regions have been actively demanding greater autonomy in both the economic and political spheres. The *akims* in these regions want to exercise greater de jure control over the activities and monetary resources of the foreign investors operating in their oblasts to "clear up" this confusion and "address" these contractual inconsistencies. The same sentiment is seen among people who are directly involved in the international companies like Tengiz Chevroil and have got access to wealth and have not shared it evenly with other partners of these contracting companies. Of course, decentralisation did not come naturally as a Kazakh government's choice. The pressure of international development agencies since the 1980s (especially UNDP and World Bank) to increase loans for the Kazakh government based on the precondition of decentralisation is something that needs to be taken into account.

Such issues of decentralisation that have turned the spotlight on the western regions have been discussed more often in the context of the expansion project of the Caspian Pipeline Consortium that was formed in 2001 and became operational through its pipeline route that extended beyond Atyrau into the Russian Federation oblasts of Astrakhan and up to the Black Sea. Nine years since its formation, i.e., in 2010, the CPC pipeline from Tengiz Oilfield to Novorissisyk, a Russian port on the Black Sea became operational. Oil started flowing towards markets in the Mediterranean and Western Europe.

This pipeline was considered to be a major breakthrough for Tengiz Chevroil. Before the pipeline was built, the only ways to ship bulk oil exports from Kazakhstan to recipient nations were through the railways or by boat or ferries across the Caspian to Azerbaijan. That was an extremely costly and time-consuming affair. The pipeline on the other hand was a big cost-saver and also raised the image of Kazakhstan as the real giver to the world's oil economy. With its expansion plans, Tengiz Chevroil was rated high because of its engineering skills.

The people's optimism was pretty high till 2010 due to the much flaunted resource nationalism agendas. Kazakhstan's open-door policy towards foreign energy companies has had a sustainable effect. Kazakhstan has attracted more foreign investment per capita than any other Commonwealth of Independent States country since 1991, with 89% of the funds going to the oil and gas sector. Western, Russian, Middle Eastern, Chinese and Indian corporations are all present in Kazakhstan; they balance each other out so that no one foreign actor has too much influence over the Kazakh oil sector. In 2012, the government launched the "People's IPO" programme, selling stakes in energy assets to domestic investors. The expectation was that half a million of Kazakhstan's 16.7 million citizens would acquire equity in the oil and gas sector over the next five years. Further initiatives were floated to build on the abilities of a diversified economy. Diversification away from oil and gas dependency is already a high priority for Kazakh government. In January 2014, Nazarbayev's ambitious "Kazakhstan-2050" programme set the objective of moving the country into the top-30 most developed nations in the world. The hydrocarbon sector and particularly the national sovereign wealth fund are expected to act as the source of financing to modernise and radically improve the quality of life. Diversifying export routes and obtaining the best purchase price in the international market have been top priorities in Kazakhstan. Overreliance on the oil sector has not detracted investors who are still hopeful about the country's energy wealth. But this high-profile pipeline project soon ran into rough weather.

Notes

1. "Launch of Eurasian Economic Union may trigger growth of salaries in Kazakhstan," *Tengri News*, July 22, 2014. http://en.tengrinews.kz/markets/Launch-of-Eurasian-Economic-Union-may-trigger-growth-ofsalaries-in-Kazakhstan-256881/
2. Gulaikhan Kubayeva, "Economic Impact of the Eurasian Economic Union on Central Asia," Central Asia Security Policy Briefs # 20, OSCE Academy in Bishkek 2015.
3. James M. Roberts, Ariel Cohen and Jonathan C. Baisdel, *The Eurasian Union: Undermining Economic Freedom and Prosperity in the South Caucasus*, The Heritage Foundation—Special report No. 148, November 26, 2013, p. 2.
4. Malika Orazgaliyeva, "Kyrgyzstan formally enters EAEU; Customs Controls to be removed," *The Astana Times,* August 17, 2015; "Kazakhstan, Kyrgyzstan Eliminate Customs Controls at Border," *Astana Calling*, Issue 418, August 14, 2015.
5. "EaEU vague future and member countries' distrust of Russia," in Emma Gabrielyan, "Armenia in a Complex Geopolitical stage," December 23, 2014, http://en.aravot.

am/2014/12/23/168279/

6. The EES came into existence on January 1, 2012.
7. There are proposals to invite countries like Bulgaria, the Czech Republic, Hungary, Finland and even China and Mongolia to join the Eurasian Union.
8. Aktoky Aitzhanova et al., *Kazakhstan 2050: Toward a Modern Society for All* (New Delhi: Oxford University Press, 2014), chapters 2 & 3. A publication of Nazarbayev University and National Analytical Centre.
9. Richard Weitz, "Sino-Kazakh Ties on a Roll," *China Brief*, vol. XIII, issue 2, January 18, 2013.
10. "US, Chinese Plans for Rail Links with Central Asia Triggering 'Railroad War' and Reducing Russia's Influence," *Eurasia Daily Monitor*, vol. 10, issue 31, February 19, 2013.
11. Dru C. Gladney, "Constructing a Contemporary Uyghur National Identity: Transnationalism, Islamicization and National Representation," *Cahiers détudes sur la Mediterranee Orientale et le monde turco-iranien,* no. 13, Jan-June 1992.
12. Ross Anthony, "The Persistence of the Nation-State at the Kazakh Chinese Border," in Franck Bille, Gregory Delaplace and Caroline Humphrey (eds.), *Frontier Encounters: Knowledge and Practice at the Russian, Chinese and Mongolian Border* (Cambridge: Open Book Publishers, 2012).
13. Ross Anthony, ibid., p. 204.
14. Alida Ashimbaeva, "Dostizhenija i problemy kazakhstansko-kitajskikh ekonomicheskikh otnoshenij" (Outcomes and problems in China-Kazakhstan economic relations), March 22, 2007. http://www.postsoviet.ru/page.php?pid=118; Konstantin Syroezhkin, *Problemy sovremennovo Kitaia I bezopasnost'v Tsentral'noi Azii,* Almaty: KISI, 2006.
15. Jacob Stokes, "China's Road Rules: Beijing Looks West toward Eurasian Integration," *Foreign Affairs* (Snapshot section), April 19, 2015.
16. Daniel Runde, "Kazakhstan: The Buckle in One Belt One Road," *Forbes*, June 29, 2015.
17. Project SEZ "Seaport Aktau" was initiated by the Decree of the President of the Republic of Kazakhstan on April 26, 2002. The duration of the project is January 1, 2003 to January 1, 2028. The main aim is to increase economic growth in the Kazakhstani sector of the Caspian Sea. The goal is to develop the production base and facilities for oil and gas industry, production of consumer goods and attracting small and medium businesses. A shipyard, a marine metal structures plant, fibreglass and metal pipes plants and production of offshore containers are functioning in the zone. http://www.traceca-org.org/uploads/media/02.-24072012_Presentation_SEZ_Seaport_Aktau_ENG.pdf
18. http://en.tengrinews.kz/industry_infrastructure/Kazakhstans-Aktau-Seaport-SEZ-to-focus-on-oil-and-gas-21055/
19. Sergei Blagov, "Gunboats doing the talking in the Caspian," *Asia Times Online,* July 9, 2002.
20. "Mangystau at the Centre of Events," http://www.iteca.kz/en/news/28-10-2009pr-mang-oil/
21. Altair Nurbekov, "Eurasian Economic Integration 'Will Continue,' Nazarbayev Says," *Eurasia & World,* April 2, 2014. *The Astana Times,* January 23, 2015.
22. Victoria Panfilova, "Nazarbayev's brand," *Vestnik Kavkaza*, April 30, 2014.
23. Michael Fuenzig, "Georgia and the Eurasian Union," *Democracy and Freedom Watch,* October 16, 2013.
24. Nino Evgenidze, "Eurasian Customs Union Crawling Closer to Georgia," *Democracy*

and Freedom Watch, January 2, 2015.

25. The foremost initiatives since Novo-Ogaryevo Process of 1991 include Central Asian Cooperation (CAC), CSTO, EurAsEC, Customs-Union I, GUUAM and in recent times Customs Union-II that developed into the Common Economic Space or the Eurasian Economic Space (CES/EES) with the prospect of developing into the Eurasian Economic Union (EEU) in 2015.
26. "Putin: All Participants Benefiting from Eurasian Economic Union," *Georgia Today,* issue no. 748, January 9, 2015-January 15, 2015.

4. Myriad Concerns

Political analysts pondering over Kazakhstan's future after President Nazarbayev's term ends tend to be concerned about the fate of Eurasian integrationist projects that were first mentored by Nazarbayev but more recently by Putin.[1] Reactions about what happens next, including Russia's pronounced authoritarian turn under Russian President Vladimir Putin, are not encouraging.[2] Risk assessment groups in Kazakhstan have pointed to a serious aberration—in Kazakhstan both domestic and foreign policies are highly personalised—the EEU is a part of Nazarbayev's personal political ambitions. Will the next Kazakh President have the same aims? Most importantly, how will Russia react? Will it try to put pressure on the Kazakh leadership as it has at times done in Belarus?

There is consensus about President Putin's vested interest that has tilted the balance in favour of the Eurasian Economic Union (EEU). Since the signing of the agreement on November 18, 2011, the EEU has become the most cited diplomatic affair as far as Eurasian multilateral engagements are concerned. The EEU is considered to be the CIS version of the European Union and there has been a lot of positive thinking about this organisation ever since the signing of the Eurasian Customs Union, which was ignored by the West for about five years. It was only when Putin with his desire of *expanding* the Eastern Partnership project by inducting newer members like Armenia, Georgia, Moldova and Ukraine with the condition that they drop their plans to sign Association Agreements with the European Union (EU) that the West started taking the Eurasian Economic Union seriously. Prior to that, the world was only marginally conscious about the Eurasian economic space and new hopes that it generated. Today the EEU seems to have breathed life due to President Putin's stance of reducing competition from the European counterparts.

Initially, there was a lot of expectation about the EEU. Within the Customs Union, most of the internal trade has been liberalised except in certain products like rice, tobacco, alcohol, sugar. Since July 2011, border controls have largely disappeared. At the same time, border controls with the non-signatory member nations that were direct neighbours within the CIS were stepped up. Member states established a common external border tariff and 85% of the import duties were liberalised. Free movement of capital and labour is expected and the Eurasian Union is expected to have a say in member states' energy policies as well as other macroeconomic policies generating competition among members.

Non-concerns

Competing levels of cultural identification have generated different notions of Kazakhness (*Kazakhshylyk*) whose implicit meaning is "rootedness." The rootedness of Kazakh tradition signifies revival of cultural practices which has an interesting character in (a) northern Kazakhstan as in Schuchinsk district, and (b) the east of Kazakhstan, especially in western Mongolia. In both cases, there are legends and fables associated with such legends that have deified the notion of rootedness and belonging. In the case of the broader Altai region, the homeland is of the Turkic tribes, which encompasses parts of Kazakhstan, Mongolia, Russia and China and which is identified as an Inner Asian identity *altyn besyk* or golden cradle. It figures in a Turkic-Mongol origin myth, where the grey wolf ancestor and the Sky God Tengri first join. The ideological drive to claim Altai as specifically Kazakh is to link that territory firmly to the nationality category and to state territory; it is supported by members of different Kazakh groups in Kazakhstan, including nationalists and Eurasianists. The desire to know one's ancestors is one way of legitimising Kazakh history. Shrine visits are a regular feature of what it means to be Muslim for most Kazakhs. One specific example is of the southern city of Taraz in Dzhambyl region, which houses eleventh-century historical shrines and sites. Pilgrimage tours in Taraz centre on the figure of Aisha Bibi, a young woman who died tragically on her way to marry her fiancé, the Kharakhanid regional ruler. Visitors typically end their tours at the site of Tektormas, an ancestor from the same era, on a hilltop overlooking the entire Taraz Valley.

Such myths and fables also exist in the Schuschinsk District of North Kazakhstan. The Burabay National Nature Park is tucked away in the town of Schuschinsk—about 50 kilometres away from Kokshetau town. Burabay is the pearl of Kazakhstan and has gorgeous pine forests and cliffs and rocks that are interspersed with serene lakes. The eco-region Burabay was created in August 2000 and is under the supervision of the Administration of Presidential Affairs. The location is a part of the Kokshetau steppe, a mixed steppe and forest and hilly upland. Every rock here has its own legend. The location is a huge mineral reserve. Among them are: Okzhetpes cliff (Inaccessible to Arrows) with a peak resembling an elephant calf and the Zhumbaktas cliff (Mysterious Stone) resembling a mysterious sphinx. Burabay is a name that is treasured by all Kazakhs, referring not only to the famous lake that lies in the middle of the mountains, but to the whole Burabay-Kokshetau National Park.

A series of Kazakh legends epitomises Burabay. The legend of the region's formation tells how God granted the Kazakhs this wonderful landscape. Another legend of the fighting spirit of a *batyr* who lost his eye fighting the Dzhungars is also very popular. There are legends about Ablai Khan fighting the Dzhungars in the eighteenth century while his warriors wanted to marry a local princess. A tall, eagle-topped monument, stands in the clearing; a large, flat-topped rock known as Ablai Khan's Throne hides in the trees behind. A tiny little museum with an exhibition hall is perched in the land that commemorates the valiant struggle of the *batyrs* of the Middle and Younger Horde.

Kazakh visitors do not claim direct genealogical ancestry to the individuals whose mausoleums, shrines and sites they visit. Rather, the lives and stories of ancestors are revisited as part of a common cultural experience. These pilgrimage practices are long-rooted in practices of ancestor worship (associated with Tengrism and Buddhism) that is characteristic of the Mongol domain of Inner Asia; they are all part of a complex cultural ecology supporting physical and spiritual health. Sites are increasingly visited for the purpose of physical and spiritual healing and help, to cope with uncertainties in the present and future. Tthese sites are also revered as the cradle of cultural unity (*Kazakshylykh*), not necessarily bounded to any one polity in space or time. Attention has been given to sacred places that are revered by people of many religions who have inherited such traditions from their ancestors. Sacred places are protected over millennia and serve as symbols of spiritual connections to nature. Today, this branch of knowledge among local and indigenous communities is gaining recognition more than ever before.

So, it is the reinvention of tradition that is central to the revivalist literature among Kazakh communities. In Western Mongolia, communities rely on semi-nomadic livestock as a means of subsistence and survival. This revival is associated with rituals of well-being performed by the *imams*. Such a role has nothing to do with the religious patrons and foreign-educated local imams who receive governmental and private donations from Turkey, Saudi Arabia, etc. Another variant is seen among a section of Kazakhs who have remained immobile, i.e., stayed back in western Mongolia and have experienced a significant increase in religious freedom. The imams in western Mongolia play an important mediating role as members of the local population who have acquired social status and try to renegotiate their identity and role as Muslim leaders with transnational connections with a broader Muslim community.

Now this trajectory is completely at odds with the discourse about religious radicalism that has infiltrated the whole of Central Asia, Afghanistan and, most recently, West Asia. Imams of western Mongolia, especially in the Mongolia-China borderland perform activities like circumcision among the Kazakh households that are settled in the grassy pastures. Islamic rituals are performed freely among these families and contribute to the well-being of the Kazakh community. Now, well-being is associated with health, happiness and prosperity. The imams through their connections with the local community belong to the tradition of celebrating health and happiness with members of the community.[3] Profiles of imams illustrate how the revival in Islam in western Mongolia has contributed to the social and material well-being of imams as Islamic missionaries. There seems to be a clear-cut distinction between relatively young imams of the post-Soviet period who have experienced social and economic well-being and traditional *mullahs* of the Soviet period who were usually elderly men who learnt and practised Islam at home. To the new category of young imams belonged (a) Alibek, the young head imam of a *sum* (State Universal Store), (b) Sabir who too was a young man in his thirties and head imam of a mosque in a *soum* centre in Mongolia with basic education in Olgii in Mongolia but also went to Turkestan (in Kazakhstan) for higher studies and (c) Zhandos who was the assistant imam in a different *soum* centre with basic education in Olgii and was supported by Turkey's Ministry of Religious Affairs for higher education. These three young men, representing the face of religious revivalism in western Mongolia, occupied a new social role in the region.

Their position and status are very dissimilar from those of the *mullahs* of the Soviet period. One such character was Kaldybai whose descent can be traced to prominent religious leaders—his grandfather was an imam who was one of the first Mongolian Kazakhs to go on pilgrimage to Mecca. His father was also an imam of a small mosque in the countryside. In 1938, the Soviet authorities of Mongolia arrested and killed his father and destroyed that particular mosque. Till the end of the Soviet era, Kaldybai avoided religious activities, living in fear of his father's past experience. He worked as a schoolteacher and also formally registered with the Communist Party. It was only after his exposure to perestroika since 1989 that he began to tread on the path of his grandfather and father. He started reading books in Kazakh that became available in the region and was successfully mentored by his uncle. In 1994 he opened his private mosque in Olgii which did not have any direct link with the Mongolian Islamic Association but did help him to generate respect among his community which contributes to the feeling of well-being which he feels responsible to impart to members of his community.[4]

Due to community closeness, the new imams of Bayan Olgii in western Mongolia have earned a great deal of respect and have also enjoyed a great amount of personal security. Besides, they also benefited from their ties with the transnational Muslim community, especially with Kazakh and Turkish. It was because of these "foreign contacts" and contacts with the diaspora imams as well as their exposure to formal Islamic education that have helped them to renegotiate their relationships in their own local spaces as well as with transnational communities. So, a dissection of their religious "journeys" helps us to understand that revival of Islam should not merely be interpreted as a negative aspect—not certainly with these imams who have had the scope to expand their opportunities by contributing to economic and social well-being. Among Kazakhs of Mongolia and Kazakhstan, religiosity is perhaps deeply embedded into the social fabric but that also entails an understanding of the cultural traditions which have varied across generations and have been nurtured by a new generation of imams.

Such explanations of well-being are different from expressions of Islamic radicalism that may have reappeared time and again across Central and West Asia in the post-Soviet period. But it seems rather simplistic to compare trends—because in Kazakhstan, religious radicalism is hardly a trend. On the contrary, due to 70 years of atheism practised by the Soviet state, one would expect egalitarian tendencies and a secular variety of Islam here. But one could also make certain inferences as major silence prevails on the subject of religious freedom. Though religiosity is not a matter of surveillance as in neighbouring Uzbekistan, in Kazakhstan as well as in

Kyrgyzstan, keeping the atheist orientation of the Soviet regime in mind, one would not be surprised to see a restriction on religious expression. It is too simplistic to expect direct results just because of an all-pervasive official rhetoric about religious harmony (exemplified in Nazarbayev's World Religions Conference initiative).

A generic idea about the growth of Islamic radicalism in West Asia has resulted in a phobia about similar trends in Kazakhstan. Though Kazakhs are typically identified as Sunni Muslim, the effect of orthodoxy in generating egalitarian attitudes still hold ground and cannot be negated by the proposition that there is significant display of intolerance by the state due to overt displays by Islamic radical groups—ostensibly because of the threats of extremism and terrorism in the surrounding region. The hypothesis here would be that in Kazakhstan there is priority for egalitarian attitudes to *economic justice* and in that context there would be preference for the imposition of *sharia* law.[5] The people's perception of the financial situation in Kazakhstan as a stable one gives rise to long-term expectations rather than short-term solutions. From that standpoint, one would find it difficult to agree with negative assessments and that an egalitarian society would be fragile due to religious extremist groups operating in its neighbourhood.

While there is praise about the economic considerations that promote egalitarianism in Kazakh society, there is also reasonable criticism about lack of Islamic education in the country which creates dangers of uncontrolled Islamic radicalism that makes the state vulnerable to sudden radical upsurges. Random news coverage by "crisis groups"[6] often create a gap in the understanding of the regime's model of social harmony. Between 2010 and 2012 a wave of armed attacks sent shock waves about Kazakhstan. Although it was initially said some attacks were the work of common criminals, very little is known about these groups. Many trials involving them are closed to the public. This gives rise to numerous conspiracy theories about their aims, targets, ideology, financial sources, hierarchy, international links, etc. One such extremist group, *Jund al-Khalifa* (Soldiers of the Caliphate), emerged in 2011 with a series of high-profile attacks for which it claimed responsibility. No one from either the political or expert community could provide clear answers about the group's origin, demands, agenda or ideology. Based on very limited official information, Kazakh security experts suggest that the individuals involved are young, religious to varying degrees. There is endless speculation about links with the Islamic Movement of Uzbekistan (IMU) or East Turkestan Islamic Movement, though the two organised movements are independent of each other and do not coordinate each other's activities. Sceptics in Kazakhstan suggest the attacks were staged by political factions who are nurturing ambitions as successors after Nazarbayev. Several Astana-based diplomats asserted that little about the attacks, or the groups alleged to be behind them, made sense. As a result, they tended to view the incidents as criminal turf wars or localised domestic political spats. However, the same diplomats also acknowledged that a growing resurgence of political Islam in the western regions especially does not bode well for long-term stability.

Those who explore the possibility of an extremist agenda behind the attacks suggest the presence and influence of a North Caucasian Salafi ideology—as alternative ideology disseminated by preachers and Arabic teachers from Turkey, Saudi Arabia, Jordan, Pakistan and Iran who reside in Kazakhstan. There are about 1,700 Islamic associations in Kazakhstan that subscribe to the spiritual-intellectual tradition in Islam.[7] They also point out a sizable number of young registered Salafiyas in western Kazakhstan, especially in Atyrau oblast. While there are differences of opinion on the ideology and agenda of the attackers, expert groups in Kazakhstan are almost unanimous about the main reason for the spread of religious radicalism: the grim socio-economic situation in the western regions. The authorities have in 2011-12 responded by what is suspected as encounter killings and detentions of suspected terrorists and suppression of extremist groups, as per the statistics of the ruling party, the *Nur Otan* Party. The year 2013 has been comparatively uneventful with effective monitoring carried out by Kazakh agencies. But the youth's leanings towards radical Islam are perhaps the greatest concern:

> Extremists do not look for young men in streets—young men find them. What leads them is a thirst for basic knowledge of *aqidah*—studies describing the beliefs of the Islamic faith—and adequate answers to various religious questions.[8]

Why and how the youth goes underground are perhaps best explained by the local media:

Owing to the Internet, today believers learn about fundamental explanations of aqidah and fiqh [Islamic jurisprudence] at home, rather than asking imams.

Then conflicts develop: an imam in the mosque tells a thing believed to be right according to DUMK, in response a young mosque-goer cites a fatwa [a juristic ruling concerning Islamic law] by ibn-Bazza, a respected Islamic scholar and former mufti of Saudi Arabia, which he saw in the web. Virtually, imam cannot answer back.

Non-acceptance of religious norms followed by the official Muslim clergy, leads to radicalisation of some young minds. As a result of disputes, independent Muslims get forced out of mosques—Pray the way Spiritual Directorate of Muslims (DUMK) approved, or leave!

Usually, outcasts go underground, where they form self-consistent communities. Ambitious young people without life experience, but with religious education obtained through self-studies join extremist communities.[9]

Even though the threat of extremism is often unexplained due to the lack of real facts and figures,[10] the rapid spread of radical religious networks is undisputed. According to a 2010 survey, 62% of Kazakhstanis indicated that they were either "very concerned" or "somewhat concerned" about the rise of Islamic extremism in Kazakhstan. Only 23% of respondents were either "not too concerned" or "not at all concerned" about the rise of religious extremism in the republic. In 2010, the governor of Atyrau Province, Bergey Ryskaliev, publicly acknowledged that religious extremism among young people was growing and therefore closer monitoring was necessary.[11]

In western Kazakhstan's oil capital Atyrau, government surveillance intensified which generated resentment among practitioners of the faith. Increasingly, they tried to practise out of sight, which, naturally, made officials more suspicious. Government surveillance expanded significantly in 2011, when Kazakhstan experienced a series of terrorist attacks that began in the western city of Aktobe.

In Aktau, one clean-shaven man in his thirties said he felt compelled to live a double-life, hiding his devout beliefs from public view. "I can't wear a beard because I am a schoolteacher," he told EurasiaNet.org. "But it's in my heart, and someday I will be able to." Another pious Muslim, a burly ex-boxer with scarred knuckles, is an adherent of *Tablighi Jamaat* (banned everywhere in Central Asia except in Kyrgyzstan) and claimed that religious-based discrimination had altered his life. He explained he was fired from a foreign operated firm in Aktau after eight years because he and his co-workers had begun to pray regularly during working hours, as Islamic practice requires. An internal migrant from Taraz, he is now unemployed and supports a wife and two children by working irregular jobs, sharing a two-bedroom apartment with two other families. He, too, would like to wear a beard, but says he cannot because prospective employers would not hire him. Members of the *Jamaat* movement in Kazakhstan say they engage in proselytising missions by relying on informal networks of family and friends to visit private homes. Though the level of government pressure on *Tablighi Jamaat* appears to be less compared to those on other movements, the fact of the matter is that its members still face regular interrogation from police and the Committee on National Security, or KNB, and are subject to administrative fines.[12]

Such diverse opinions about real and imagined concerns are increasing by the day. I would tend to consider manifestations of religiosity in Kazakhstan as a two-way process: positioning between Islamic education and religious freedom[13] on the one hand and ancestral traditions and spirituality on the other hand.

Transboundary Rift: Water Woes

a. Ili River Issue

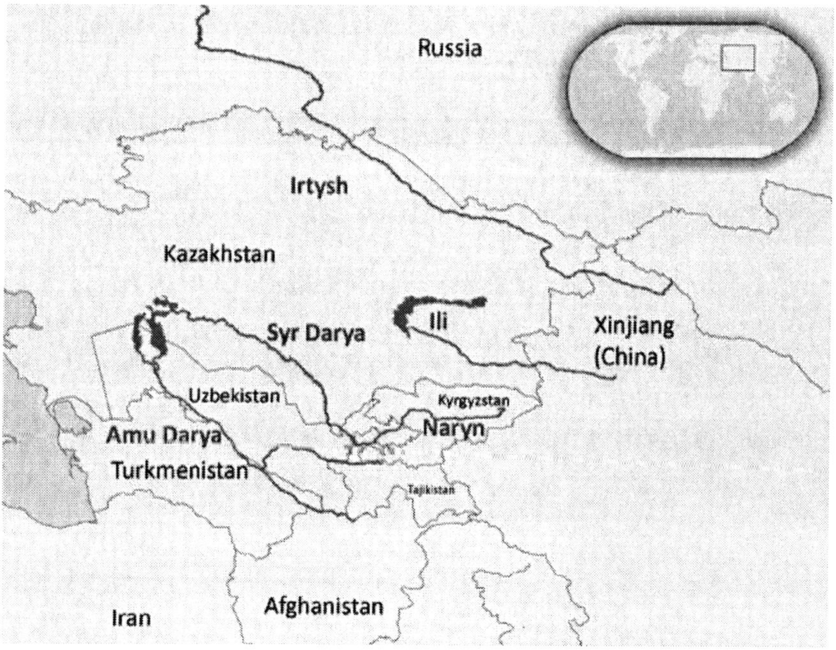

Water and cross-border river management is a major unresolved issue and remains one of the stumbling blocks in the ensuing relationship between

Kazakhstan and China.[14] Two of Kazakhstan's main rivers, the Ili and the Irtysh, originate in China, the former in the Tian Shan Mountains and the other in the Chinese Altai mountains. The Chinese authorities draw water off upstream from both rivers, without seeking Kazakhstan's consent, a situation that worsened after the initiation of the "Far West Development programme." This programme aims to foster the rapid expansion of Xinjiang's agricultural industry, especially for cotton and wheat which are water-intensive crops. Population growth in Xinjiang has also created the urge for greater water consumption. In order to implement these projects, China has planned intensive water-extraction from the Ili and the Irtysh. In the 1990s, it had announced the construction of the Kara Irtysh-Karamay Canal, intended to redirect 10-40% of the Irtysh water to Ulungur Lake. The purpose was not only to irrigate adjoining agricultural fields but also to transport the water to the Karamay oilfields about 400 kilometres from Urumqi. The expectation is that the water diversion will be fully functional and reach the fullest operational limit by 2020. This ambitious plan has affected Kazakhstan's agricultural and industrial development and is said to influence regions in Siberia, because Irtysh is the main tributary of the Ob River which flows through Omsk district.

Kazakhstan is concerned because the Irtysh is the source of life of the country's rising population of 16 million. Important towns of northeast Kazakhstan like Karaganda, Pavlodar and Semey are dependent on the Irtysh water while Astana's development is reliant on the Ishim, Irtysh's main tributary. The navigable conditions of Irtysh are also satisfactory and make it usable during the summer months, also enabling movement of water transport between northeast Kazakhstan and the Siberian region of Omsk. The Ili river in the south is equally an asset for Kazakhstan especially the Kapchagai hydroelectric station. Ili's location between the Chinese border and Lake Balkhash also makes the river a chief source of irrigation for the fields adjoining Grand Almaty Canal.

From the standpoint of resource usability, Kazakhstan argues against China's strategy of redirecting water from the rivers. Another argument is the degradation of the fragile ecosystem due to diversion of upstream water which is rich in minerals. Concerns have been expressed regarding the damage of Lake Zaysan. Similarly, the Ili will be faced with greater damage as the Lake Balkhash which gets the main supply of Ili water will be badly affected with pollutants and chemicals that come in with the

Kapchagai hydroelectric power station. With the building of the dam in the 1960s and 1970s, the damage has already set in. With the water shortage, the fish species of the river seem to have decimated and the lives of the people of the border region seem to have been badly affected. There is widespread speculation in the West and among the UN agencies about the Ili water issue becoming a case of environmental tragedy, almost comparable with the Aral Sea tragedy.[15]

Here is a description of the environmental hazards by a noted environmentalist Eleusizov in the surroundings of the city of Yining, a two-hour drive from the Kazakh border which despite being lush and green is at the heart of the battle for one of Central Asia's most overlooked resources: water.

Eleusizov described a nightmare scenario of Balkhash's division into several smaller lakes and the spread of desertification throughout the area. Worse still, he said, the Aral disaster showed that airborne salt from the evaporation of Balkhash would land on glaciers and make them melt all the more quickly. He emphasised that glaciers supplying water to Almaty and many parts of Xinjiang would be at risk.

> "One needs to approach this from the interests of the entire basin. [The Chinese] need to understand that if Balkhash dies, so do China's glaciers," Eleusizov said. The people moving into Xinjiang as part of the Go West campaign, he said, "will also be left without water."[16]

Another report also describes the hazards of development projects along transboundary rivers like the Irtysh, also called Kara Irtysh, which runs along 672 kilometres northwest through the border with Kazakhstan:

> China plans to build new canals, reservoirs, dams, hydroelectric power stations on the Irtysh River and on other smaller sources of transboundary rivers, which threatens an environmental catastrophe for Eastern and Central Kazakhstan.
>
> According to the Federal Agency for Water Resources of the Russian Federation, until recently, China took from the Black Irtysh 1-1.5 km^3 of water a year, Kazakhstan—3.8 km^3, Russia—0.43 km^3. From 1997, China began increasing water intake from the watercourse of the Black Irtysh for

> irrigation of arid lands. The destabilising factor was the construction of a 300-km irrigation canal Black Irtysh–Karamay, intended for irrigation of areas, expansion of areas under cotton and corn in the Xinjiang Uyghur Autonomous Region (XUAR), and for the needs of the oil industry. With the commissioning of the channel into design capacity, China's water intake from the river increased almost 5 times to 5 km^3 per year.
>
> Experts are observing a shallowing of the 300-km Irtysh–Karaganda canal, and a sharp deterioration in the biological value of the water. Russia's Omsk Region has also been classified as one of the regions facing water scarcity. On the Irtysh River near Omsk, there is massive formation of new islands and shoals, salinisation of the floodplain, concentration of harmful substances in water, degradation of flora and fauna, and exposure of drinking and industrial water intakes.[17]

On Astana's initiative, an agreement on cooperation in the use and protection of transboundary waters was signed with China in 2001 and a Kazakh-Chinese joint commission was established. In 2008, China and Russia signed an Intergovernmental Agreement on the rational use and protection of transboundary waters. But there are serious allegations of China backtracking on the issue of a solution to the transboundary water woes:

> The Russian-Chinese and Kazakh-Chinese agreements set aside the issue of the parties' liabilities. Articles 5, 6, 7 of the Russian-Kazakh document talk about coordination of any work on cross-border facility, while Article 8 declares "compensation of the injured party" of harm caused by "any action taken" by the other party. The preamble of the Russian-Chinese document refers to "conduct of friendly consultations and taking of coordinated actions," refers to the need to inform the other party in the case of "water management activities that could lead to significant transboundary effects," Article 3 of the Kazakh-Chinese agreement limits the efforts of the parties and talks about taking appropriate actions only "as a result of flood disasters and man-made accidents." Article 4 is ambiguous: "None of the parties shall limit the other party to rationally use and protect water resources of transboundary rivers, taking into account mutual interests."[18]

b. Water Sharing Issue in Chu and Talas Basin of Kyrgyzstan

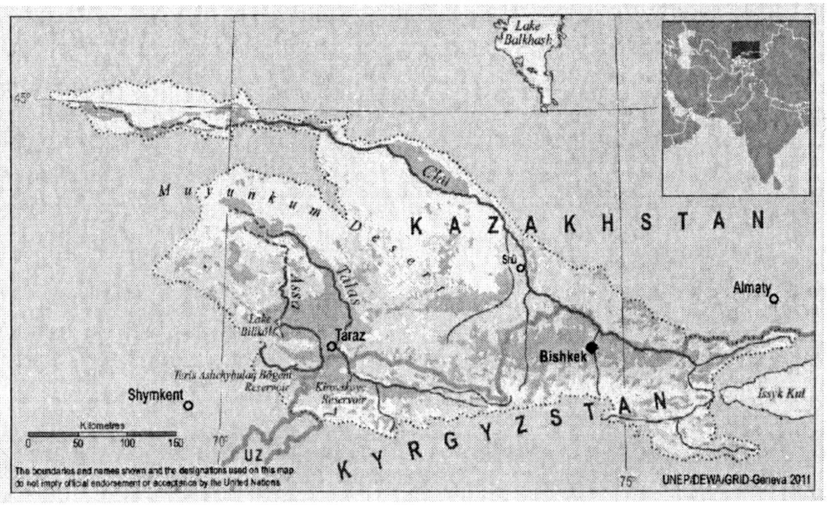

Chu and Talas river basins are located between the northern Tian Shan mountains and the eastern margin of the Turan lowland. The administrative division of the mountain basin belongs to the Kyrgyz Republic; the plain, to the Republic of Kazakhstan. The rivers flow entirely within the territory of the Kyrgyz Republic.

The success story promoted for Central Asian water cooperation involves the Chu and Talas basin and the 2000 agreement between the riparian states, Kazakhstan and Kyrgyzstan. Under the agreement, Kazakhstan and Kyrgyzstan agreed to share the operation and maintenance costs of the transboundary infrastructure. After the agreement was ratified by Kazakhstan in 2002, the international organisations started to support the operationalisation of the agreement—the establishment of a joint commission.

Until its promotion as a success story, the Chu-Talas basin received hardly any attention in international literature. An exception was the US Agency for International Development (USAID) report[19] on cost-sharing for the operation and maintenance of transboundary infrastructure in different basins in Central Asia. It was only in the early 2000s that the Chu-Talas basin appeared in the academic literature. Sievers mentions about the 2000 agreement on the Chu-Talas between Kazakhstan and Kyrgyzstan, shortly after its ratification in 2002. Since then, this agreement and the Chu-Talas basin have received more attention, especially from the international community—the UN Special Programme for the Economies of Central Asia (SPECA), the Organisation for Security and Cooperation in Europe (OSCE), the Asian Development Bank which started to celebrate the agreement as a breakthrough for Central Asia. With the international agencies involved, the internationally shared knowledge about the Chu-Talas basin increased.

On July 7, 2013, over 200 residents of Kara-Buura District, Talas region, Kyrgyzstan, blocked the canal "Ahmed" by building a makeshift stone dam, preventing the flow of water into Kazakhstan. According to Kyrgyz reports protesters blocked the canal to demonstrate their opposition to a border demarcation agreement between Kyrgyzstan and Kazakhstan that became functional four years ago. Negotiations aimed at unblocking the canal were unfruitful. The treaty *On the Delimitation and Demarcation of the Kazakh-Kyrgyz Border,* signed by the two countries on December 15, 2001, and ratified by the Kyrgyz parliament in 2008 stands challenged as Kyrgyz villagers feel that the handover of Kok Sai territory in Talas region to Kazakhstan was not a correct decision. They resented the sharing of pastures and also accused the previous regime of Askar Akayev of depriving his own citizens of their land rights. The blocking of the canal has also had deplorable results—eleven kilometres of Kyrgyz territory feeding into other villages in Kyrgyzstan's Kara-Buura District downstream of the makeshift dam.

The makeshift dam built by Kyrgyz villagers in Kara Buura District.

There were heated reactions over the incident:

On the Kyrgyz side:

"V Kyrgyzii pravit tolpa" (In Kyrgyzstan, the mob rules!)

"Tam ne tolpa pravit a grazhdanskoe obshchestva." (A civil society rules Kyrgyzstan, not the mob.)

On the Kazakh side:

Voobshe dazhe obidno ot "bratev" Kyrgyzov nozh v spino polutit. Sto chelovek portyat avtoritet millionov. (It hurts to get a knife in the back from our "brothers," the Kyrgyz. A hundred people spoil the reputation of millions.)[20]

Notes

1. According to Dosym Satpaev, the most critical analyst of Nazarbayev's government, EEU was President Nazarbayev's pet project—envisioned by him way back in 1994. But his emotional and subjective perception of the EEU prevents him from having a balanced view of all the risks and threats inherent in Kazakhstan's membership of the EEU. Dosym Satpaev, "Kazakhstan and the Eurasian Economic Union: The View from Astana," *European Council on Foreign Relations,* January 12, 2015.
2. "Kazakhstan: Waiting for Change," Brussels: International Crisis Group, Asia Report No. 250, September 30, 2013.
3. Cynthia Werner, Holly Barcus and Namrata Brede, "Discovering a sense of well-being through the revival of Islam: profiles of Kazakh *imams* in Western Mongolia," David. W. Montgomery (ed.), *Negotiating Well-being in Central Asia* (UK: Routledge ThirdWorlds Book Series, 2015).
4. Montgomery, *Negotiating Well-being in Central Asia,* ... pp. 114-15.
5. Azamat K. Junisbai, "Understanding Economic Justice Attitudes in Two Countries: Kazakhstan and Kyrgyzstan," *Social Forces*, vol. 88, no. 4, June 2010, pp. 1684-85.
6. "Kazakhstan—Waiting for Change," Asia Report No. 250, September 30, 2013, International Crisis Group, Brussels.
7. Aktolkyn Kulsarieva et al., "The Religious Situation in Kazakhstan: Main trends and Challenges." *World Applied Sciences Journal,* 25 (11), 2013, pp. 1612-18. www.idosi.org/wasj/wasj25(11)13/15.pdf
8. Azamat Maitanov, "Why Kazakh youth join extremists?" *Ak Zhaik,* February 28, 2013.
9. Azamat Maitanov, ibid.
10. John C. K. Daly, "How Real is the Jihadi Threat to Kazakhstan?" *The Central Asia-Caucasus Analyst,* September 17, 2014.
11. Dilshod Achilov, "Islamic Education in Central Asia: Evidence from Kazakhstan," in *Asia Policy*, no. 14, July 2012.
12. Nate Schenkkan, "Kazakhstan: Government Pressure on Devout Muslims Generates Resentment," March 20, 2012, http://www.eurasianet.org/node/65156
13. Dilshod Achilov, ibid.

14. Transboundary water issues have revolved round a series of conventions related to the International Water Law which influence the signatory states. While joint projects and water management seem to offer opportunities for improving the regional economic profile, there are occasions when states tend to use the principles of international law as a tool for conflict regulation. Aidar Amrebayev and Aigul Akhanova, "Water disputes in Central Asia and its influence on social conflict potential," presentation in international conference, *Protest and the State in Eurasia and West Asia*, November 26-27, 2014, organised by Maulana Abul Kalam Azad Institute of Asian Studies, Kolkata.
15. Marlene Laruelle and Sebastien Peyrouse, *The Chinese Question in Central Asia: Domestic Order, Social Change and the Chinese Factor* (London: Hurst and Company, 2012), pp. 17-19.
16. Jack Carino, "Water woes in Kazakhstan," *China Dialogue,* April 1, 2008.
17. Ksenia Muratshina, "The Irtysh River in the hydro policy of Russia, Kazakhstan and China," Russian International Affairs Council: Central and South Asia Analysis, May 29, 2012.
18. Ibid.
19. Adrian O. Hutchens, "Final Report—Example Allocations of Operating and Maintenance Costs of Interstate Water Control Facilities Employing the Use-of-Facilities Method", Prepared for Central Asia Mission, US Agency for International Development, December 1999.
20. "Kyrgyz Block Water to Kazakhstan, Demanding the Return of 'Their' Land," *Global Voices,* posted on July 17, 2013.

5. Impressions

During 2012-14, field trips to Kazakhstan were undertaken to understand Kazakh conscience that is reminiscent of *zhuz* legacy, colonial, Soviet and post-Soviet dispensations. Aspects of lineage and tribal traditions of the *Kishi Zhuz* have come across in revisionist writings as well as in the regional museums of north Kazakhstan. Similarly, a Soviet hangover that combines memories of collectivisation, deportation and War is discernible throughout the Akmolinsk oblast. There is also an image of a loosening of the federal structure of government as well as ruptures in the social fabric as one travels to the western regions of Kazakhstan. The urban spectacle is also very different in different cities—the spatial growth of urban centres like Almaty and Astana is a stark contrast to the fringe status of oil towns like Atyrau despite the growing popularity of Tengiz Chevroil with its headquarters located in Atyrau. TCO and the Kashagan oil project (now dumped by the government) are the rallying point of several Western companies as well as collaborative projects that are being showcased in a major way by President Nazarbayev, much to the apathy of dissenting voices in Atyrau. Atyrau's Caspian character is different from Astana's capital look. Also attractive is the Russian environment in northern Kazakhstan with Kokshetau emerging as the regional centre and the city *akimat* exercising a lot of authority that is beyond the President's control. The place is a grim reminder of the Soviet past as well as *Kishi Zhuz* tribal connections. Much of that memory has waned today. It thrives as an eco-region with government's development programmes on the priority list. Mixed reactions also exist among the oralman communities in southeast Kazakhstan as well as non-titular nationalities like the Germans and the Koreans who have had sad experiences of deportation during the Stalinist regime. But there are also Kazakhs who share the pride of belonging to the *zhuz* culture but are also critical about the official decision of renaming Kazakhstan as *Kazakh Yeli* because that term very loosely binds Kazakh people belonging to various nationalities and lineages but tends to disregard people's histories prior to the formation of Kazakhstan.

Kazakh conscience has found expression in multiple responses about zhuz legacy, tribal lineages, relational patterns among nationalities. There has been awareness about various phases of "victory" and "defeat/disaster"—some of which have either been silenced or revived in new Kazakh historiography. The Kazakh psyche is represented by a unique combination of at least two sets of tribal tradition, one that is strongly ingrained in public memory as belonging to the princes and elite of the Middle Horde and the other representing the *Kishi Zhuz* comprising unsuccessful warriors, and that has almost faded from public memory. The selective rewriting of Kazakh history is unacceptable to the new generation of Kazakhs. They tend to tilt more towards aspects of collaboration, e.g., the union of Oirats and the Kazakhs. Even while talking about confrontation or encounter, regional history-writing are vocal about internal tribal dissensions and singles out the Kalmyks and the Dzhungars—i.e., tribes from the east—as their main competitors and arch rivals. So, Kazakhstan's inherited intellectual tradition as an adaptation of the Eurasian ideology of the colonial period is a glorified chapter in Kazakh history. The other part is about forgotten links in the Kazakh steppe and allegiance of minor allies in the Kazakh union about whom much less has been spoken about till date.

Much of that revised thinking has percolated among the new generation in Kazakhstan that is sensitive to issues of spirituality and awakening and is "organically integrated into Kazakhstan's popular culture." This generation of intellectuals and scholars seek to distance themselves from the world-class urban ambience of Astana or Almaty. Alexey Zelenskiy, an Almaty-based scholar argues that New Age thinking is breaking new grounds—and through approaches and perspectives that are indifferent to all kinds of political challenges. The New Age approach transcends disciplinary spaces and challenges nation-building hypotheses of the post-Soviet Kazakh state. It decentres itself from statist premises of ethnicity and religiosity and creates a new space for collectives and networks, building on the traditional ideals of ethics, plurality and diversity.

The purpose of the first study trip in 2012 was to get a sense of the lofty image of Kazakhstan as a post-Soviet Central Asian country not only with enormous resource potential but also with the vision and the ability to position itself reasonably well within the international arena by establishing its status as a negotiator and partner in regional alignments and also by adjusting itself internally with her ethnic communities and her co-ethnics like the Uyghurs and the Mongols in the neighbouring regions. In recent times, Kazakhstan's adjustments with China and Kyrgyzstan over water-sharing issues have attracted a lot of global attention. Such assessments reflect Kazakhstan's ability to balance her Central Asian partners. A related question that comes to mind is the people's response.

The research trip in 2012 was centred round these questions. In the specific case of Almaty, one does see the nostalgia about the former capital's academic potential and university scholarship is extremely commendable. But the difference lies with the new generation that is somewhat inclined to the new opportunities in Astana which is heavily funded by the Government. In Astana, the Nazarbayev University aspires to be a university of world-class category and has attracted a lot of foreign scholars (Beatrice Penati, Alexander Morrison from University of Cambridge and University of Liverpool, respectively and also John Schoberlein who is the Founder Director of Harvard Forum of Central Eurasian Studies) who, as mentors, have set up their own specialised units of research. Almaty, by contrast, retains its classical character and in the realm of education, is more vision-oriented, and not business-oriented. The al Farabi Kazakh National University reflects this different mood.

The Almaty trip had two basic purposes: to gather data from prime academic institutions like R. B. Suleimanov Institute of Oriental Studies and al Farabi Kazakh National University which since the Soviet days have been administered by the main educational body of the government, i.e., the Academy of Sciences. An exception to this model of classical research is Kazakhstan Institute for Strategic Studies which is a think tank and is under the direct supervision of the office of the President and reflects the policy priorities of the Republic of Kazakhstan. Astana's voice is somewhat reflected in Almaty through KISI—which showcases the Republic's priorities and achievements, either in terms of the new unions within the CIS, or from the viewpoint of the Eurasianist model taking into account vertical as well as horizontal options, i.e., South East Asian countries on the one hand, as well as China. KISI's scholars are optimistic of Kazakhstan-monitored regional integration beyond the scope of the SCO. From the standpoint of South Asian and Indian research, it would be useful to study how the SCO's options and limitations can be compared with those of the ASEAN or the SAARC. In such comparative analysis, the question of integration needs to be addressed.

Al Farabi Kazakh National University under the Ministry of Science and Education of the Republic of Kazakhstan is an oriental showpiece in terms of scientific investigation and academic collaboration. The various departments of the Institute of Oriental Studies (e.g., Manuscripts Division, International Relations, Korean Studies of Central Asia, Uyghur Studies Department, etc.) of the University and departmental publications provide useful insights into Kazakhstan's oriental set-up since the Soviet period. Research based on Arabic-Turkic-Persian textual sources is very significant in these publications. The articles on Central Asian history and historical sources, Central Asian Islam are mostly in Russian; but there seems to be an increase in the use of Kazakh and Uyghur in most of the publications that are the products of MOUs and academic collaboration. It was interesting to get an idea about diaspora project in the time and space model in Kazakhstan in the course of interaction with German Kim, the principal investigator of the Korean Studies Institute and chief researcher at KISI. His articles on Korean diaspora in the post-Soviet space add to the knowledge about diaspora linkages, which in the case of the Korean diaspora, remains miniscule, asserted Kim. Diaspora narratives especially in the context of war and conflict have an enduring effect on the minds of the readers. There have been reflections of the Korean War of 1950-53 in the accounts of the prisoners of war.

Kazakhstan Institute for Strategic Studies (KISI) represents a completely different domain of research. It is primarily a think tank and is armed with policymaking decisions of the Kazakh government. Leila Muzaparova, the Deputy Director of the institute, is one of the main spokespersons of Kazakhstan's multi-vector foreign policy. The new universities of Kazakhstan like Turan University and Nazarbayev University have opened up prospects for academic collaboration with foreign universities. Historical workshops, for example, are conducted during long summer holidays (June-August) by Turan University which is basically a new university that represents a tie-up between Kazakh historians and Western historians with specialisation in Kazakh history. During my visit in July 2012, the University organised its Summer School, "Writing History from Below: New Social history of Central Asia," in which scholars with expertise in archival research participated. Diverse subjects, for example, looking at colonialism from below, or colonial practices, etc., were taught. Beatrice Penati lectured on the methods of tax collection in colonial Turkestan. The tax registers are indeed a valuable source of research about colonial practices and agricultural norms in colonial Turkestan. A search for revivalist projects like Islam in Central Asia and Kazakhstan and alternative histories led me to the publishing house, Daik Press, that is useful because it mainly disseminates research work of scholars of KazNU.

Almaty's cosmopolitan character is well evident in the employees' job profiles. Not all aspired for nor got highly prestigious KazNU education. During casual conversations, Mukhambet, Editor-in-Chief of the local newspaper *Delovaya Nedelya*, and Aizhan, a young employee of an American freight company, a postgraduate student of al Farabi National University shared views about options for Kazakh children belonging to multi-ethnic communities in Almaty. The former candidly said that a Dungan representation in the London Olympics actually helped Kazakhstan to win as many as 7 gold medals in the tournament in 2012! Aizhan helped me to get a visual idea of Barakholkha, a massive trade district in Almaty's environs in which labour migrants and enterprising shuttle traders belonging to mostly Uyghur, Uzbek and Dungan ethnic backgrounds participated in a network of trading activities whose principal ownership was in the hands of an ethnic Kazakh.

The primary research questions that I addressed during the second research trip in 2013 were as follows: (a) changing urban space of the new Kazakh capital, Astana and (b) responses of minority communities in Kazakhstan like the Uyghurs, Dungans and the Koreans in the former Kazakh capital, Almaty. An added interest was in the varied representation of Kazakh history, the primary one that was based on *zhuz* (horde) legacy. Besides data collection in university libraries, my intention was interaction with scholars and dispersed nationality groups and communities in Almaty. Data collection was concentrated in the main library of Lev Gumilev Eurasian National University in Astana where entries on subjects like the Kazakh horde—Large, Middle and Small *Zhuzes* [1] are pretty significant in terms of Kazakhstan's engagement with its tribal heritage. Special care has been taken to preserve Soviet research material on subjects like "ethnography" and spirituality. The Kazakh intellectuals' cosmopolitan ideas have received uninterrupted attention. The most celebrated Kazakh writer is E. A. Masanov and his works on *zhuz* legacy, Kazakh territoriality are hugely popular among the scholar community. Another subject that has been critically examined is the collectivisation programme under Stalin that had dispossessed a huge section of Kazakh peasants. Similarly, there have been reassessments on the subject of deportation of Kazakh minority nationalities (the Koreans, for example). A large section of post-1991 literature is on the republican status of Kazakhstan highlighting momentous decisions like multilateralism, regional integration and economic interdependence. Scholarly interest in demographic patterns is reflected in seminar and conference volumes that are published by the Ministry of Education and specialised institutions on historical sciences. There has been a renewal of interest in the writings of Kazakh orientalists like Chokan Valikhanov, especially on the subject of Kazakh territoriality. There is a reason for this special interest—to indicate the extent of *zhuz* control to the lower banks of the Syr Darya which were later overrun by the Kalmyks, Dzhungars and the Bashkirs. The leadership of the *batyrs* (hero warriors) like Bogenbay Batyr, Kabanbay Batyr, Taylak Batyr and Naurzibai Batyr in the anti-Dzhungar movement before the advent of the Russians is a special narrative in Kazakh historiography.

The summer of 2013 was a good time in terms of academic interaction in Astana: the trip's timing coincided with ESCAS XIII Conference that was hosted by Nazarbayev University. The lectures were based on the metanarrative as well as sub-narratives of Kazakh history. There were engaging debates on (a) the alteration of social space of Kazakhstan with the presence of Polish, German and Jewish minorities in Alma Ata (Almaty) during 1945-1989, (b) encounters with Islam in Kazakhstan during the Tsarist period with sub-themes like the content and form of institutionalised Islam in the Orenburg Muftiyat, the negotiations between Tsarist officials and indigenous leaders (like Srym Batyr) in the Kazakh steppe, the features of Islamic hagiography, the representation of Islam in poetry, verses, etc. The continuing debate about Russian colonisation of the steppe acquired a new dimension with noticeable new trends of research on the "Kazakh new way of life." Sociological research conducted by Public Opinion Research Institute and its research reports were shared during the round table discussions. Aspects of internal and external migration were discussed at length by this group. What is very interesting is the study about urban development and the case study of Astana as a modern capital where building material like granite tiles have been used and new elements like metal surfaces have given a completely new look to the capital which in Soviet times was known as Akmolinsk or Akmola. A retrospective analysis about Astana in the newspaper *Subbota* (dated June 26, 2010) points to archival documents on Akmolinsk *uezd* as a rich trading mart that was frequently visited by Tashkent and Bukharan caravan merchants. It was the nomads' rich cattle reserve and the cattle were brought from Semipalatinsk, Semirechinski, Syr Darynskyi oblasts.

The previous year's visit to Kazakh National University (KazNU) in Almaty enabled an access to the classical Oriental domain that focuses on oriental subjects and classical learning like manuscripts, languages and dialects, textual representation, ethnology, etc. Mereurt Abusseitova, Laura Yereksheva, Larisa Dodkhudoeva and Dilorom Alimova were the scholars who collaborated with their European and Indian partners in disseminating knowledge about what was discussed in the course of a round table meeting: *Central Asia: From Shared History to Shared Future*. Allied subjects were discussed during a UNESCO workshop on *Transformations of the Societies of Central Asia: Socio-Cultural Aspects* during the same period. The essence of both the meets was that Central Asia represented a cultural mosaic. Global attention is directed towards Central Asia's cultural diversity which is considered to have laid the foundations of the region's shared future, conditioned by local and global factors. The convergent and divergent economic interests as well as policy planning are also destined to impact on the region's future. It is this confluence of ideas about the region's shared heritage and visions about a common future that contemporary scholars are attentive to. There has also been growing awareness about the ways in which the Central Asian states have positioned themselves vis-à-vis the neighbouring states, including India. As participant in this meet, I spoke about the India factor and the necessity to engage in the study of connected histories and transnational identities of Central Asia and South Asia.

Cityscapes

Astana

Changing cityscapes have been a continuing source of interest of my field visits. Aims of achieving buoyancy by converting the new capital into a dream city not by continuing Soviet-style economic development of the post-War period and fulfilling Khrushchev's mission of transforming Akmola into the machine-based capital city Tselinograd (meaning virgin land city) but by bringing in a new element—that of restoration of steppe settlements of the medieval period like Bozok (of the Kipchak Khanate), and rather conformed to the poetic compositions of Kazakh poet, Olzhas Suleimanov. With the transfer of capital to Tselinograd, now Astana, the moment of choice for the Kazakhs had appeared—i.e., the right to decide their own history.

The new capital Astana is more than 15 years old and is striking at first sight to the visitor because of the city's grandiose architectural designs (the 5-storeyed *Khan Shatyr* shopping mall built in the shape of a giant yurt and has a marble slope, *Kazak Yeli* [Kazakh Country] column, *Bayterek* and all governmental buildings including the Kazmunaigas office straddled along the *Nourzhol Boulvard* or The Radiant Path, Palace of Peace and Harmony which has the structure of a Giant Pyramid with a stained-glass conference room with fluttering dove-prints at the top, the alabaster white pillar called the Kazakh people's Monument that has a golden eagle or *Samruk* at the top is a major attraction for ethnic Kazakhs). The new urban landscape is dotted with governmental buildings that are high-rises (all situated on the left bank of the Esil River) or tall towers of apartments stretching on the entire stretch of Tuelsizdik Avenue approaching the bridges that connect the old part of the city with the new part of the city. This picture is a strong contrast to the worn-down wood-and-plaster dwellings of the Soviet era that are holed up in remote corners of Soviet-period "microregions." Critics argue that this is a city of architectural follies and has been built with specific intentions only—to deck up the President's Palace grounds using money that could have been better spent developing economically distressed areas of Kazakhstan. The right bank of Esil river is reminiscent of the old city, Aqmola. Since the renaming of the city as Astana, there has been a complete transformation—featured by shimmering skyscrapers and grandiose civic structures. The biggest attraction is the Tuielsuzdik Avenue cutting the city horizontally, with major buildings of the Left Bank up to Nazarbayev University falling in sight as one travels right from the micro-region where the modest but friendly Astana Hotel is located—a clear 40 minutes drive up to, say, Kabanbay Batyr or Nourzhol Boulevard area.

A major disconnect is seen between Left Bank and Right Bank environment. The Right Bank is the "village" part or the "aul" part and does not match with the high-tech Left Bank environment. Citified Russians who have been here for a long time refer to the city as *bolshaya derevnya* (big village). They refer to village migrants as poor and sick, having no will to improve their quality of living. So, regional differences within Kazakhstan actually suggest north/south dichotomy and urban/rural dichotomy. This binary division of society can be seen since Soviet times—and the Astana project should be reviewed not as state-society relationship but as people-to-people relationships. It is the people's reactions that constitute the "bordering mentality" of Astana.

I got a glimpse of the glitzy world of Astana during my third visit. This dazzling beauty is showcased through a series of landmark events and vision statements, namely, *Vision 2030, Vision 2050, Kazakh Mangalik Yel, Expo 2017* and *Silk Way*—all that make Astana Asia's most sought-after global capital. Architectural designs of the Pyramid and the Palace of Peace and Reconciliation reflect the desire to recreate the magic of the Louvre in Paris. The latest addition to the cultural bonanza this year is the National Museum which stands in sprawling Independence Square and has been advertised in a major way since its inauguration on Astana Day, i.e., on the sixth of July 2014. Most of the artefacts in this museum are from the restoration work that the Kazakh Government has conducted all over the steppe country. Some of these artefacts have also been directly brought in from the Central State Museum in Almaty or from the already existing Museum of the First President of the Republic of Kazakhstan. The new museum has 12 rooms and the maintenance of the exhibition is supported by Kazakhstan's national oil and gas company, KazMunaiGaz. The Museum commemorates the heritage of the Silk Route and the transition from Akmolinsk to Tselinograd to Astana. Also interesting are galleries portraying ancient settlements of the city of Astana that have been unearthed—e.g., Bozok settlement and Botai settlement. New projects like the Green Belt around the city of Astana are projected through laser beams.

The Palace of Independence, situated in Independence Square, is, like any new architecture in Astana, jumbo-sized with three floors, each floor having a spacious Congress Hall, a Ceremonial Hall and a Press Centre with an attached mega-size restaurant respectively. A major characteristic of the building was the exhibition floor—with criss-crossed galleries filled with classical and new age paintings by Kazakh artists. This was the venue of the signing of the Eurasian Economic Union on May 29 between Russia, Kazakhstan and Belarus heralding the creation of an economic union in the Eurasian space.

The Nourzhol Boulevard is a spectacular sight at night. The majestic walkway right up to Ak Orda (the administrative quarter right up to the

President's Palace), in the midst of a huge square is a major draw for Astana's citizens. On both sides of the Boulevard are the modern administrative and commercial quarters, residential buildings and monuments all that went into the making and re-making of Astana as Kazakhstan's new urban district. This part of the city with other landmarks at a distance that can be seen from here (like Nazarbayev Centre, Pyramid, Palace of Peace and Reconciliation, etc.) represents the grand edifice of the city of Astana. The construction here is phenomenal, laden with granite slabs, marble, gypsum—all that lend material value to this huge space. Cultural anthropologists have been struck with the outlandish relation between state building and materiality[2]—a bizarre showpiece of grandiose construction that makes Astana Asia's most sought-after global capital.

Almaty

Tucked into the southeast corner of the country, Almaty is bordered to the south by the Alatau spur of the Tien Shan range and to the steppe in the north. The most sought-after residential areas are at the city's edge where it begins to climb towards the mountains. Chimbulak is the sports zone and Medeu is the ski resort. The air is comparatively fresh here and the mountain streams flow with clear water and the view of the city from the mountains is spectacular. Almaty until recent times has been famed as the third greenest city in Soviet times. Almaty's roads were planted with trees that ran as channels to obstruct the strong winds from the mountains. The snow fed rivers could not be contained by the concrete channels and seismic activity had devastating effects like mudslides (as in 1976) that brought in boulders to the broad streets like Lenin Street, renamed as Dostyk Avenue. The city's location in a seismic zone posed a series of difficulties for the city's administration that faced ego problems with centralised industrial ministries during the Soviet period. The decision to locate heavy industry in the city was inappropriate, according to Almaty's residents. The post-Soviet reconstruction of the city has inflicted more damage—asphalt roads, heavy decor, sports centres, endless number of grocery shops in the ground floors of apartment blocks, hotels, casinos, flower stores, restaurants, kiosks and the warehouse/containers' cheap shopping marts are an eyesore to this green city which otherwise retains its traditional Central Asian character. Outside the city centre are the micro-regions where the labour population and their housing have sprung up and these maintain the character of a neighbourhood city. Almaty's environs represent the typical Garden Cities of the Soviet period and were separated from the city by the green band. With post-Soviet mega-housing projects, this green band vanished and private housing looking out into open fields became the prize catch of the elite who built dachas here. Villa owners were not to be controlled by the *Akimat* and were such a contrast to the shacks that were built in a makeshift manner. In both cases, the housing was devoid of serious planning and basic minimum infrastructure was lacking in these micro-regions. There have been lamentations among citizens of Almaty about how the state stopped being paternalistic and even refused to play its previous role as service provider and welfare provider. Water, for instance, has become very costly in Almaty. The *aryks* (canals) do not work well in the post-Soviet period due to lack of maintenance. Plants, trees, gardens are dying everywhere due to the dust. So, the present city may be privatised but has fallen into disarray. The city Akimats seem to be exercising a lot of influence.[3]

The other casualty was the apple gardens. The name "Almaty" means "the father of apples"—referring to the fruit-bearing orchards in and around the city that became noteworthy in the eighteenth century due to a special kind of apple that became extremely popular in the agricultural and nomadic settlements. These were introduced by Russian settlers from southern Russia. Apple-growers from England, in their fascinating research about "apple culture," narrated the unmatched variety of the Tian Shan apple, the seeds of which became the focus of the trade that developed from China in the east to Mediterranean in the west.[4] While the wild variety of apples in the Tien Shan evoked a lot of enthusiasm, the city of Almaty has not been as lucky. Today, during summer travels to Almaty's mountainous environment, the apple plantation areas are well in sight, but the commercial intention to set up resorts in the eco-friendly surroundings is unbearable. With the arrival of "big money," apple orchards in the neighbourhood of Almaty, which had strengthened the mountain region, seem to have disappeared. In their place came the expensive houses and mansions which were destroyed in course of time, along with the orchards, by the mudslides and avalanches—noticeable in the mountain game resort of Medeu in the Chimbulak region which was showcased as the "roof of Almaty" during the 2011 Winter Olympic Games.

The place, situated at 1,691 metres above sea level, was highly rated as a competition rink during the event. To maintain an artificial ice rink has proved to be extremely costly for the Kazakh government. These events are more attractive in terms of the global population that visits the region for entertainment. Such is the irony—the people no longer feel attracted by the apples from Kazakhstan. What have arrived at the market are modified, flavourless apples from China. The citizens of Almaty have been preserving their vegetables for their own consumption with their meagre pensions, and have been selling the durable but tasteless apples to the tourists for making money.

But it is Almaty that is a city that has experienced the negative effects of relational shifts. Rural to urban migration started in the Soviet period and this was due to the spread of education and vertical social advancement—and it was a gradual and controlled process.[5] Rural Kazakhs who live in close-knit *aul* communities preserved a patriarchal set-up. The dissolution of the Soviet Union is associated with a massive influx of Kazakhs into the cities. These newly urbanised Kazakhs preserved their tradition in cities—which gave the city its composite character—and tradition has remained as a cultural artefact which the contemporary Kazakh government has tried to preserve. Officials are keen to identify themselves with the Almaty mentality, which has been vibrant and living since the Soviet days. In the later Soviet period, Almaty was inundated with more and more Kazakh settlers coming from small towns who became increasingly aware of their privileged status as members of the titular nationality and were also being inducted into the administrative elite. This group faced competition from the rural impoverished Kazakhs who, after 1991, settled in the free land around the city (*raiony*) and became the source of dispute with their Kazakh brethren or had trouble with the local authorities. The constant penetration of this section of rural Kazakhs who posed themselves as the upholders of Kazakh tradition, representatives of the concept of "being Kazakh," created a rupture in the Soviet fabric. To overcome criticism of the ruptures within, Nazarbayev emphasised a permissive environment, showcasing a sense of tolerance and endurance among the Kazakhs. The ambience in Almaty was always attractive with numerous options as housing, investment, education, lifestyle and living, fairs and exhibitions, media opportunities, etc.[6]

The perennial attraction about Almaty is its composite character. The appeal lies in Almaty's academic environment. Al Farabi Kazakh National University has since the Soviet days been administered by the main educational body of the government, i.e., the Academy of Sciences. An exception to this model of classical research is Kazakhstan Institute for Strategic Studies (KISI) which is a think tank that is prospering under the direct supervision of the office of the President and reflects the policy priorities of the Republic of Kazakhstan. Astana's voice is somewhat reflected in Almaty through KISI—which showcases the Republic's priorities and achievements, either in terms of the new unions within the CIS, or from the viewpoint of the Eurasianist model taking into account vertical as well as horizontal options, i.e., South East Asian countries on the one hand, as well as China. KISI's scholars are optimistic of Kazakhstan-monitored regional integration beyond the scope of the SCO. So, here were two institutions in Almaty—with two wide angles of research.

Al Farabi Kazakh National University which is under the Ministry of Science and Education of the Republic of Kazakhstan is very attentive to its Indian partners. Since Soviet times, the University has been administered by the main educational body of the government, i.e., the Academy of Sciences. An exception to this model of classical research is Kazakhstan Institute for Strategic Studies (KISI) which is a think tank that is prospering under the direct supervision of the office of the President and reflects the policy priorities of the Republic of Kazakhstan. Astana's voice is somewhat reflected in Almaty through KISI—which showcases the Republic's priorities and achievements, either in terms of the new unions within the CIS, or from the viewpoint of the Eurasianist model taking into account vertical as well as horizontal options, i.e., South East Asian countries on the one hand, as well as China. KISI's scholars are optimistic of Kazakhstan-monitored regional integration beyond the scope of the SCO. So, here are two institutions in Almaty – with two different perspectives of research.

Beyond the academic space is a world of young fortune-seekers. The enthusiasm of local employees (Mukhambet, Editor-in-Chief of the local newspaper *Delovaya Nedelya*, Aizhan, a young employee of an American freight company) was a revelation about Almaty's young job seekers. Almaty celebrated her victory in London Olympics, as contestants from at least two non-titular nationalities secured as many as 7 gold medals. But it was Yulia Goloskokova, the young MA student of Turan University who practised as a young trainer in the English language and was a happy-go-lucky character always interested in full-time activity. Here was an example of a young Russian based in Almaty—a native to the region with a passion for language learning—Hindi being one of them—which has helped her to be popular as an easy and no-nonsense travelling companion. Despite her eccentric choices in terms of travel destinations, she made it a point to come back to her hearth and home—to spend time with her ailing mother (who passed away this summer) and tell the visitors that Almaty was a place worth living in. Another young Kazakh aspirant whose home and education is in Almaty but who works as Researcher and Moderator in the European Union's Delegation Office in Astana is Elnara Bainazarova. Elnara is suave, professional and formal in her one-to-one exchanges in Astana where people are mostly businesslike. She is a committed worker who is nostalgic about her Almaty University education and is respectful of the Oriental Department's faculty who trained her in International Relations. But she aspires to go global and make it big—which is why she is committed to her job of preparing a dossier of agreements and meetings between *Ak Orda* (the Presidential office) and the European Union's ministerial delegations from Finland and Brussels. And it is her educational background in Oriental Studies in Almaty that she fondly nurtures. Combined with this is her indomitable spirit and energy that make her a smart, easy-going and adorable travelling companion. Her ability to weave a Kazakh story based on site visits with remarkable easiness is worth appreciating. Her experiences as an urban youth bring out an insider's story about changing fortunes of the iconic cities in the north and the south of Kazakhstan—Almaty, Astana, Kokshetau, Pavlodar. These cities have a character of their own and are worth a visit, she says. Elnara's sentiments about Russians in Kazakhstan came across during our conversations, visuals of city tours and libraries' data collection. There are 2.3 times as many Russians as Kazakhs in industry. And vice versa, there are three times as many Kazakhs as Russians in agriculture. Businessmen, entrepreneurs, corporate people of small companies are heavily reliant on Russian supplies (literally from nails to cars—every component of metal which cannot be sourced locally).[7] Like many Kazakhstanis, Mantai Tulegenev, managing director of a construction company in Almaty, refers to Kazakhstan as a former colony of Russia.

> Because our republic was, to put it mildly, a colony of Russia, that is Moscow, only the extraction and refining industry developed in the republic. We have virtually no machine-building. For us, all of the final manufacturing of products is done in Russia, and therefore the economy of Kazakhstan is closely connected with the Russian economy. At the present time we have become a politically free republic, but economically

> we cannot say that, because our economy without the economy of Russia cannot move. Therefore, we are always looking at the political stability of Russia. If everything is fine in Russia, then our economy will develop normally.[8]

So, economic prosperity took top priority in post-Soviet Kazakhstan. Kazakhstan is undoubtedly one of the most consistently pro-Russian and post-Soviet countries and has been identified by the Russian President Putin as a country "worthy of special respect and attention." A Russian presence in Kazakhstan also has the merit of keeping a strategic partnership between the two sides well in place. The main pillar of this partnership is resource exploitation. Russia's energy activities in Central Asia are closely focused on Kazakhstan, which remains firmly anchored to Russia in terms of the energy industry. The Russian company LUKOIL, for example, is active in seven oil and gas onshore and three offshore exploration projects in the Kazakhstan sector of the Caspian shelf. In addition, the majority of Kazakh exports pass through pipelines located on Russian territory. However, cooperation in the energy sector is not as smooth as one might expect and it is still dominated by major friction between Astana and Moscow. Disputes over the direction of oil and gas pipelines, which occasionally occur, lead some Kazakh experts to consider Russia and Kazakhstan as competitors rather than partners in the energy market.

Soviet Memories

ALZHIR, A Soviet Gulag

The memorial complex ALZHIR or Aqmola Deportation Camp for Wives of Traitors of the Revolution, situated in Malininka village about 40 kilometres west of Astana bears testimony to broken families and sorrows of women and children of Kazakh, Uzbek, Azeri, Polish, German, Korean backgrounds who were forced into a life of seclusion in this camp in the Kazakh steppe in the 1930s. The camp was in operation from the 1930s through to the early 1950s (more precise figures claim from 1937 to 1946) and was one of the most notorious camps in central Kazakhstan—not just because of its special role as a women's camp within the gulag system, but also because it had several high-profile prisoners, including artists and actresses. Living conditions were just as harsh as in any gulag. Hardest for most, however, was the fact that they had been separated from their loved ones—not only husbands (who were considered the actual traitors and often sent to other gulags as far away as eastern Siberia, never to return) but also from their children.

The ALZHIR memorial museum at Malinovka was opened as late as 2007 by President Nazarbayev. The introductory film shown to visitors on arrival at the museum makes the claim that the Soviet Union was the only country ever to have done this sort of thing to its own people. The role that Kazakhstan has assumed in aiming to come to terms with its gulag history is a bit of an over-celebration. The same can be said about Karlag memorial near Karaganda. In fact, the new history of Kazakhstan has sections devoted to the gulag history in Kazakhstan—and these are painstaking efforts to unearth the regional archives and sometimes even private collections and memoirs of that period provide interesting information about Kazakh stories of deportation.

Often referred to as "dark tourism" in the popular western websites, ALZHIR memorial museum does represent commendable effort on the part of the Kazakh state to at least bring out certain archival details about the deportation programme and the social layers that survived or perished during the 1930s.

Within the complex, there are the following: (a) Arc of Sorrow/Arc of Grief (b) Statue of Hope (c) Statue of Despair. A model of the notorious barrack (Barrack No. 26) is at the side of the memorial complex and has a plaque in front of it describing how the women prisoners built these barracks that had flat roofs. The roofs would be heated by reeds that had to be collected from the fields in huge quantities. Each barrack had a capacity of 200-300 persons. The model was designed by a Kazakh artist belonging to the Union of Artists of the Republic of Kazakhstan.

The documentary film has recorded some of these narratives about Uzbek, Azeri, Kazakh, Polish and German women prisoners.

Inside the museum, at the ground floor there is a central atrium that has a wired sculpture at the ceiling with wooden doves inside it—as if to reflect the bondage of those trying times. The photo gallery on the ground floor focuses on the background history, as well as on activities of personalities like Mustafa Shoqai who were associated with the Turkistan national movement of 1918-20 (also called the movement for Kokand Autonomous Government). It is intriguing that people's protests of all hues and shades, irrespective of the context, were categorised as "movements." The Zheltoqsan uprising of 1986 was an example of protest in modern times. On the first floor, the depictions are a bit more graphic—here the focus is on the conditions in the ALZHIR camp itself, as well as the system of repression.

Inside the complex, there are monuments that are more symbolic than real—a watch tower and a red star that is about to fall off the ground.

Kokshetau, Unvisited Heritage City

"Monuments are powerful because they appear to be permanent markers of memory and history."[9] Kokshetau and Atyrau are places which have a strong Soviet memory and are relatively "unvisited." Here, Soviet-era monuments and memorial sites that exist as in several post-Soviet cities, Lenin's statue in the city park of Kokshetau, Ablai Khan's statue in the central square of the Akimat, or Victory Park in Atyrau are glorious reminders of the past—be it the battle cry of tribes belonging to the Middle and Lesser Hordes or the Soviet victory over German aggressors in 1941. It is interesting that although many statues of Lenin were removed in Moscow and St. Petersburg, they still remain in most smaller, provincial Russian cities, towns, and villages, Kokshetau being one of them. One would tend to believe that these memorials are also a means of connecting with the people. Scholars feel that memorials have enormous symbolic power because they invoke a sense of timelessness, fear, awe and uncertainty. In the search for a post-Soviet identity, Kazakhstan, like other states, was trying to make the past usable. So, besides being spiritual and community-oriented, an intimate connection with the Kazakh landscape was considered useful. Here, the *akimat* of Kokshetau has a far more significant role to play by bringing to the public domain historical episodes or warrior legends that constitute a part of the Kazakh people's history. As part of post-War reconstruction measures, Communist Party ideologues emphasised the heroic phases of Kazakh history to encourage soldiers of the Red Army. A reappraisal of the former Kazakh Communist Party officials like Zhumabai Shayakhmetov (1902-1966) indicates the tendency to reassess the role of ideologues as facilitators of a modernisation project instead of viewing them as representatives of a repressive regime.[10] In a remarkable rehabilitation drive,[11] Shayakhmetov became a friendly name whose patriotic fervour was associated with Soviet propaganda machinery that published booklets about heroism of

Kazakh chieftains against Dzhungars and Oirots, Russian imperialists and Central Asian competitors. This was 1941-43—that is, wartime—and the Party did everything to evoke heroic sentiments among their own people. Kazakh soldiers of the Red Army were called *batyrs*. At the local level, too, heroic narratives percolated into mainstream writings about the Kazakh nation. Al'kei Margulan's texts inspired soldiers who were recruited for the War and helped in propaganda activities in Kazakh towns, mines and collective farms. Another historian, Viatkin, addressed nineteenth-century uprisings. Viatkin tried to present a people's history, and his aim was to cover all episodes in the struggle for national independence, right from the time of the Kipchak Khanate to the twentieth century. In Viatkin's outlay of what appears to be a Kazakh narrative, the people's mood gets highlighted.[12] All these efforts were initiated before Moscow's historians launched the project *The History of the Kazakh SSR* in 1943. The fact of the matter is that alternative thinking was noticeable in history-writing during the War period and cosmopolitanism today is about such variations in approach.

In the quaint provincial town of Kokshetau in Akmola oblast is the regional historical Museum. At the front gate of the Museum is inscribed a a decree of the Presidium of the Supreme Soviet of the USSR from 1958, awarding Kokshetav Oblast the Order of Lenin by virtue of its success in surpassing the yearly plan for bread production. Following independence, the Soviet name for the city, Kokshetav, was altered to the more Kazakh-sounding Kokshetau. The museum is blessed with worthwhile contributions of the Soviet period in the domain of science, industry and agriculture. The museum is a reminder of Kokshetau's role as a centre of provincial administration. The broad streets with pot-holed pavements are flanked by magnificent Soviet-style buildings, a relief to the eye amidst the skyscrapers of Astana and the multi-storeyed residential blocks of a post-Soviet transient cityscape, many abandoned industrial complexes in the city and on its outskirts hardly contribute in making the place look cheerful. The regional *akimat* is located in the central square comprising a monument of the seventeenth-century Kazakh hero Ablai Khan. There is a central park with Lenin's full-size monument as well as a war memorial with an inscribed wall dedicated to war heroes of the 1918-20 period.

However, it is the location of the city beside Lake Kopa, which seems to have shrunk considerably over the two centuries since the building of the

1824 Cossack fortress in Kokshetau, but has given the place its own sleepy character. In the post-independence years, Kokshetau has suffered more than many other towns in the north due to the exodus of a large number of ethnic Russians, and the town is estimated to have lost one-fifth of its population. Kazakhs today are unlikely to realise the historical worth of Kokshetau. It is rather unfortunate that the government chooses to project it as a gateway to Kazakhstan's high-profile eco-tourism destinations like Burabay.

Burabay, In Tune With Tradition

The emphasis on inherited tradition takes us on the trail of the medieval Kazakh khanate. There is a mapping of Kazakh khans' activities in and around 1628—not only did they reform their political apparatus and judicial system with adequate support from the three *zhuzes* but also established themselves as representatives of an amalgam of authorities of the highest order (referred to by the metaphor *ak suiek* or white bone). A Council of Elders advised the *sultans* in decision-making. It was "steppe democracy" that got a fresh lease of life in the re-evaluation of Kazakh history. Images of a mighty Kazakh khanate with illustrious names like Kasym Khan, Tauke Khan and Ablai Khan who tried to unite all tribal groups under a single military slogan *Uran Alash!* tend to get highlighted in the regional museums.

In the eco-region Burabay in the Schuchinsk district, there are fables and legends about Kazakh nomad warriors and leaders of the *zhuzes* who not only convened tribal conventions but also were careful about safeguarding tribal tradition. The region comes to life with tales surrounding Ablai's rock empire and the Zhumbaktas Rock memory of the woman who was unsuccessful in getting a suitor from Ablai's tribal chiefs. Ablai Khan's memory evokes a lot of sentiment about the Kazakhs' war history. Discussions have touched upon other aspects of Kazakh-Kyrgyz nomadic dispensation—for example, fragmentation, encounters with the common enemy—that is, the Kalmyks and subsequently integration with the Russian camp—a reminder of such ups and downs in Kazakh tribal union reflected in a 1927 account of Mukhamadjan Tynyshpaev.[13]

What is hinted here is the alternative mapping of steppe history—an account of war and disunion followed by aggression and rejuvenation of the Middle Horde partially due to partnership deals with lesser allies—an image which is much different from those narratives that recount historical milestones in the 300-year relationship between the Russians and the

Kazakhs. This brings us to another lesser known aspect of the Kazakh tribal confederacy—and this time this relates to the Little Horde and its trade and diplomatic ties with the Russians that resulted in a far greater control of Abul Khair in the Ural region. The local history museums of Kokshetau and Atyrau have filled this gap—their collections tell a different story—of the role of warriors of the Little Horde that was used very conveniently by the Middle Horde tribesmen. So this story differs completely from the narrative that Middle Horde tribes were sole beneficiaries of a convenient arrangement with the Russian colonists. Thus we see a fairly broad spectrum of narratives that point to the enigma of Kazakh tribal tradition.

The Burabay National Nature Park is tucked away in the town of Schuschinsk—about 50 kilometres away from Kokshetau town. Burabay is the pearl of Kazakhstan and has gorgeous pine forests and cliffs and rocks that are interspersed with serene lakes. The eco-region *Burabay* was created in August 2000 and is under the supervision of the Administration of Presidential Affairs. The location is a part of the Kokshetau steppe, a mixed steppe and forest and hilly upland. Every rock here has its own legend. The location is a huge mineral reserve. Among them are: Okzhetpes cliff (Inaccessible to Arrows) with a peak resembling an elephant calf and the Zhumbaktas cliff (Mysterious Stone) resembling a mysterious sphinx. Burabay is a name that is treasured by all Kazakhs, referring not only to the famous lake that lies in the middle of the mountains, but to the whole Burabay-Kokshetau National Park.

A series of Kazakh legends epitomises Burabay. The legend of the region's formation tells how God granted the Kazakhs this wonderful landscape. Another legend of the fighting spirit of a *batyr* who lost his eye fighting the Dzhungars is also very popular. There are legends about Ablai Khan fighting the Dzhungars in the eighteenth century while his warriors wanted to marry a local princess. The princess was brought to Burabay who agreed to give her hand to the first warrior who could shoot an arrow to the top of Okzhetpes. All failed, hence the name Okzhetpes which means "Unreachable by Arrows." The distraught princess then drowned herself in the lake, thus creating *Zhumbaktas* (Mysterious Stone). *Polyana Abylay Khana* (Abylay Khan's Clearing) is a location in the heart of the meadows where the warrior hero is thought to have reputedly once assembled his forces during his Dzhungar campaigns. A tall, eagle-shaped monument, stands in the clearing; a large, flat-topped rock known as Ablai Khan's Throne hides in the trees behind. A tiny little museum with an exhibition hall is perched in the land that commemorates the valiant struggle of the *batyrs* of the Middle and Younger Horde.

Atyrau, An Oil Fountain

Atyrau is a place from where the river (Ural) flows into the sea (Caspian). This city in western Kazakhstan is a major draw for most of the oil companies from the West but it is China and its oil companies CNPC, SIMOCO that are in the driver's seat. Major competition is from Tengiz Chevroil (TCO, the Kazakh-American multinational giant) and its Caspian variant—KASPICHEVROIL. My interaction with engineers and language consultants of TCO (Aidar Zhangaliev and Nurbergen Dnekeshev) gave me the impression of a dual force in this oil-rich zone which aspires to have an identity of its own and not only be regarded as Astana's prize catch or as Western investors idealise as "a geologist's dream."

Uniquely poised as a location that is stretched between Europe and Asia due to the Ural River (*Ak Zhaik*) that flows through its midst, Atyrau has a life of its own. That life belongs to the people who live in the old part of the city—the Zhilgorodok and the Balarshe. Memories of the old city are thriving in the city museum. Here, like in Kokshetau, people are nostalgic about their Horde legacy—that of the Younger Horde. The 1941 Victory Square immortalises the victory of the Fatherland. No less is their pride about the trading genius of the seventeenth-century Russian trader Gurev and his caviar business that gave Atyrau its identity as a fishing settlement in the Caspian, and the Ust-Zhaisky fortified town which once belonged to the Cossack warriors. Today the buzz about Atyrau is not only about its fishing area but also about its oil refineries, petrochemical plant, metalworking and construction-material industries and ship-repair yards which have attracted a large section of foreign entrepreneurs. The other point of attraction is its longest pedestrian bridge on the Ural River. But a very interesting feature was Atyrau's old railway station that brought local goods from various parts of CIS to Atyrau to be carried by cargo ships along the Ural River to Europe.

Some of these distinctive features of transformation of a prosperous fishing village to an oil-rich gateway that is now coveted by industrial and investing giants of Western Europe as well as China are depicted through the narratives of local people. Their interest in their local museums reflects their pride in indigenous traditions and occupations. Their pride lies in their warriors who fought real wars and battles—be it the *batyrs* who fought the Dzhungars or the Soviet military men who fought during Second World War.

Zarya Vostoka, Bordered Conscience

Narratives about the margins and from the margins belong to a completely different genre. They represent "bordered conscience" and can be studied within the framework of "decentring of narratives."[14] Interaction with marginal communities like the Uyghurs and the Dungans in the Zarya Vostoka region on the southeastern fringe of Almaty district suggests the presence of actors of social change.[15] These positive opinions featured in Uyghur Studies during the 1990s and the 2000s. The Kazakh city of Almaty had become in many respects the centre of an evolving transnational Uyghur community by the mid-1990s. The city of Almaty posed as a city with opportunities for a number of non-titular nationalities including the Uyghurs. Almaty, only a few hours distance by car from China, has been a city of cross-border interaction for the Uyghurs and they have found themselves in the city negotiating between divergent influences emanating from respective sides of the border for over a century.

The Uyghurs of Kazakhstan have different tales of belonging. Certain myths and phobias about Chinese presence do haunt the Central Asian region and sometimes there are attitudinal issues, despite the fact that attitudes towards Beijing are changing. Seldom do they feel alienated from their host country, Kazakhstan. Transnational sentiments are also evident because of shared historical memories. The Uyghurs and the Dungans are China's Central Asian minorities who have displayed their trading skills to a major extent but whose competitiveness in Kazakhstan remains modest. These cross-border minorities play a significant role in the development of Sino-Central Asian economic relations and in the cultural mediations between the two worlds.[16] Sometimes, there are nuanced views which cannot be considered within the narrow framework of a "Yellow Peril" that is traced back to the Dzhungar period. Interactive social behaviour is a unique quality for which Almaty is always "home" to its resident nationalities. A visit to a Uyghur home in the Zarya Vostoka micro-region of Almaty in 2012 unfolded this minority community's social behaviour which was so much in tune with the permissive environment that Nazarbayev showcased among his global partners.

Sometimes the blanket word Dungan refers to people of Hui ethnicity, i.e., the Uyghurs, the Kazakhs and the Kyrgyz who settled down and lived in the Xinjiang region since the 1760s. The Dungans of Central Asia (and Kazakhstan) call themselves *Huizu*. I sensed some of these distinctive approaches during my field trip to Astana and Almaty in August 2013. It is these perceptions that have imparted a dynamic profile to the Russo-Chinese borderlands that overlap with Kazakhstan and Ili prefecture of China.

A Kuldja Narrative: "In-betweenness" of the Uyghurs of China and Central Asia

Ablet Kamalov, a Uyghur historian from Kuldja region is nostalgic about his roots. His Kuldja experience was a nice memory—he is clearly unhappy to be dislocated from his country of origin in East Turkestan. Kuldja's history is deeply embedded in Ablet's mind. The state-managed commercial contacts today are so different from the Oriental market places in the past. His fairy tale musings of Urumqi and Kuldja are in sharp contrast to the corporate profile of Xinjiang today. Ablet's generation find it difficult to come to terms with the major shift in priorities. Today, the focus has shifted to big business. The trade networks among relatives across borders have become relatively unimportant.

Ablet's nostalgia for his Kuldja home was no less despite the fact he was closely associated with the classical Oriental faculty in Kazakhstan—where he moved after his intensive training in St. Petersburg. Kamalov moved from the Kuldja region in China to Kazakhstan in 1963 at the age of two with his parents and two sisters. His father knew both the Uyghur and Kazakh languages. Ablet's mother only knew the Uyghur language. For such a family, there was a lot of difficulty in a Russian environment. His sisters were trained in Uyghur schools. Also, most of the indigenous products were available in Kuldja—so moving hearth and home was not easy. Zarya Vostoka continued to have a Uyghur school but his sisters could not adjust much there. Ablet and his brother were put into a Russian school to avoid exclusion.

Ablet was inducted to the youth wing of the Communist Party, or the Komsomol, and was educated in the premier organisation MGIMO in Moscow. The central institutions were sensitive about Ablet's birthplace, China. Ablet was interested to study in Novosibirsk but his family was not keen because it was a Russianised environment. But Ablet was sent to Tashkent where he studied in the Department of Chinese Studies in the Faculty of Oriental Studies. His options after that were Academy of Sciences in Kazakhstan (in continuity with his Tashkent training) and Defence organisations (for example, several intellectuals had military corps training). A Uyghur Studies Department was initially set up in 1949 which was distinct from Dungan Studies. Then he spent a year in Leningrad as *asperantura.* His study in Leningrad was on Medieval Uyghur History based on Uyghur sources. This fact is quite interesting as Soviet journals laid emphasis on *istochnikovedenie* or source studies. His supervisor and head of Turkic-Mongol group in Leningrad was Klyshtorny, a leading exponent in Chinese studies. Ablet defended his dissertation in 1990. Post-1991, the relations between China and the Soviet Union improved following which he undertook his first tour to his birthplace, Kuldja. Till then, Kuldja was a memory—he had heard of Muslim celebrations and legends in Kuldja. There was a romantic notion of Kuldja and much of Kuldja's history was disseminated by his parents. Ablet compared his Kuldja experience to another historical event, i.e., that of the Russian Revolution in St. Petersburg. The image of Kuldja in history seems to be deeply embedded in Ablet's mind. In Ablet's narrative, memories are also associated with place names—Xinjiang in China is either Dihua (less used) or Ulumuchi. But the name Kuldja is used universally by Kazakhs, Uyghurs and other small nationalities of Central Asia and China, though Yining is the official name of Kuldja in China. There are therefore many memories associated with place names Kuldja and Yining and these are seldom recorded.

Summing Up

The various narratives suggest variations in Kazakh mood in different locations and different dispensations. Popular perceptions reveal strong attachment to Kazakh tradition and *zhuz* legacy. At the same time, reminiscences of the Soviet past are quite revealing. Myriad concerns and expectations in a post-Soviet set-up are extremely varied. Popular perceptions and social behaviour in different regions of Kazakhstan are also different. The northern region's steppe tradition is deeply entrenched in Kazakh memory. At the same time, reminiscences of the Soviet past reveal selective appreciation of Soviet order. Town-planning in Astana, which observers have either praised or criticised,[17] does bear a strong resemblance to the Soviet city plans. The oil towns of Kazakhstan like Atyrau have a status symbol because of its oil wealth which has attracted a great deal of foreign investment. Almaty, a bit out of pace due to Astana's global visions, still continues to be appealing because of its composite character. The cosmopolitan profile of Kazakhstan is featured by such regional varieties and variant approaches.

Notes

1. M. S. Mukanov, *Etnicheskaya territoriya Kazakov v XVIII-XV vekov,* Alma Ata, 1991.
2. Mateusz Laszczkowski, "State Building(s): Built Forms, Materiality and the State in Astana," Madeleine Reeves, Johan Rasanayagam and Judith Beyer (eds.), *Ethnographies of the State in Central Asia: Performing Politics* (Bloomington: Indiana University Press, 2014), p. 149.
3. "Almaty—Rethinking the Public Sector," in Catherine Alexander, Victor Buchli and Caroline Humphrey (eds.), *Urban Life in post-Soviet Asia* (University College, London: UCL Press, 2007).
4. John Selbourne, "Sweet Pilgrimage: Two British Apple Growers in the Tian Shan," *The Steppe Magazine*, Winter 2011/2012.
5. J. B. Abilhojin, *Ocherki sotsial'no ekonomisheskoi istorii Kazakhstana-XX vek*, Almaty: Universitet Turan, 1997.
6. Aleksandra Babkina, "Kazakhstan to modernise housing and public utilities—country drawing on Europe's experience," *Central Asia Online,* January 17, 2012; Alima Bissenova, "Post-socialist dreamworlds: Housing Boom and urban development in Kazakhstan," Cornell University Doctoral Research, 2010.
7. Keith Rosten, *Once in Kazakhstan: The Snow Leopard Emerges* (Lincoln: iUniverse Inc., 2008), pp. 22-23.
8. Rosten, in conversation with Tulegenev, ibid., p. 23.
9. Benjamin Forest and Juliet Johnson, "Unravelling the Threads of History: Soviet-Era Monuments and Post-Soviet National Identity in Moscow," *Annals of the Association of American Geographers*, August 2001.
10. Harun Yilmaz, "History writing as agitation and propaganda: the Kazakh history book of 1943," *Central Asian Survey,* vol. 31, no. 4, December 2012.
11. Shayakhmetov's name was chosen for renaming a street in Astana and Shymkent. In 2011, in an official function of young politicians, the vice-rector of the Eurasian National University in Astana named Shayakhmetov as an example of good managerial abilities.
12. M. Viatkin, *Ocherki po istorii Kazakhskoi SSSR do drevneishykh vremen po 1870 gody,* Tom pervyi, Ogiz Gospolitizdat, 1941.
13. The intricacies of an internal break-up before the eastern Kazakhs merged with the Russians are available in this account. Recalling the historical struggle between the Kazakhs and the Kalmyks, Mukhamadjan Tynyshpaev refers to the rise of the Mongol tribes which formed the Oirat Union under the name "Kalmyk/Kalmak" during 1399-1408. The extent of control of the Kalmyks in Kyrgyz-Kazakh territory gave solid competition to the Kazakh khan Esym, the brother and successor of Taueke Khan. The Kazakhs increased their power under Tauke-khan, who from the end of seventeenth to the beginning of eighteenth centuries was involved in bitter struggle with the Kalmyks. The idea behind this narrative is that the Kazakhs were engaged in internal strife and disputes and had to succumb to the pressure of the Kalmyks with boundaries between the two tribal competitors being drawn up along River Irtysh, Lake Balkhash, and the strip of land between the rivers Chu and Talas. So around 1723 or 1733, the Kazakh Union disintegrated.

14. "In from the margins," D. L. Wallace, "Alternative Rhetoric and Morality: Writing from The Margins," www.ncte.org/library/NCTEFiles/.../CCC0612Alternative.pdf, 2008; Barbara Estelle Verchot, "Creating Marginality and Reconstructing Narrative: Reconfiguring Karen Social and Geopolitical Alignment," MSc Thesis, Department of Interdisciplinary Studies, University of Central Florida, Spring Term, 2008.
15. By eschewing the view of the centre, van Schendel brings borderlands at the centre of the discussion and perceives them as active rather than passive agents of the nation-state. Michiel Baud and Willem van Schendel, "Towards a comparative history of Borderlands," *Journal of World History*, vol. 8, no. 2, 1997, pp. 211-42.
16. Konstantin Syroezhkin, "Social perceptions of China and the Chinese: A View from Kazakhstan," *China and Eurasia Forum Quarterly*, vol. 7, no. 1 (2009).
17. Natalie Koch, *The Monumental and the Miniature: Imagining "Modernity" in Astana*,Department of Geography, University of Colorado at Boulder.

Conclusion

In dealing with the "appearance" of a post-Soviet set-up, the notion is about new forms rather than old forms: there is an overall tendency to believe that there has been a sudden break from past political and social traditions. The polarised views of the ethno-nationalists and the cosmopolitans emanate from this fixed notion of binary social relationships. But varied interpretations and opinions about historical and contemporary events indicate a remarkable shift in the analysis of Kazakhstan's post-Soviet dispensation. The Kazakh borderlands discourse has evolved as an interesting trajectory especially since China's entry as the new global partner in the Central Asian region. The pressure of neighbouring China as a demographic giant has been replaced by a new perception of China as an effective partner. There is a fixed set of questions related to Chinese presence in the region. But cultural mediations between the two worlds—the Chinese Kazakh and the Central Asian Kazakh—need serious introspection. In the context of Sino-Kazakh or Kazakh-Mongolian relations, there seems to be no definitive research data or foolproof evidence about apathy towards Chinese influence in Kazakhstan. Sometimes the views of the people are also varied and diffused which generate a lot of complications. The most tolerant attitude is demonstrated by Almaty residents as well as in the northern regions, whereas the central region of Kazakhstan seems to be less tolerant. The most indifferent are the western, eastern and southern regions. All these shades need to be carefully examined instead of making blanket suggestions about an all-pervasive Chinese competition that is inimical to Kazakhstan.

The feel-good approach towards the Kazakh repatriation programme seems to have ebbed in the 2000s. Experiences of repatriation have been far from satisfactory for many non-titular groups who have tried to return from their diaspora venues in the early 1990s. While some non-titular groups of Kazakhs (Koreans and Germans) are of the opinion that "a homeland is forever" and are optimistic about the land of the Kazakhs as the future for their children and grandchildren, younger generations of Kazakhs have preferences for transnational spaces like Mongolia or Western countries like Turkey, Germany and Australia. There is also an intrinsic urge to identify diaspora as an imagined community that constantly reinvents and reinvigorates itself through cultural contact (language, food, art and religion). In the present context in which younger generations try to relate to their surroundings rather than to their rootedness, there is a need to revisit the diaspora framework. In fact the position of "going back home" needs to be reconsidered.

Though not too many, Kazakhstan has had to take a call on her domestic priorities without however loosening her alliance with the former Soviet bloc. In fact, one needs to appreciate Kazakhstan's stance in CIS affairs—especially in the context of events in Ukraine since when a new geopolitical drama unfolded in the entire region that lay between European Union (EU) and Russia. It became obvious that Kazakhstan, like most others, were pinning their hopes on the Commonwealth of Independent States (CIS), however loose the structure might have become with numerous fault lines held over from a union of many republics and regions, i.e., the former USSR. Since 2013, Ukraine's east-west divide directly affected its relations with Russia which in a way was considered to have put a brake on Putin's dream project—the Eurasian Union. The last two years' events in Ukraine turned out to be the real game-changer as far as the Eurasian Union was concerned. Since 2010, Russia started using the ECU as the driver for exporting competition with the European Union (EU) and that too in the shared neighbourhood.

Behind the scenes, another government that is quietly working in this complex set of diplomatic equations is Kazakhstan, which well understands Russia's mindset in a way that Western European nations cannot. The Kazakh President Nursultan Nazarbayev enjoys warm personal relations with all the major diplomatic players involved in efforts to resolve the Ukrainian crisis and has quietly worked to use that influence to further peace efforts. European leaders seem to view Nazarbayev as a potential mediator. Kazakhstan also has a unique non-European, post-Soviet political forum to exercise its quiet diplomacy. On December 18, 2014, Kazakhstan took over the presidency of the Commonwealth of Independent States[1] from Belarus. Engaging in shuttle diplomacy, Nazarbayev paid an official visit to Ukraine on December 22. Here he met President Petro Poroshenko and Prime Minister Arseniy Yatsenyuk. He assured them of Kazakhstan's readiness to provide a forum for dialogue, telling the press in Kiev that he was committed to trying to end the conflict in Donbass. His next stop was Moscow where he reiterated his message to Putin. Nazarbayev's attempts to convince the European Union's principal stakeholder—Germany—fell flat but his telephone diplomacy with his Western partners is still continuing. Kazakh efforts are viewed in Europe as a possible means of breaking the diplomatic gridlock.[2]

Nazarbayev's main gain was his ability to link the Ukrainian issue to that of the Eurasian Economic Union. Playing the role of an independent intermediary yields substantial dividends for Nazarbayev. First, it insures him against excessively sharp political moves on Russia's part. Secondly, Nazarbayev's stance indicates to Russia's Western opponents that Astana should not be identified with Moscow's policies, and thus there is no point in pressuring Kazakhstan in any way. At the same time, the Kazakh President has an advantage here too by emphasising that the sanctions against Russia do not work, adding that that there is nothing good about them because "Russia is our [Kazakhstan's] partner." So, Nazarbayev's stance reflects his shrewd diplomatic strategy: turning the competing parties to his favour. Apart from mediating between Russia and Ukraine, Nazarbayev's mission has another, less publicised aspect: the Kazakh leader serves as a bridge between Russia and the European Union, seeking to improve understanding between the sides. Third, Nazarbayev demonstrates that no matter how the Ukraine crisis develops, Kazakhstan's relations with the European Union will remain normal.[3]

While diplomatic hawks are pretty optimistic about Nazarbayev's diplomatic gains in putting military issues regarding Ukraine on hold, it is the lack of unity among EEU's partners that is actually giving him a lot of trouble. The decision to go ahead for a snap presidential poll in April 2015, a year ahead of the original schedule, comes in the wake of Putin's proposal for a currency union which is anathema to both Kazakhstan and Belarus. Nazarbayev's caustic remarks about keeping Ukraine's territories stable were a pinprick to Russia's egocentric image and created a dent to the image of this fledgling Union.[4] Kazakh-Russian relations have come under the scanner since the Ukraine crisis of 2013-14.

Notes

1. Formed after the 1991 disintegration of the USSR, the CIS consists of members—Armenia, Azerbaijan, Belarus, Kazakhstan, Kyrgyzstan, Moldova, Russia, Tajikistan and Uzbekistan—and two participants, Turkmenistan and Ukraine.
2. John C. K. Daly, "Behind the scenes, Kazakhstan seeks to resolve Ukrainian stalemate," Analysis: UPI, February 8, 2015. http://www.upi.com/Top_News/Analysis/Outside-View/2015/02/08/Analysis-Behind-the-scenes-Kazakhstan-seeks-to-resolve-Ukrainian-stalemate/8141423010362/
3. Alexey Malashenko, "Nazarbayev as Mediator," http://carnegie.ru/eurasiaoutlook/?fa=57771, Carnegie Moscow Centre, January 21, 2015.
4. "Kazakhstan: Eurasian Union Troubles Obvious as Putin Visits Astana," http://www.eurasianet.org/taxonomy/term/1724

Bibliography

Books

Abilhojin, J. B. *Ocherki Sotsal'no Ekonomicheskoi Istorii Kazakhstana-, XX Vek*, Almaty: Universitet Turan, 1997.

Aitken, Jonathan. *Nazarbayev and the Making of Kazakhstan: from Communism to Capitalism.* London: Bloomsbury Academic. Brubaker, Rogers. *Nationalism Reframed: Nationhood and the National Question in New Europe.* Cambridge University Press, 1996.

Aitzhanova, Aktoky et al. *Kazakhstan 2050: Toward a Modern Society for All.* New Delhi: Oxford University Press. A publication of Nazarbayev University and National Analytical Centre, 2014.

Baubock, Rainar and Thomas Faist, eds. *Diaspora and Transnationalism—Concepts, Theories and Methods.* Amsterdam University Press, 2010.

Bustanov, Alfrid K. *Soviet Orientalism and the Creation of Central Asian Nations.* London: Routledge, 2015.

Chatterjee, Suchandana. *The Steppe as History: Essays on a Eurasian Fringe.* Delhi: Manohar, 2010.

Cheah, Peng and Robbins, Bruce, eds. *Cosmopolitics: Thinking and Feeling Beyond the Nation.* University of Minnesota Press, 1998.

Dave, Bhavna. *Kazakhstan: Ethnicity, Language and Power.* London: Routledge, 2007. *Istoriya Kazakhstana.* Volume 4. Almaty: Atamura, 2010.

Diener, Alexander C. *One Homeland or Two? The Nationalization and Transnationalization of Mongolia's Kazakhs.* Woodrow Wilson Center Press, 2009.

Kabirov, M. N. *Ocherki istorii uigurov Sovietskogo Kazakhstana.* Alma Ata: Nauka, 1975.

Kabirov, M. N. *Pereselenie Iliiskikh Uigurov v Semirechie.* Alma Ata: Nauka, 1951.

Laruelle, Marlene and Sebastien Peyrouse. *The Chinese Question in Central Asia: Domestic Order, Social Change and the Chinese Factor.* London: Hurst and Company, 2012.

Lipman, Jonathan N. *Familiar Strangers: A History of Muslims in Northwest China.* Seattle and London: University of Washington Press, 1997.

Shayakhmetov, Makhmud. *The Silent Steppe.* London: Stacey International, 2008.

Tolybekov, S. E. *Kochevoe Obshchestvo kazakov v XVII-nachale XX veka: politico-ekonomicheskii analiz.* Alma Ata: Izdatel'stvo Nauka, Kazakhskoi SSR, 1971.

Kotkin, Stephen. *Magnetic Mountain: Stalinism as a Civilization.* University of California Press, 1997.

Olcott, Martha Brill. *Kazakhstan: Unfulfilled Promise.* Carnegie Endowment for International Peace, 2010.

Rosten, Keith. *Once in Kazakhstan: The Snow Leopard Emerges.* New York: iUniverse, 2005.

Syroezhkin, Konstantin. *Problemy sovremennovo Kitaia I bezopasnost'v Tsentral'noi Azii.* Almaty: KISI, 2006.

Uehling, Greta Lynn. *Beyond Memory: Crimean Tatars' Deportation and Return.* New York: Palgrave Macmillan, 2004.

Book Chapters

Anthony, Ross. "The persistence of the Nation-State at the Kazakh Chinese Border," Franck Bille, Gregory Delaplace and Caroline Humphrey (eds.), *Frontier Encounters: Knowledge and Practice at the Russian, Chinese and Mongolian Border* (Cambridge: Open Book Publishers, 2012).

Appiah, Kwame. "Cosmopolitan patriots," in Peng Cheah, Bruce Robbins (eds.), *Cosmopolitics: Thinking and Feeling Beyond the Nation.* University of Minnesota Press, 1998.

Laruelle, Marlene. "The Three Discursive Paradigms of State Identity in Kazakhstan," in Mariya Omelicheva (ed.), *Nationalism and Identity Construction in Central Asia: Dimensions, Dynamics and Directions* (London: Lexington Books, 2015).

Laszczkowski, Mateusz. "State Buildings: Built Forms, Materiality and the State in Astana" in Madeleine Reeves, Johan Rasanayagam and Judith Beyer (eds.), *Ethnographies of the State in Central Asia: Performing Politics* (Bloomington: University of Indiana Press, 2014).

Rovisco, Maria and Magdalena Nowicka. "Introduction" in *The Ashgate Research Companion to Cosmopolitanism* (Surrey, England: Ashgate, 2011).

Soni, Sharad. "Moving beyond nomadism: emerging equations in Kazakh-Mongol relations," in Anita Sengupta and Suchandana Chatterjee (eds.), *The state in Eurasia: performance in local and global arenas* (a MAKAIAS publication) (Delhi: Knowledge World, 2013).

Vertovec, Steven and Robin Cohen. "Conceiving cosmopolitanism," Introduction in Steven Vertovec and Robin Cohen (eds.), *Conceiving Cosmopolitanism: Theory, Context and Practice* (Oxford: Oxford University Press, 2002).

Vertovec, Stevan and Robin Cohen (eds.). *Migration, Diasporas and Transnationalism* (UK: Edward Elgar, Cheltenham, 1999).

Vertovec, Steven. "Transnationalism and Identity," *Journal of Ethnic and Migration Studies,* Vol 27, No. 4, 2001.

Walker, Kirsty. "Intimate Interactions: Eurasian Family Histories in Colonial Penang," in Tim Harper and Sunil Amrith (eds.), *Sites of Asian Interaction: Ideas, Networks and Mobility* (Cambridge: Cambridge University Press, 2014).

Yessengalieva, Anna. "The Role of Language in Forming Modern Society in Kazakhstan," in Anita Sengupta and Suchandana Chatterjee (eds.), *Eurasian Perspectives: In Search of Alternatives* (a MAKAIAS publication) (Delhi: Shipra Publications, 2010).

Journal Articles

Anacker, Shonin. "Geographies of Power in Nazarbayev's Astana," *Eurasian Geography and Economics,* 45, No. 7, 2004.

Ayşegül, Aydıngün and Yıldırım Erdoğan. "Perception of Homeland among Crimean Tatars: Cases from Kazakhstan, Uzbekistan and Crimea," *Bilig,* 54, Summer 2010.

Baigazin, Meiram. "The Migration Situation in Kazakhstan," *Central Asia and the Caucasus*, No. 5 (29), 2004.

Barcus, Holly and Cynthia Werner. "The Kazakhs of Western Mongolia: Transnational Migration from 1990-2008," *Asian Ethnicity,* Vol. 11, No. 2, June 2010.

Baud, Michiel and Willem van Schendel. "Towards a Comparative History of Borderlands," *Journal of World History,* Vol. 8, No. 2, 1997, pp. 211-42.

Beyer, Judith. "Settling Descent: Place Making and Genealogy in Talas, Kyrgyzstan," *Central Asian Survey*, Nos. 3-4, September-December 2011.

Bonnenfant, Isik Kuscu. "Constructing the Homeland: Kazakhstan's Discourse and Policies Surrounding Its Ethnic Return-Migration Policy," *Central Asian Survey,* Vol. 31, No. 1, March 2012.

Brubaker, Rogers. "The 'diaspora' diaspora," *Ethnic and Racial Studies,* Vol. 28, No. 1, January 2005.

Brubaker, Rogers. "Nationalizing States Revisited: Projects and Processes of Nationalization in Post-Soviet States," *Ethnic and Racial Studies,* 2011.

Cohen, Mitchelle. "Rooted Cosmopolitanism," *Dissent,* Fall 1992.

Cerny, Astrid. "Going where the grass is greener: China Kazakhs and the *Oralman* immigration policy in Kazakhstan," *Pastoralism,* Vol. 1, No. 2, July 2010.

Delanty, Gerard. "The cosmopolitan imagination: critical cosmopolitanism and social theory," *The British Journal of Sociology,* Vol. 57, Issue No. 1, 2006.

Diener, Alexander C. "Kazakhstan's Kin State Diaspora: Settlement Planning and the *Oralman* Dilemma," *Europe-Asia Studies,* Vol. 57, No. 2, March 2005.

Diener, Alexander C. "Problematic Integration of Mongolian-Kazakh Return Migrants in Kazakhstan," *Eurasian Geography and Economics,* Vol. 46, No. 6, 2005.

Eitzen, Hilda. "Refiguring ethnicity through conflicting genealogies," *Nationalities Papers,* 26 (3), 1998, pp. 435-38.

Gabriel, Sharmani P. and Fernando Rosa. "Introduction: "Lived Cosmopolitanisms" in *Littoral Asia, Cultural Dynamics,* 24 (2-3), 2012.

Gladney, Dru C. "Constructing a Contemporary Uyghur National Identity: Transnationalism, Islamicization and National Representation," *Cahiers détudes sur la Mediterranee Orientale et le monde turco-iranien,* No. 13, January-June 1992.

Huttenbach, Henry R. "Whither Kazakstan? Changing Capitals: From Almaty to Aqmola/ Astana," *Nationalities Papers,* Vol. 26, No. 3, 1998.

Junisbai, Azamat K. "Understanding Economic Justice Attitudes in Two Countries: Kazakhstan and Kyrgyzstan," *Social Forces,* Vol. 88, No. 4, June 2010, pp. 1684-85.

Kamalov, Ablet. "The Uyghurs as Part of Central Asian Commonality: Soviet Historiography on the Uyghurs," in Ildiko Beller Hann et al. (eds.), *Situating the Uyghurs Between China and Central Asia* (Surrey: Ashgate, 2007), pp. 31-48.

Kamalov, Ablet. "Úighur community in 1990s Central Asia: a decade of change," in Touraj Atabaki and Sanjyot Mehndale (eds.), *Central Asia and the Caucasus: Transnationalism and Diaspora* (Routledge, 2005).

Kreindler, Isabelle. "Ibrahim Altynsaryn, Nikolai Ilminskii and the Kazakh national awakening," *Central Asian Survey,* 2 (3), 1983.

Kuscu, Isik. "Constructing the homeland: Kazakhstan's discourse and policies surrounding its ethnic return-migration policies," *Central Asian Survey,* Vol. 31, Issue 1, 2013, pp. 31-44.

Muratshina, Ksenia. "The Irtysh River in the hydro policy of Russia, Kazakhstan and China," *Russian International Affairs Council: Central and South Asia Analysis,* May 29, 2012.

Mun, Lee Chai. "The Lost Sheep: The Soviet Deportations of ethnic Koreans and Volga Germans," *The Review of Korean Studies,* Vol. 6, No. 1, 2003.

Reeves, Madeleine. "Introduction: contested trajectories and a dynamic approach to place," *Central Asian Survey,* Vol. 30, Nos. 3-4, September-December 2011.

Regev, Motti. "Cultural Uniqueness and Aesthetic Cosmopolitanism," *European Journal of Social theory,* Vol. 10, No. 1, 2007.

Roberts, Sean R. "Imagining Uyghurstan—Re-evaluating the birth of the modern Uyghur nation," *Central Asian Survey,* Vol. 28, No. 4, 2009.

Sarsanbayev, A. "Imagined Communities: Kazakh Nationalism and Kazakification in the 1990s," *Central Asian Survey*, 18/3, 1999, pp. 319-46.

Subrahmanyam, Sanjay. "Connected histories: notes towards the reconfiguration of early modern Eurasia," *Modern Asian Studies,* 31, 1997, pp. 735-62.

Trepavlov, Vadim. "Altytuly: ostatki Nogaiskoi ordy v kazakhskikh stepyakh," *Viestnikh Evrazii,* No. 2 (13), 2001, pp. 33-44.

Tussupova, Dinara. "Mass media and Ethnic Relations in Kazakhstan," *Problems of Communism,* November/December 2010.

Schiller, Nina Glick, Darieva, Tsypylma and Gruner-Domic, Sandra. "Defining cosmopolitan sociability. An Introduction," *Ethnic and Racial Studies,* Vol. 34, No. 3, March 2011.

Waldron, Jeremy. "What is cosmopolitan?" *The Journal of Political Philosophy*, 8 (2), 2000, pp. 227-43.

Weitz, Richard. "Sino-Kazakh Ties on a Roll," *China Brief,* Vol. XIII, Issue 2, January 18, 2013.

Dissertations, Reports, Working Papers

Achilov, Dilshod. "Islamic Education in Central Asia: Evidence from Kazakhstan," *Asia Policy*, Number 14, July 2012.

Anderson, Bridget and Blanca Hancilova. "Migrant Labour in Kazakhstan: A Case for Concern?" Working Paper No. 69, University of Oxford, 2009.

Badalov, Ulugbek. "The Oralmans: Migration of Ethnic Kazakhs from China to Europe" [excerpts from PhD dissertation in political anthropology, School for Advanced Studies in Social Sciences (EHESS), Paris (2011)].

Bissenova, Alima. "Post-socialist Dreamworlds: Housing Boom and urban development in Kazakhstan."

Faugner, Kari. "Chinese Perspectives on the Dungan People and Language. A Critical Discourse Analysis on the Ambiguousness of Chinese Ethnicity," Masters' Thesis in East Asian Linguistics, Department of Culture Studies and Oriental Languages, Spring 2012.

Hutchens, Adrian O. "Final Report—Example Allocations of Operating and Maintenance Costs of Interstate Water Control Facilities Employing the Use-of-Facilities Method," Prepared for Central Asia Mission, US Agency for International Development, December 1999.

"Kazakhstan: Waiting for Change," Brussels: International Crisis Group, *Asia Report* No. 250, September 30, 2013.

Kuscu, Isik. "Kazakhstan's Oralman Project: A Remedy for Ambiguous Identity?" ProQuest, 2008.

Muratshina, Ksenia. "The Irtysh River in the hydro policy of Russia, Kazakhstan and China," *Russian International Affairs Council: Central and South Asia Analysis,* May 29, 2012.

Oka, Natsuko. "Transnationalism as a threat to state security? Case studies on Uighurs and Uzbeks of Kazakhstan,"
http://src-h.slav.hokudai.ac.jp/coe21/publish/no14_ses/14_oka.pdf

Sadovskaya, Elena. "Chinese Labour Migration to Kazakhstan at the beginning of the twenty-first century," Norwegian Institute of International Affairs, 2012.

Sadovskaya, Elena. "Migratsionnaia Situatsiya v Respublike Kazakhstan v 2005 g., Analiticheskii obzor i rekomendatsii," Report commissioned by ILO, 2005.

Satpaev, Dosym. "Kazakhstan and the Eurasian Economic Union: The view from Astana," European Council on Foreign Relations, January 12, 2015.

Schatz, Edward. "When Capital Cities Move: The Political Geography of Nation and State Building," Working Paper No. 303, February 2003.

Rybina, Liza et al. "Patriotism, cosmopolitanism, consumer ethnocentrism and purchase behaviour in Kazakhstan," *Organisations and Markets in Emerging Economies,* Vol. 1, No. 2, 2010.

Web Articles

Amerkulov, N. and N. Masanov. "Kazakhstan ne imeyet budutshego bez Rossii," *Caravan*, February 4, 1994.

Ashimbaeva, Alida. "Dostizhenija i problemy kazakhstansko-kitajskikh ekonomicheskikh otnoshenij" (Outcomes and problems in China-Kazakhstan economic relations), March 22, 2007,
http://www.postsoviet.ru/page.php?pid=118

Auezova, Zifa Alua. "Conceiving a People's History: The 1920-1936 discourse on the Kazakh past," https://www.academia.edu/6873274/4_Conceiving_a_peoples_history_The_1920_1936_discourse_on_the_Kazakh_past

Babkina, Aleksandra. "Kazakhstan to modernise housing and public utilities—country drawing on Europe's experience," *Central Asia Online,* January 17, 2012.

Brauer, Birgit. "Rebranding Kazakhstan by Changing Its Name," Jamestown Foundation *Eurasia Daily Monitor*, Vol. 11, Issue 30, February 14, 2014, available at http://www.refworld.org/docid/5301c7814.html [accessed March 6, 2014].

Carino, Jack. "Water woes in Kazakhstan," *China Dialogue,* April 1, 2008. Kamziyeva, Gulmira. "Astana develops new Oralman repatriation programme," *Central Asia Online,* November 2, 2011.

Kelaart, Lucy and Genya Vasyuta. "Crimean Tatars: Crimean Tatars struggle to leave Uzbekistan," *EurasiaNet,* June 26, 2004.

"Kyrgyz Block Water to Kazakhstan, Demanding the Return of 'Their' Land," *Global Voices*, posted July 17, 2013.

Lillis, Joanna. "Kazakhstan: Astana Lures Ethnic Kazakh Migrants with Financial Incentives," *Eurasianet.org*, February 26, 2009.

Nandy, Ashis. "Defining a new cosmopolitanism: Towards a Dialogue of Asian Civilizations," http://vlal.bol.ucla.edu/multiversity/Nandy/Nandy_cosm.htm

"The Shanyrak Crystallizes Kazakh Culture and History," [As eloquently described by the Embassy of the Republic of Kazakhstan to Canada], *KazakhWorld,* http://kazakhworld.com/the-shanyrak-crystallizes-kazakh-culture-and-history/

Fitzpatrick, Sheila. "Kazakhstan's City of Gold: All that Glitters," http://www.themonthly.com.au/issue/2013/october/1380549600/sheila-fitzpatrick/kazakhstan-s-city-gold

http://registan.net/2014/02/10/nazarbaev-and-kazakh-yeli/

"Kazakhstan: One Last Time for Nazarbayev," *The Diplomat,* March 16, 2015.

Laszczkowski, Mateusz. "'City of the Future'—the politics, pragmatics and aesthetics of the future in Astana, Kazakhstan," http://www.ucl.ac.uk/mariecuriesocanth/

"A City of Change," November 10, 2010.
https://onesteppeatatime.wordpress.com/category/almaty/page/2/

"Mangystau at the Centre of Events," http://www.iteca.kz/en/news/28-10-2009pr-mang-oil/

Parmer, Michael Hancock. "Nazarbaev and Kazakh Eli," October 2, 2014, http://registan.net/2014/02/10/nazarbaev-and-kazakh-yeli/

"US, Chinese Plans for Rail Links with Central Asia Triggering 'Railroad War' and Reducing Russia's Influence," *Eurasia Daily Monitor*, Volume 10, Issue 31, February 19, 2013.

www.dark-tourism.com/index.php/.../498-alzhir-memorial-kazakhstan

Wallace, D. L. "Alternative rhetoric and morality: writing from the margins," www.ncte.org/library/NCTEFiles/.../CCC0612Alternative.pdf , 2008.

http://en.tengrinews.kz/industry_infrastructure/Kazakhstans-Aktau-Seaport-SEZ-to-focus-on-oil-and-gas-21055/

http://www.traceca-org.org/uploads/media/02.-24072012_Presentation_SEZ_Seaport_Aktau_ENG.pdf

Newspaper Articles and Magazine Articles

"Anger at devaluation hints at a broader malaise," *The Economist*, February 22, 2014.

Assanov, E. "Uzbekskoe Plemya Naiman," [Section Compatriots. Frontier], *Mangilik El,* June 3, 2014.

"Astana. Retrospektiva," No. 73, *Subbota*, 26 Iuniya, 2010 goda.

Blagov, Sergei. "Gunboats doing the talking in the Caspian," *Asia Times Online*, July 9, 2002.

Evgenidze, Nino. "Eurasian Customs Union Crawling Closer to Georgia," *Democracy and Freedom Watch*, January 2, 2015.

Feigenbaum, Evan A. *Asia Unbound*, November 15, 2010.

First World Kazakhs' Qurultay, "Qushaghymyz Bauyrlargha Aiqara Ashyq," *Egemen Qazaqstan*, October 2, 1992.

Fuenzig, Michael. "Georgia and the Eurasian Union," *Democracy and Freedom Watch*, October 16, 2013.

Jacobsen, Jax. "Kazakhstan Braces for 2015 Elections," *Silk Road Reporters*, February 17, 2015.

"Kazakh elections Raise the Spectre of Unrest," *Stratfor Global Intelligence*, February 25, 2015.

Maitanov, Azamat. "Why Kazakh youth join extremists?" *Ak Zhaik*, February 28, 2013.

Nurbekov, Altair. "Eurasian Economic Integration 'Will Continue,' Nazarbayev Says", *Eurasia & World*, April 2, 2014. *The Astana Times,* January 23, 2015.

Panfilova, Victoria. "Nazarbayev's brand," *Vestnik Kavkaza*, April 30, 2014.

"Putin: All Participants Benefiting From Eurasian Economic Union," *Georgia Today*, Issue No. 748, January 9, 2015-January 15, 2015.

Scott, W. M. Stephen. "The Ideal Soviet Suburb: Social Change Through Urban Design," *Panorama, 2009.*

"Tsentr Evrazii," www.republika.kz, 5 Iuliya 2012.

"Why Celebrate 550 Years of Kazakh Statehood?" Editorial, *The Astana Times,* February 28, 2015.

Zhao, Shengan Ciu Jia. "Oil and money: a match made in Kazakhstan," *China Daily* (European Weekly Edition), September 12, 2011.